Theodore Johnson

**Imperial Britain**

A Comprehensive Description of the Geography, History, Commerce, Trade, Government, and Religion of the British Empire

Theodore Johnson

**Imperial Britain**
*A Comprehensive Description of the Geography, History, Commerce, Trade, Government, and Religion of the British Empire*

ISBN/EAN: 9783337168193

Printed in Europe, USA, Canada, Australia, Japan

Cover: Foto ©ninafisch / pixelio.de

More available books at **www.hansebooks.com**

# THE IMPERIAL LIBRARY

IMPERIAL BRITAIN

# The Imperial Library,

## CONDUCTED BY FRANCIS GEORGE HEATH,

Will be issued in a series of Volumes which, elegantly bound, will be published from time to time.

---

"The Imperial Library" is to consist of works of far-reaching interest, giving information upon every subject concerning our great Empire—all designed to aid the noble movement, now progressing, for strengthening the ties which unite the Mother Country to the splendid Colonies which are the power and the pride of "Greater Britain."

The great and far-reaching object for which "The Imperial Library" has been founded is to bring home to the minds of the millions of our splendid Empire a knowledge of what they, as citizens in their huge commonwealth, are so proud to possess; and thus, it is hoped, may be built up, by gradual means, and at a cost that may come (by easy instalments) within the pecuniary resources of the humblest of intelligent readers, a storehouse of information collected with one object and under one system; and ultimately, it may reasonably be hoped, there will be produced an Encyclopædia Britannica such as no private person at present possesses.

---

LONDON: THE IMPERIAL PRESS, LIMITED, 21 SURREY STREET, VICTORIA EMBANKMENT, W.C.

*Her Most Gracious Majesty, Queen Victoria.*

# THE IMPERIAL LIBRARY

# IMPERIAL BRITAIN

A Comprehensive Description of the Geography, History, Commerce, Trade, Government, and Religion of the British Empire.

In Two Volumes. With Maps and Illustrations.

VOL. I.

The British Empire in Europe, etc., etc.

BY THE

REV. THEODORE JOHNSON,

Late Chief Diocesan Inspector of Schools for Rochester Diocese.

Author of "The Parish Guide," "A Geography and Atlas of the British Empire," "Handbook of English History," etc., etc.

London

THE IMPERIAL PRESS, LIMITED

21 SURREY STREET, VICTORIA EMBANKMENT, W.C.

1898

(All Rights Reserved.)

# GENERAL

"Britannia needs no bulwarks,
   No towers along the steep;
  Her march is o'er the mountain wave,
   Her home is on the deep."
        —"*Ye Mariners of England.*"
            —THOMAS CAMPBELL.

"A land of settled government,
  A land of just and old renown,
  Where freedom broadens slowly down,
From precedent to precedent."
        —Lyric, "*You ask me why, etc.*"
            —LORD TENNYSON.

"This royal throne of kings, this sceptr'd isle,
This earth of majesty, this seat of Mars,
This other Eden, demi-paradise;
This fortress, built by Nature for herself,
Against infection and the hand of war;
This happy breed of men, this little world;
This precious stone set in the silver sea,
Which serves it in the office of a wall,
Or as a moat defensive to a house,
Against the envy of less happier lands;
This blessed plot, this earth, this realm, this England."
            —WILLIAM SHAKESPEARE.

### Dedicated

TO

ALL TRUE AND LOYAL
SONS AND DAUGHTERS
OF THE
VAST DOMINIONS
OF
IMPERIAL BRITAIN
THROUGHOUT THE
WORLD.

"Righteousness
exalteth
a
Nation."
—*Prov. xiv., 34.*

# IMPERIAL BRITAIN.

## PREFACE TO VOL I.

UNDER this comprehensive and noble title, the author has endeavoured to represent the Geography, History, Commerce, Trade, Government, and Religion of the vast territories and possessions of the British Empire, which now comprises one-sixth of the earth's surface, with a population numbering one-fifth of the inhabitants of the whole world.

The present aim is not so much to add yet another volume to the existing list of Geographies of the British Empire, as it is to present to the general reader, in a popular form, statistics and facts relating to the descriptive nature; the progress and wealth; and the general position and resources of Imperial Britain. The range is therefore made considerably wider than that generally taken for ordinary purposes of study, by the introduction of such subject matter as:—Her national position and relationship to foreign powers; her belt of defences, powerful safeguards, and means of communication, both external and internal; her navigation and foreign markets; together with the numerous links, National, Social, Commercial, and Religious, that bind her vast foreign possessions to the Mother Country, however distant they may be situated from it.

In all instances where quotations have been made from other works, the same has been fully acknowledged so far as the Author could do so. Should there, however, be any omissions, he now begs to offer his apologies for the same, and he will gladly have the corrections made in all future editions of this work.

That "Knowledge is Power" and "Union is Strength" are two well-known truisms. May they be realised and acted upon by Britain's sons and daughters in every clime and in every station. The units make up the grand whole, so that while her children remain loyal to her Government and Laws; strong and courageous in their labour and aims; true and faithful in their Religion; so long will Britain's Greatness and Glory shine among the many nations of the earth, and in the noble words of Shakespeare :

> "Naught shall make us rue,
> If England to itself do rest but true."

THEODORE JOHNSON.

BODIAM RECTORY,
SUSSEX, 1898.

# CONTENTS OF VOL. I.

## PART I.

|  | Page |
|---|---|
| THE BRITISH EMPIRE—GENERAL DESCRIPTION— | |
|    1. NAME AND POSITION | 1 |
|    2. INHABITANTS | 1 |
|    3. POPULATION | 2 |
|    4. EMIGRATION AND IMMIGRATION | 2 |
|    5. AREA | 3 |
|    6. NATIONAL EXPENDITURE OF POSSESSIONS | 3 |
|    7. NATURAL PRODUCTIONS | 3 |
| FOREIGN POSSESSIONS— | 3 |
|    1. HOW ACQUIRED, ETC. | 4 |
|    2. GOVERNMENT AND ADMINISTRATION | 5 |
|    3. CONSTITUTION | 6 |
|    4. LAW | 7 |
|    5. HOME CONTROL | 8 |
|    6. AGENTS GENERAL | 8 |
|    7. COLONIAL INSTITUTE AND IMPERIAL INSTITUTE | 9 |
|    8. ADVANTAGES AND USES OF COLONIES | 10 |
| FUTURE GROWTH AND PROSPECTS OF FOREIGN POSSESSIONS— | 13 |
|    1. NEW OVERLAND ROUTE TO INDIA | 13 |
|    2. IMPERIAL AND COMMERCIAL FEDERATION OF THE EMPIRE | 15 |
| SHORT HISTORY OF BRITISH COMMERCE | 19 |
| TABLE OF BRITISH POSSESSIONS, WITH DATES, ETC. | 30 |
| MAIL INTELLIGENCE, POST AND CABLE RATES | 34 |
| PASSENGER STEAMSHIP LINES | 38 |
| TABLE OF DISTANCES FROM LONDON TO SYDNEY, P. & O. LINE | 42 |
| ETHNOLOGY—ORIGIN OF BRITISH PEOPLE | 43 |

## PART II.

**THE BRITISH ISLANDS—GENERAL INFORMATION—**

| | Page |
|---|---|
| 1. INTRODUCTION | 48 |
| 2. CONNECTION WITH THE CONTINENT | 49 |
| 3. CLIMATE | 49 |
| 4. POSITION | 50 |
| 5. SHAPE AND EXTENT, INCLUDING SMALLER ISLANDS | 50 |
| 6. CENSUS NOTES, 1891 | 51 |
| 7. ANNUAL EXPENDITURE AND REVENUE | 52 |
| 8. GOVERNMENT AND ADMINISTRATION | 52 |
| 9. ARMY AND NAVY, COMPARED WITH FOREIGN POWERS | 56 |
| 10. INTERNAL COMMUNICATION, INCLUDING:— | |
|    (a) RAILWAYS OF GREAT BRITAIN AND IRELAND | 60 |
|    (b) POST AND TELEGRAPH | 67 |
|    (c) CANALS AND NAVIGABLE RIVERS | 69 |
|    (d) ROADS | 70 |
| 11. EXTERNAL COMMUNICATION, INCLUDING:— | |
|    (a) COMMERCE | 71 |
|    (b) IMPORTS AND EXPORTS | 72 |
| 12. FISHERIES AND FISHERMEN | 73 |
| 13. LITERATURE AND THE PRESS | 76 |
| 14. RELIGION | 77 |
| 15. EDUCATION | 80 |
| 16. ROYAL FAMILY, ETC. | 82 |
| 17. ROYAL RESIDENCES | 84 |
| 18. PATRON SAINTS AND NATIONAL SYMBOLS | 84 |
| 19. NAVAL BATTLES SINCE 1066 | 84 |
| 20. PRINCIPAL WARS SINCE 1066 | 86 |
| 21. LANGUAGES OF THE BRITISH ISLES | 87 |
| 22. GENERAL HISTORY—NOTABLE EVENTS | 87 |
| 23. TRADE STATISTICAL NOTES, COMPARED WITH FOREIGN POWERS | 90 |
| 24. AGRICULTURAL RETURNS, 1896 | 92 |
| 25. TABLE OF CHIEF FEATURES OF BRITISH ISLANDS | 94 |

## PART III.

ENGLAND AND WALES, PHYSICAL AND POLITICAL—

| | Page |
|---|---|
| 1. SHAPE AND EXTENT | 95 |
| 2. AREA AND POSITION | 95 |
| 3. BOUNDARIES | 95 |
| 4. COASTLINE, SHOWING CAPES AND HEADLANDS, BAYS AND INLETS | 95 |
| 5. STRAITS AND ROADSTEADS | 100 |
| 6. ISLANDS | 102 |
| 7. COAST DEFENCES AND SAFEGUARDS | 108 |
| 8. CINQUE PORTS | 109 |
| 9. PHYSICAL FEATURES—SURFACE (GENERAL DESCRIPTION), | 109 |
| 10. MOUNTAINS AND HILLS | 110 |
| 11. PLAINS AND LOWLANDS, INCLUDING VALLEYS | 116 |
| 12. RIVERS | 118 |
| 13. LAKES, INCLUDING BROADS AND MERES | 124 |
| 14. CLIMATE | 126 |
| 15. NATURAL PRODUCTIONS:— | 127 |
| (*a*) MINERAL, INCLUDING MINERAL SPRINGS AND NATURAL CURIOSITIES | 128 |
| (*b*) VEGETABLE | 132 |
| (*c*) ANIMAL | 136 |
| 16. POPULATION AND PEOPLE | 138 |
| 17. TABLE OF DETAILED IMPORTS AND EXPORTS | 139 |
| 18. TRADE AND MANUFACTURES | 141 |
| 19. PRINCIPAL SEAPORTS | 143 |
| 20. POLITICAL DIVISIONS, WITH TABLES (ENGLAND AND WALES) | 143 |
| 21. ENGLAND—DERIVATION OF COUNTY NAMES | 147 |
| 22. CONCISE DESCRIPTION OF ENGLISH COUNTIES:— | |
| (*a*) MARITIME (20) | 149 |
| (*b*) INLAND (20) | 155 |
| 23. THE COUNTY COUNCIL | 161 |
| 24. CHIEF TOWNS | 162 |
| 25. WALES—COUNTIES:—MARITIME (9); INLAND (3) | 172 |
| 26. CHIEF BATTLEFIELDS (ENGLAND AND WALES) | 175 |

## PART IV.

| | Page |
|---|---|
| SCOTLAND— | |
| 1. NAME | 177 |
| 2. POSITION | 177 |
| 3. AREA AND EXTENT | 177 |
| 4. POPULATION—CENSUS, 1891 | 177 |
| 5. BOUNDARIES | 178 |
| 6. COASTLINE, INCLUDING CAPES AND HEADLANDS, BAYS AND INLETS | 178 |
| 7. STRAITS | 179 |
| 8. ISLANDS | 180 |
| 9. PHYSICAL FEATURES—SURFACE | 185 |
| 10. MOUNTAINS | 187 |
| 11. PLAINS | 190 |
| 12. RIVERS | 190 |
| 13. LAKES | 194 |
| 14. CLIMATE | 196 |
| 15. SOIL AND AGRICULTURE | 197 |
| 16. NATURAL PRODUCTIONS:— | |
| (*a*) MINERAL | 197 |
| (*b*) ANIMAL | 198 |
| (*c*) VEGETABLE | 199 |
| 17. MINERAL SPRINGS AND NATURAL CURIOSITIES | 200 |
| 18. PEOPLE, RACE, AND LANGUAGE | 201 |
| 19. RELIGION | 202 |
| 20. EDUCATION | 202 |
| 21. GOVERNMENT | 202 |
| 22. NAVAL AND SEAPORTS | 202 |
| 23. INTERNAL COMMUNICATION | 203 |
| 24. COMMERCE, INCLUDING IMPORTS AND EXPORTS | 203 |
| 25. POLITICAL DIVISIONS, WITH TABLE | 204 |
| 26. CONCISE DESCRIPTION OF COUNTIES | 205 |
| 27. CHIEF TOWNS | 216 |
| 28. TRADE AND MANUFACTURES | 221 |
| 29. CHIEF BATTLEFIELDS | 221 |
| 30. SHORT HISTORICAL NOTES | 222 |

## PART V.

IRELAND—                                                      Page
   1. NAME - - - - - - 223
   2. SHAPE, AREA, AND EXTENT - - - 223
   3. POSITION - - - - - - 223
   4. COASTLINE, INCLUDING CAPES AND HEADLANDS, BAYS AND INLETS - - - - 223
   5. STRAITS - - - - - - 225
   6. ISLANDS - - - - - - 226
   7. PHYSICAL FEATURES—SURFACE - - - 228
   8. MOUNTAINS AND HILLS - - - - 228
   9. PLAINS - - - - - - 229
 10. RIVERS - - - - - - 229
 11. LAKES - - - - - - 231
 12. CLIMATE - - - - - - 233
 13. SOIL AND AGRICULTURE - - - - 233
 14. NATURAL PRODUCTIONS :—
      (*a*) ANIMAL - - - - 234
      (*b*) VEGETABLE - - - - 235
      (*c*) MINERAL - - - - 236
 15. MINERAL SPRINGS AND NATURAL CURIOSITIES - 237
 16. RACE AND LANGUAGE - - - - 238
 17. POPULATION, NOTES, CENSUS, 1891 - - 238
 18. POLITICAL DIVISIONS - - - - 238
 19. COUNTIES, WITH TABLE - - - - 240
 20. TRADE AND MANUFACTURES - - - 241
 21. SEAPORTS - - - - - - 241
 22. NAVAL AND MILITARY STATIONS - - - 241
 23. CHIEF TOWNS - - - - - 242
 24. GOVERNMENT - - - - - 248
 25. RELIGION - - - - - - 250
 26. EDUCATION - - - - - - 250
 27. REVENUE - - - - - - 250
 28. INTERNAL COMMUNICATION - - - 250
 29. COMMERCE, INCLUDING IMPORTS AND EXPORTS - 250
 30. HISTORICAL NOTES - - - - - 251
 31. BATTLEFIELDS - - - - - 252

xvi                    CONTENTS.

## PART VI.

|   |   | Page |
|---|---|---|
| BRITISH POSSESSIONS IN EUROPE— | | |
| 1. ISLE OF MAN | | 255 |
| 2. CHANNEL ISLANDS:— | | 262 |
|     (*a*) JERSEY | | 264 |
|     (*b*) GUERNSEY, WITH HERM AND JETHOU | | 266 |
|     (*c*) ALDERNEY AND THE CASQUETS | | 267 |
|     (*d*) SARK, LITTLE SARK, ETC. | | 268 |
| 3. GIBRALTAR | | 269 |
| 4. MALTA, WITH GOZO AND COMINO | | 275 |
| 5. CYPRUS | | 282 |
| INDEX | | 289 |

## LIST OF ILLUSTRATIONS

| | Page | | Page |
|---|---|---|---|
| THE IMPERIAL INSTITUTE, LONDON | 11 | THE TRONGATE, GLASGOW | 217 |
| HOUSES OF PARLIAMENT, LONDON | 53 | THE UNIVERSITY, GLASGOW | 219 |
| PORTSMOUTH | 59 | KINGSTOWN HARBOUR, IRELAND | 242 |
| WINDSOR CASTLE | 85 | CHRISTCHURCH CATHEDRAL, DUBLIN | 243 |
| THE THAMES — WOOLWICH REACH | 121 | ST. PATRICK'S CATHEDRAL, DUBLIN | 244 |
| IN THE MERSEY | 123 | SACKVILLE STREET, DUBLIN | 245 |
| THE ROYAL ALBERT DOCKS | 163 | THE CASTLE, DUBLIN | 247 |
| MILWALL DOCKS | 165 | LONDONDERRY | 249 |
| THE PORT OF LIVERPOOL | 167 | BRADDA HEAD, ISLE OF MAN | 257 |
| LIME STREET, LIVERPOOL | 169 | SOUTH STACK LIGHT, HOLYHEAD | 259 |
| QUEEN'S DOCK, HULL | 171 | CORBIÈRE LIGHT, JERSEY | 265 |
| SOUTHAMPTON DOCKS | 173 | SARK, FROM THE WEST COAST | 268 |
| BASS ROCK | 181 | STRAIT OF GIBRALTAR | 269 |
| FORTH BRIDGE | 189 | GIBRALTAR | 270 |
| TAY BRIDGE | 191 | STREET IN GIBRALTAR | 273 |
| BEN AND LOCH LOMOND | 193 | PLAN OF VALETTA HARBOUR | 275 |
| LOCH KATRINE | 195 | GRAND HARBOUR, VALETTA | 277 |
| ABERDEEN | 207 | MARINA, LARNAKA, CYPRUS | 283 |
| EDINBURGH, FROM CASTLE HILL | 213 | LIMASOL, CYPRUS | 285 |
| UNIVERSITY, EDINBURGH | 215 | | |

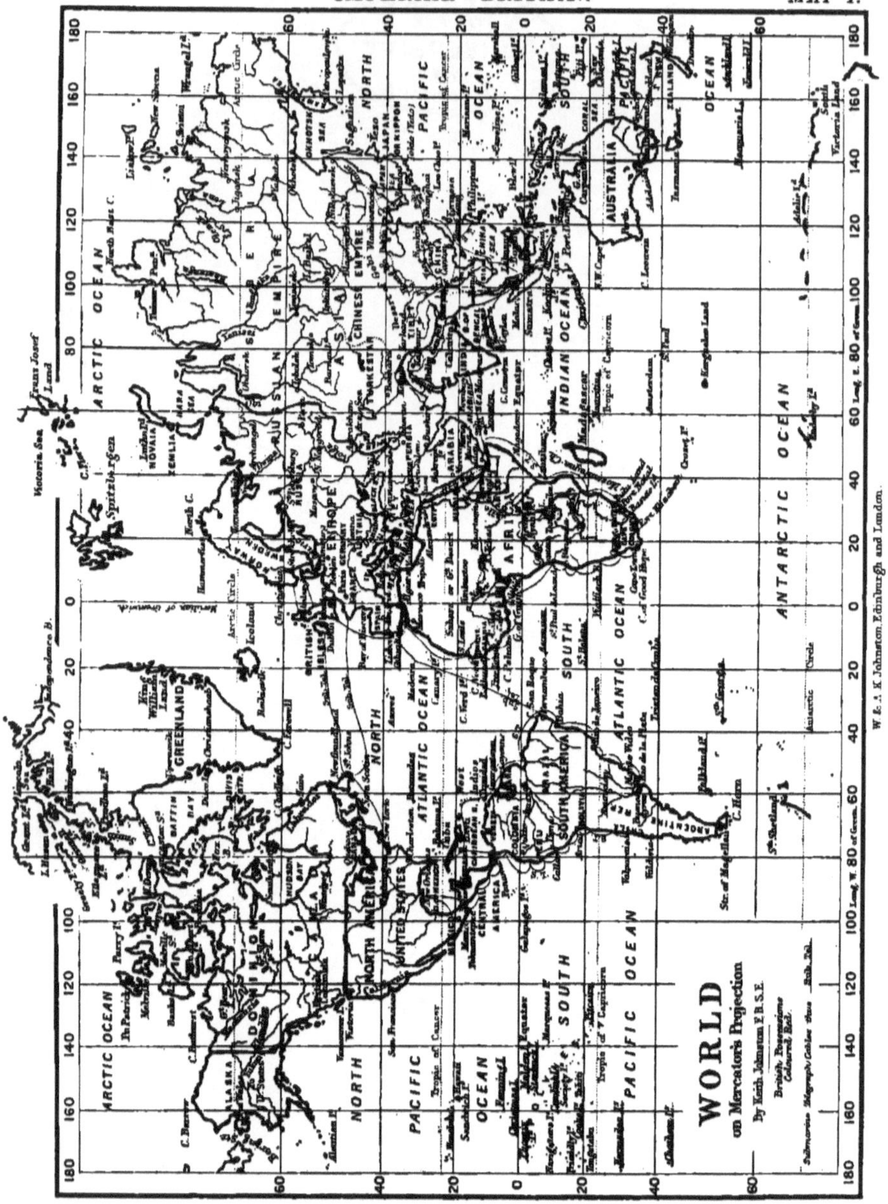
WORLD
on Mercator's Projection
By Keith Johnston F.R.S.E.
British Possessions Coloured Red.
W. & A. K. Johnston, Edinburgh and London.

# IMPERIAL BRITAIN.

## PART I.

### THE BRITISH EMPIRE.

NAME AND POSITION.—Under this name is included not only the United Kingdom of Great Britain and Ireland, but the vast and numerous foreign possessions—known as Colonies or Dependencies—scattered throughout every part of the world, so that the familiar proverb, "The sun never sets upon the British Empire," is absolutely a fact, for the British dominions are to be found throughout the five great divisions of the world—Europe, Asia, Africa, America, and Australasia.

INHABITANTS.—This immense territory comprises people of every race, colour, religion, and language, varying widely in habits, and appearance, according to the position they occupy upon the earth's surface, *e.g.*, the British flag has been planted from the burning plains of the Equator to the frozen regions of both the Arctic and Antarctic Circles, or, as Cotton has quaintly described it :—

"The Colonial Empire of Britain is as varied in its composition as it is vast in its extent. The Colonies proper vary in character from a settled country, with a civilisation more than a century old, like Lower Canada, to an unexplored wilderness of savages, like New Guinea; from the Continent of Australia to the Rock of Gibraltar; from Hong-Kong, the emporium of Chinese trade, to Heligoland,[1] the favourite watering-place of Hamburgers."

POPULATION.—Thus we find the inhabitants of the British Empire to be about 327,000,000. This multitudinous mixed race of many nations, including about *one-fifth* of the inhabitants of the whole world, are represented in our different possessions under the names of Hindoos, Mahommedans, Chinese, Parsees, Burmese, Malays, Cingalese, and Cypriots in Asia; Negroes, Kaffirs, Zulus, Hottentots, Soudanese, and Arabs in Africa; Indians of various tribes in North and South America; Maories and Bushmen with other mixed island Melanesian races in Australasia; and English, Scotch, Welsh, Manx, Irish, Genoese, and Maltese in Europe. To the native population of our vast foreign possessions must be added the millions of emigrants and settlers, which, beyond those of our own nationality, include most of the European nations—the principal peoples being the French, Germans, Dutch, Spanish, Portuguese, Jews, Italians, and Danes.

EMIGRATION. — Later on will be found fuller information relating to emigration, but here it will suffice to mention that recent statistics show that since the year 1815, or during the past eighty years, more than seventeen millions of the British peoples have left their homes as emigrants to our Colonies. And by far the greater portion have found new life and employment in the United States, Canada, Australia, and South Africa.

The average number of persons emigrating each year

---

[1] N.B.—Heligoland is no longer a British possession; it was ceded to Germany in 1890.

from Great Britain is about 250,000. Of this number nearly three-fourths are bound for our greater Colonies.

The Immigration of persons of foreign or colonial birth is small compared with this number. In 1891, the Census only showed 400,629 foreigners residing in the British Isles, but this number has of late years increased.

Another system of emigration exists by which the Coolie labourers, chiefly from India and China, are transported to Mauritius and the West Indies, in place of the old slave traffic, which happily, has been abolished. To a certain extent also, the Polynesian islanders emigrate, for purposes of labour, to Queensland, and some other of our Australian Colonies.

Area.—The area of the British Empire throughout the world now stands at nine millions of square miles, or about one-sixth of the land surface of the globe; whereas, the area of the British Islands is only 123,000 square miles.

Professor Meiklejohn states, in his "Comparative Geography of the British Empire," that "the Empire is equal to three Europes, but that Great Britain alone is only $\frac{1}{100}$ part of the whole Empire."

Expenditure.—The annual expenditure of Great Britain, on account of her Colonies, has been estimated to be £100,000,000.

Natural Products.—The vast dominions of the British Empire include some of the most fertile countries in the world, so that if the rest of the civilised countries of the world closed their ports against us, we could easily supply all our needs from our own possessions; *e.g.*, Britain stands first among the corn-growing countries of the world; her forests of timber, and her wool supplies, are unrivalled, and the output of her minerals exceeds that of any other nation, more especially in coal, iron, copper, and salt.

Foreign Possessions of Great Britain.—The foreign

possessions of the British Empire, which date from the reign of Queen Elizabeth (Newfoundland, so called from the discovery of Sir Humphrey Gilbert in 1583), may be classed under four heads, *viz.* :—

1. THE EMPIRE OF INDIA, which began in 1757 under *George II.*
2. Crown Colonies, as GIBRALTAR, 1704, etc.
3. Those possessing a representative Government, as CANADA, 1623-1760, etc.
4. Protectorates, as BECHUANALAND, 1885, etc.

HOW ACQUIRED.—These world-wide and valuable possessions have been acquired either by conquest, purchase, or settlement, since the reign of Queen Elizabeth, as shown by the following table :—

1. *Conquest by War*, as Canada from the French in 1760.
2. *Cession by Treaty*, as Florida from Spain in 1763.
3. *Colonisation by Settlers*, as South Australia in 1836.
4. *Discovery by Navigators*, as Newfoundland in 1583.
5. *Exploration by Travellers*, as interior of Australia and Africa.
6. *Purchase by Treaty*, as Singapore from the Maharajah of Johore in 1824.
7. *Exchange with Foreign Powers*, as Malacca for Sumatra, from the Dutch, in 1823.
8. *Trading Ports and Districts established*, *e.g.*, the East India Company, as portions of India, and Further India since 1600, and Hudson's Bay Company, Canada, etc.
9. *Presentation*, as Malta given by Charles V. of Spain, 1530, to the Knights of St. John, who in 1798 capitulated to Napoleon, but after two years it was again taken by the English, and its possession finally confirmed by the Treaty of Paris, 1814.

10. *Annexation* to existing or neighbouring possessions, as Bermuda in 1609, and Oudh in India, 1856.
11. *Royal Dowry*, as Bombay to Queen Catherine of Braganza, wife of Charles II., who allowed the East India Company to rent it as a trading port for £10 a year.
12. *Missionary Enterprise*, as Central Africa, New Guinea, and South Pacific Islands, where trade and annexation have followed the work of religion.

N.B.—Other possessions have been added as penal settlements, as Port Blair for Indian convicts in the Andaman Islands.

GOVERNMENT AND ADMINISTRATION.—We must here distinguish between the two terms *Colony* and *Dependency*.

(*a*) A COLONY, in the strictest sense of the name, is a settlement by people sent from the Mother Country (Latin, *colonia*), to possess and cultivate the soil, and to open up commercial relations and trade with the parent country, besides forming a new home as an important provision against the excess of population, *e.g.*, Australia, etc.

(*b*) A DEPENDENCY (from the Latin *dependeo*, *in subjection to*), is a foreign land acquired by conquest, cession, etc., where the native population are in subjection to another country, and receive their support and protection from that country, *e.g.*, India, etc.

Thus it is that in our Colonies the inhabitants are called colonists or settlers, who are strangers to the country, but who have been sent there as emigrants from the Home Country, where emigrants from other lands have joined them, and so they make a mixed and varied population in their new home; whereas, in our Dependencies, the original native population remains unchanged, without these additional settlers from the parent country — the majority of Europeans in our foreign Dependencies being those who hold appointments as Government officers in the army and navy, or others engaged in trade and commerce.

CONSTITUTION.—The Government and Constitution of the vast and scattered Empire of Great Britain is naturally of the highest importance. The Imperial control and supervision of such an immense territory, with its many millions of subjects, is vested under the administration of the British Government acting for the Sovereign, Queen, and Empress; but the general administration of our foreign possessions, with the exception of the Indian Empire and its Dependencies, including Aden, Perim, and the Kuria Muria Islands, Socotra, the Somali Coast Protectorate, the Laccadive, Andaman, and Nicobar Islands, is vested in the Colonial Office; and the British Empire in India is governed by the Viceroy, or Governor-General, and his Legislative Council, among whom the Commander-in-Chief, or head of the Indian army, holds a prominent place. They are represented at home by the Secretary of State for India, and his numerous staff of officials at the India Office, Whitehall, London.

Beyond this the foreign possessions of Great Britain have but three different kinds of constitution :—

 (*a*) *Crown Colonies*, that is Colonies ruled by Crown officers, who are alone held responsible to the British Government at home. Most of these have a native population, as Ceylon, Gibraltar, Jamaica, Gold Coast Settlements, New Guinea, etc. etc.

 (*b*) *Colonies under Representative Government*, that is, Colonies possessing their own legislature or representative institutions, but they have no responsible

Government, inasmuch as their chief public officers are appointed and controlled by the Crown, or Home Government, which also retains a veto on legislation through the Colonial Office in London, *e.g.*, Natal, Barbadoes, etc. etc.

(*c*) *Colonies possessing a Responsible Government*, such as Canada, Cape Colony, the Australian Colonies, New Zealand, etc. In these countries the Home Government appoint but one officer, the Governor, who possesses for the Crown a veto on legislature, which happily is seldom exercised. Such Colonies elect their own Government, *i.e.*, ministers and parliament, independently of the Home Government.

(*d*) In addition to the above-named classes of Colonies, the Island of Ascension in the Atlantic is treated as an Admiralty possession under the direct control of a naval officer as Governor.

LAW.—The Criminal and Civil Law of Great Britain extends throughout all those Colonies which have been annexed by settlement, and which are peopled for the most part by British subjects; but in those Colonies which have been acquired by force of arms, or treaty, etc., the native laws found there are allowed to remain with such modifications, alterations, and additions as may be considered to be necessary to uphold justice, peace, and order among the inhabitants.

The Duke of Devonshire, as Lord Hartington, ably described the Government of the British Empire in 1890. He said : " Our Government, like other Governments, has a great deal to do besides making laws. It has to administer the affairs of an enormous Empire. It has to conduct the foreign relations of an Empire not less powerful than any Empire in the world. It has to conduct the relations of that Empire with every foreign State—civilised or uncivilised—all over the world. It has to administer the affairs of a great Indian Empire—a task the like of which does not devolve upon any other Government in the world. It has to regulate the relations of the Mother Country with vast self-governing Colonies; to provide to a certain extent for the government of those great communities; to watch over their interests, and to regulate their relations with each other and with ourselves. Our Government has vast naval and military departments to administer, not to speak of such unconsidered trifles as the post-office and telegraph department, which are in themselves departments as great as any of those railway or industrial companies with whose affairs we are acquainted. Above all, it has to superintend the collection and the expenditure of an enormous annual revenue."

HOME CONTROL.—The vast foreign possessions of Imperial Britain are controlled and directed by the Home Government acting for the Sovereign as Imperial Ruler under the following Government Offices :—

1. Admiralty, Whitehall, S.W. (*See Ascension Island.*) *Chief Officer*, The First Lord of the Admiralty.
2. Colonial Office, Downing Street, S.W. *Chief Officer*, Secretary of State for the Colonies.
3. Crown Agents for the Colonies, Downing Street, S.W. Three Chief Crown Agents.
4. Home Office, Whitehall, S.W. Secretary of State for Home Affairs. (*See The Channel Islands.*)
5. India Office, St. James' Park, S.W. Secretary of State for India.
6. Emigration Information Office, 31 Broadway, Westminster, S.W.

AGENTS GENERAL.—Before passing away from the administration and government of our Colonies in every part of the world, it may be well to point out the important work of the Agents General in London. Each principal Colony has an Agent General at home to represent its interests, and to act as an Ambassador to the Home Government. All matters relating to politics, commerce, law, and government, are thus placed directly before the authorities, so that the Secretary of State for the Colonies is able to discuss these important matters at first hand, while the particular interests and needs of each Colony represented must receive individual attention.

A stroll along Victoria Street, leading from the Houses of Parliament, will reveal the principal Agents General Offices in close proximity to the centre of Government. Here the latest information and statistics of our large dominions of Canada, the Cape, Natal, and Australasia may be obtained at these Colonial Offices.

COLONIAL INSTITUTES.—Two other institutions have of late years been founded as strong links to bind our foreign possessions into closer union with the Mother Country, viz:—

*The Colonial Institute in Northumberland Avenue, Charing Cross, London, W.C.*, founded in 1868, with its staff of officers, its valuable library of colonial literature, its interesting lectures and discussions, and its stream of visitors, from every distant quarter of the British dominions, which daily meet within its walls, is no mean factor in representing the power and value of colonial life and enterprise.

*The Imperial Institute at South Kensington*[1] is now known far and wide for its many-sided representation of all matters relating to the Empire of Greater Britain. Here may be found valuable and costly specimens of native and colonial produce, arts, and manufactures in the museums;

---

[1] The Outcome of the Indian and Colonial Exhibition of 1886.

a second library of books upon Imperial subjects; offices of enquiry upon matters concerning colonial life, work, and government in every quarter of the globe, with photographs, maps, and diagrams exhibited upon a scale of magnificence not to be met with elsewhere.

ADVANTAGES AND USES OF COLONIES.—1. The secret of Britain's wealth, power, and prosperity lies in a great measure in her vast foreign possessions, for by means of her numerous Colonies and Dependencies, she commands the highways of the ocean, and proudly owns the title of "Mistress of the Seas." As an example of this, Professor Meiklejohn states in his interesting and able volume, "The British Empire: Its Geography, Resources, Commerce, Landways, and Waterways, 1895," on page 5, when discussing the commercial position of Great Britain, "Of the TONNAGE of all the ships that pass through the Suez Canal, Great Britain has 79 per cent.; France has only $5\frac{1}{2}$ per cent.; Germany, $4\frac{1}{2}$. This is sufficient proof of the leading commercial position of Great Britain, since the Suez Canal is the highway to the whole East."

2. Again, our Colonies furnish a new home, with a better means of living, for the surplus population of this country.

3. They enable us to trade with other distant lands, for we import from these lands not only food supplies and general produce, but the raw materials of those countries provide us with home manufactures, both for consumption and use here, as well as for export in the form of manufactured goods; e.g., British India and the Australian Colonies are among the largest markets in the world for the sale of our manufactured goods.

4. They form stations and forts to protect our ships of war and commerce, so that a commercial belt of navigation has been gradually formed by our steamship and tele-

*The Imperial Institute.*

graphic communication by sea, and the connecting railway systems on land.

5. They are continuous and extensive markets for the sale of English goods and produce.

6. They form calling-ports and stations where our ships may be replenished with fuel, food, and water supplies.

7. By increasing the export and import trade of Great Britain they materially increase the revenue. It has been estimated that nearly one-half of our commercial trade is with India and our Colonies.

8. They are powerful aids in the spread of civilisation and religion. Although, in certain districts in Africa and elsewhere, Christianity has led the way for the planting of the English flag as a protection to the natives against oppression and slavery, yet as a rule our missionaries follow the flag, and their powers of teaching both religion and civilisation are a hundred-fold strengthened when this is so.

9. They offer protection, and attract both the British capitalist and workman to a new sphere of labour, so that the Colony receives the full benefit of these powerful influences, and the links of commercial, social, political, and religious life are thus strengthened both at home and abroad.

Professor Seeley, in writing upon the growth and commercial prospects of our colonial possessions, says, "The time is certainly not far distant when of these new States, some of which are of yesterday, many will equal the European States, which they will surpass in natural wealth and equally-diffused prosperity."

It will be seen from the above-named advantages and uses of our Colonies and Dependencies that it would have been impossible for Great Britain to have attained her present great position in the world of trade, commerce, or politics without them.

FUTURE GROWTH AND PROSPECTS OF OUR FOREIGN POSSESSIONS.—Among the more important matters relating to the future of our Colonies may be mentioned :—

(*a*) The New Overland Route to India.
(*b*) Imperial Federation.

## THE NEW OVERLAND ROUTE TO INDIA.

The following is a short abstract of a paper written by Colonel A. T. Fraser, R.E., and published in the *Journal of the Society of Arts*, on "An Egypto-Assyrian Railway as the New Overland Route to India." The Sublime Porte has long ago conceded a railway right athwart Asia Minor, from the Bosphorus into the heart of Assyria, and this is already open as far as Angora, the exact course to be taken after reaching Mosul being as yet undecided. The line thus conceded, when prolonged to Kurrachee, is evidently the straightest that can be made between the English Channel and India. But owing to the insistence of the Porte that railroad concessions can only be given to Turkish subjects, great delay is occurring on the Syrian lines. It would be of great advantage if the distance between India and the Mediterranean were reduced to a quick and cheap five days' journey. The existing route *via* the Red Sea is liable to be blocked, and British trade would then be diverted again round the Cape. Laying a railway between Ismailia and the head of the Persian Gulf would at once alter the whole complexion of affairs, at a cost of some £5,000,000, and steamers already trading to India could then do the remainder of the work. There are no special engineering difficulties to be encountered. From Ismailia there would be a plunge into the winding valleys and sublime desolation of the desert of Sinai, and then the line would make for the head of the Gulf of Akaba, for convenience of access and protection by the British fleet in Indian seas. The only serious engineering operations would be in crossing the deep valley above Akaba, which is a continuation of that of the Jordan, and getting upon the tableland of Arabia. The route across Arabia is the most favourable possible for a railway; it crosses an insignificant amount of drainage, and is remarkably clear of settled inhabitants. The few Arab tribes will warmly welcome the line, as it will give them access to markets, and its safety can be ensured by fixed payments to the tribal sheiks. It will be necessary to carry the line 80 miles south of Bussorah, to the deep water anchorage of the port of Koweit, and clear of the muddy bar at the mouth of the Shatt-el-Arab, which is at present impracticable for large steamers. The new route will then have Alexandria at one extremity and Koweit at the other. Fast vessels can run down the Persian Gulf to Kurrachee in less than three days, so that the time of journey from the Mediterranean to India will be reduced from ten to four days, thereby lessening the cost of transit. For private interests and commerce there would be the great advantage of a daily mail (six times a week) to India. As it is, there is almost daily steam communication between continental ports and Alexandria. The Persian Gulf is not long and is easily navigated, though it has the reputation of being, in summer, the hottest sea in the world. But in a well-appointed steamship the inconvenience of extreme heat, lasting barely three days, would be scarcely noticed. Colonel Fraser recapitulates the advantages resulting from the construction of this railway as follows :—1st, the virtual extension of the commercial frontier of India westward by 20 degrees of longitude; 2nd, a daily mail to India, and cheaper passages; 3rd, an economical trooping service; 4th, the salubrious port of Kurrachee taking the place of Bombay as a depôt for mails and passengers; 5th, Alexandria becoming practically the port for Western India; 6th, the opening of a coalfield in Mesopotamia; and lastly, the termination of all uncertainty with respect to our Egyptian policy. The construction of these railways to Mesopotamia would be speedily followed by an extension of the British line from Bussorah along the northern shores of the Persian Gulf and the Mekran coast, to meet the Indian system of railways converging in Kurrachee. There is no difficulty in taking a railway over the low strips of land at the base of the chain of mountains which bounds the plateau of Persia, and the whole length of line would be under the observation of our fleet in Indian waters, giving Great Britain a material stake in the Persian littoral. Branch lines of railway would bring down the trade of Southern Persia to its old centre at the Straits of Ormuz, connecting the port of Bunder-Abbas with Bagdad *viâ* Shiraz and Ispahan, and giving Indian passengers a cool alternative route for a section of the journey. But the directness and advantages of the Egypto-Assyrian route over that advocated by the Euphrates Valley Railway are so marked that the new overland route has to be considered apart from the extensive system of Persian lines to which it must inevitably lead, and those railways in Turkish territory with which India has no present concern.—*Reprinted by special permission from " The Imperial Institute Journal," Vol. II., No. 22, October, 1896, p. 363.*

IMPERIAL FEDERATION.—Since the year 1867, when Canada became the leader in the van of federation, there has been a growing desire among the dominions of Great Britain for Imperial Federation. Throughout the greater Colonies of Australasia and South Africa the feeling is a strong one for a federal constitution or union; the only difficulty is how best to formulate a successful scheme of Imperial Federation which shall both strengthen the home powers and the scattered lands and peoples of Great Britain. Through the kindness of the author, Mr. J. G. Colmer, C.M.G., Chief Secretary to the High Commissioner for Canada in London; and the Librarian of the Imperial Institute, Mr. H. H. Hebb, I am enabled to give the following synopsis of the prize essay on Commercial Federation as published in *The Statist* of May 2nd, 1896.

## THE COMMERCIAL FEDERATION OF THE EMPIRE.

The following is a synopsis of the prize essay written by Mr. J. G. Colmer, C.M.G., on the Commercial Federation of the Empire in connection with *The Statist* thousand guineas competition on the subject. The essay was published in full in *The Statist* of May 2nd. The scheme may be divided into four parts : (1.) The granting of preferential treatment to Colonial and Indian products in the United Kingdom. (2.) Preferential treatment of British products in the Colonies and India. (3.) The additional revenue so derived to form a fund, if the Mother Country and the Colonies and India agree, with a view to improve and supplement the defences of the Empire outside the United Kingdom. (4.) The formation of a Colonial Council to give the Colonies a greater voice in Imperial affairs, and to provide for the administration of the fund.

1. It is suggested that in the United Kingdom small specific duties should be placed on certain enumerated articles, about twenty in number, when imported from foreign countries—similar imports from the Colonies and India to remain duty free, as at present. That the proposals are moderate in their nature will be understood when it is stated that the duties, with one or two exceptions, are equivalent to an *ad valorem* duty of about 3 per cent. on foreign imports of the

articles specified. On foreign wheat and flour a revival of the duties in force up to 1869, of about 1s. per quarter, is recommended. The imports in 1894 of the enumerated articles from foreign countries were valued at £85,539,794, and from the Colonies and India at £44,958,350. The duties, it is anticipated, would realise about £2,700,000. The enumerated articles are live animals, meats, cheese, butter, wheat, flour, hemp and other fibres, ivory, undressed leather, sugar, unrefined and refined; wool, tallow, seal skins, fish oil, logwood, mahogany, and nuts and kernels for oil. It would have been easy to mention many other articles produced in the Colonies, on foreign imports of which duties might be imposed, such as india-rubber, indigo, farinaceous substances, ornamental feathers, fish, fruits, gutta-percha, hides, palm oil, rice, furs, skins, silver and tin ore, wine, and wood. But, in the judgment of the writer of the essay, Commercial Federation will have a greater chance of immediate adoption and success if it is inaugurated on a moderate basis. It is also proposed to reduce by one-half the existing duties on imports, from the Colonies and India, of cocoa, coffee, and tea, the duties on the foreign imports of those articles to remain as at present. This rearrangement of the existing tariff, with a reduction of 5 per cent. in the duties on tobacco from all countries, would mean a decrease in the revenue to the extent of about £2,000,000. It will be seen, therefore, that the scheme involves, roughly speaking, a net increase in the revenue of the United Kingdom of about £700,000. It is urged that an increase in price is not likely to result from the placing of duties on foreign imports of the enumerated articles, at any rate to the extent of the proposed duties. In every case there would still be a considerable importation of the different commodities from the Colonies and India. As they would remain duty free, the supplies coming from within the Empire would dominate the market, and with the foreign competition, have a tendency to prevent the increase in prices which perhaps might follow if duties were placed upon such imports from all countries.

2. As the fiscal systems in the Colonies and India are so varied, and the nature of their trade-exchanges so different, it has apparently been found difficult to make any proposal for giving preferential treatment of a uniform character to British imports in those markets, in return for the concessions suggested on the part of the United Kingdom. It is, therefore, recommended in the essay that the Mother Country should take the initiative in the matter, inform the Colonies and India what advantages the United Kingdom is prepared to offer to the imports of the articles enumerated from within the Empire, and ask what concessions of a preferential character they would be prepared to extend to imports from the United Kingdom over imports from foreign countries.

It is believed that correspondence of this nature would pave the way for an Imperial conference, at which the details of the proposals could be discussed, and definite arrangements agreed upon, by which in every part of the Empire there would be preferential treatment, on a moderate scale, for Inter-Imperial trade. The scheme, which is essentially in the nature of a "family arrangement" between the Colonies and Possessions and the Mother Country, would naturally be subject to alteration from time to time, as required, in the interests of all the parties concerned.

3. Assuming that the Colonies were prepared to grant preferential treatment to British trade (upon which no doubt appears to exist, in view of the resolutions of the Ottawa Conference); assuming also that India was ready to follow their example, and that they re-arranged their tariffs in favour of British Trade in a manner satisfactory to the United Kingdom, and that the formation of a fund for defence purposes was agreed upon as part of the scheme, it is fair to suppose that the Colonies and India would be able to contribute, as partly or entirely the outcome of their preferential treatment of British imports, according to their local circumstances, a sum equal in the aggregate to the net amount of additional revenue (£700,000) to be raised in the United Kingdom. In one of the appendices of the essay a suggestion for the apportionment of the £700,000 among the Colonies and India is offered. This would provide a fund of nearly £1,500,000 per annum, the joint contribution of the Colonies and India and the United Kingdom, which, it is suggested, could be used to supplement and improve the existing defences, including graving docks and coaling stations, in the outlying parts of the Empire. Among other things the maintenance of guard-ships in the leading ports of the Empire is proposed. These vessels would be useful not only for harbour defence, but in connection with the training of naval militia, which, it is believed, could readily be formed in the leading maritime ports of the Empire. This force would not only be valuable locally, but would also be available for drafting on Her Majesty's ships that might be operating in the neighbourhood of the Colonies in the time of war.

4. In order to give the Colonies a larger voice in the affairs of the Empire than they now have, and to enable them to participate in the administration of the proposed fund for defence, the formation of a Colonial Council is suggested. It would consist of the Secretaries of State for the Colonies, Foreign Affairs, India, and War, the First Lord of the Admiralty, and the Chancellor of the Exchequer, the Colonial Secretary being President. The High Commissioner for Canada and the Agents-General of the self-governing Colonies—or such other persons as the Colonies might appoint—would be members of the

Council. It would be, as its name implies, a Council in which the Colonies would have a voice through their representatives in regard to any matters arising out of the preferential trade arrangements, and upon all other subjects in which the Colonies they represented had the right to consult, or to be consulted by, the Imperial Government. The only serious obstacle of an international character in the way of carrying out the scheme is contained in the restrictive clauses of the commercial treaties with Belgium and Germany, which oblige the Colonies to admit imports from those countries on the same terms as those from the United Kingdom. By the action of the most-favoured-nation clauses in other treaties this obligation is made more or less general. As British imports from Belgium and Germany are greater than British exports to those countries, and as, even if the objectionable clauses were cancelled, the Colonies could still be made amenable to the general most-favoured-nation clauses, which form part of the treaties, it is suggested that if the proposition were made to the countries in question they would prefer the modification of the treaties rather than their abrogation. The treaties are terminable in any case on twelve months' notice. Retaliation on the part of foreign countries is not anticipated as the result of the adoption of the scheme, because their import duties are now as high, generally speaking, as they can be made, and any increase would react on the countries themselves. Besides, with the Imperial Customs Union in existence, a policy of retaliation would hardly be lightly undertaken. The following are some of the advantages which, it is claimed, would be derived by the Mother Country on the one hand, and the Colonies and Possessions on the other, from the adoption of the scheme of Commercial Federation. It would bring the Mother Country into closer union with the Colonies. By giving preferential treatment, on a moderate scale, to British trade within the limits of the Empire, the bond of unity would be material as well as sentimental. By such preference the doctrines of Free Trade that prevail in the United Kingdom would not be seriously endangered, and freer trade than at present would be made possible within the Empire. On the other hand, the British manufacturer would retain the control of the rapidly increasing Colonial markets. There would be a unity for the defence of the outlying parts of the Empire, and a Colonial Council for mutual consultation on matters of general interest. Greater attention than ever would be attracted to the Colonies. Emigration would flow in larger numbers to their shores and increase the demand for British goods. The investment of capital in the Colonies would be encouraged, and their powers of production be so increased that the United Kingdom would, year by year, depend less upon foreign sources for her food supplies.—

Attached to the essay are several statistical appendices, illustrating the commercial affairs of the Empire, and showing that, relatively speaking, the trade of the United Kingdom with the Colonies has been increasing in a greater ratio than the trade with the other parts of the world.—From "*The Imperial Institute Journal*," Vol. II., No. 18, June, 1896.

A SHORT HISTORY OF BRITISH COMMERCE.—British Commerce really commenced during the Plantagenet period. Then it was that England was first made an *entrepôt* for foreign goods, and many foreigners—chiefly craftsmen and traders—were encouraged to settle here, in order to pursue their trades. To aid them in this object they were specially protected by Statutes and Acts of Parliament. Thus, at this early period, we find the following trading companies existing:—

1. German Merchants of the Steelyard.
2. Merchants of the Staple.
3. Brotherhood of St. Thomas-à-Becket.
4. Italian and Flemish Merchants.

HENRY I., 1100-1135.—Commerce, even as early as Henry I., was encouraged by the Lords selling their charters to guilds and townsmen in order to raise money for the wars of the Crusades. In 1108 a colony of Flemings settled at Worsted, near Norwich, to introduce the woollen cloth manufacture into this country.

HENRY II., 1154-1189.—The Royal Navy of England was first established in 1166, under Henry II., the first Plantagenet King.

JOHN, 1199-1216.—Under King John, the Magna Charta, signed at Runnymede, June 19th, 1215, provided that "Cities and Towns should be protected in their liberties, and foreign merchants should be free from exactions. A year previous to this, 1214, commerce had been greatly encouraged by the charter given to London City to elect its own Mayor and Corporation Officers. For a lengthened period the English people were prohibited from exporting articles of merchandise, or home goods. This was somewhat disastrous to British trade, but the object desired was to retain here all goods for home consumption or use.

HENRY III., 1216-1272.—In 1261 the exportation of raw wool and the importation of manufactured cloth were forbidden. Owing to the Hanseatic League, which consisted of the steelyard merchants from the Rhineland and the Baltic having settled in London in 1220, and having so greatly increased their trade by attending the fairs in the chief towns of England, which at this period were the general places of sale and merchandise, commerce increased.

Hallam says, "The English had also their factories on the Baltic Coast, as far as Prussia, and in the Dominion of Denmark."

EDWARD I., 1272-1307.—The Company of Merchant Adventurers was formed in 1296 with the object to improve the manufacture of woollen goods in England, and to sell cloth at Antwerp, and other towns on the Continent of Europe.

In Edward I.'s reign, foreign merchants received a charter of justice to improve commercial interests.

EDWARD II., 1307-1327.—Under Edward II., commerce received but little assistance beyond the regulation by Treaty, 1325, of Trade with the Venetian Republic.

EDWARD III., 1327-1377.—Under Edward III., by reason of the expensive foreign wars, Parliament granted Tunnage and Poundage in 1340. This greatly hampered commerce, inasmuch as two shillings were levied upon every tun of wine imported by foreigners, and sixpence upon each pound of merchandise, either as imports or exports, and all English ships were charged according to their tonnage.

Yet it was to Edward III. that Hallam gives the title of "Father of English Commerce"—inasmuch as commerce now became, next to liberty, the leading object of Parliament; and Prof. Longman adds:—" Commerce, indeed, became so important that, following the example of his father, Edward felt the necessity of summoning a Commercial Parliament—apparently more numerous than the National Parliament itself—to discuss questions of trade. Merchants soon became so rich, and were held in such high esteem, that in the year 1363, one, Picard, Mayor of London, entertained Edward the Third, the Black Prince, and the Kings of France, Scotland, and Cyprus, with many of the nobility in London, at his house in the Vintry, where the foreign wine merchants carried on their business."

RICHARD II., 1377-1399.— During Richard II.'s reign, commerce rapidly increased in wealth, and the first Navigation Act, 1382, required, for the first time, all merchandise to be imported and exported in English ships only.

The Mariner's Compass, invented in Henry III.'s reign, so aided geographical discovery, that we note the following new places found in Africa during this reign:—

 1344—Madeira, by one Robert Macham.
 1345—Canary Islands, by the Genoese.
 1364—The Guinea Coast, by the French.
 1392—Cape of Good Hope, by the Portuguese.

HENRY IV., 1399-1413.—The great wealth of the foreign merchants caused Parliament, under Henry IV., to impose some restraint upon them, as follows:—

1. Foreign money forbidden to be circulated in England.
2. Foreign goods to be sold three months after exportation.
3. English goods to be bought with the profits.

HENRY V., 1413-1422.—In Henry V.'s reign the Royal Navy was improved, and the first *Great Harry* built.

Tunnage and poundage were again granted by Parliament during the King's life, with an additional subsidy on wool and leather.

Henry VI., 1422-61.—In the time of Henry VI., far greater progress than has hitherto been noted was seen in the growth of British Commerce; our merchant ships now exceeded 900 tons burden.

All importation of manufactured articles was forbidden by statute in 1463, under Edward IV.; and to export British coin, or plate, without the royal sanction, was treated as a felony. During this reign the trading classes remained remarkably prosperous.

Edward V. and Richard III., 1483-85.—Little was done to benefit commerce or trade under the next two reigns of Edward V. and Richard III.

Henry VII., 1485-1509.—To the Tudor monarchs belong the full glory of an extended system of British Commerce. As our Colonies date from the reign of Henry VII., who was the first English monarch to fit out an expedition of enterprise and discovery to the New World, so one of the greatest events in European history is linked with his name.

The new world of America was given to commerce, to civilisation, and to Christianity.

Christopher Columbus, the servant of Queen Isabella of Castile, was the first to discover the new continent in the West India Islands in 1492; and, five years later, John and Sebastian Cabot and others, the fearless navigators employed by Henry VII., made the important discovery of the Mainland of North America and its islands, *viz.*, Newfoundland, Labrador, New Brunswick, Nova Scotia, and Cape Breton, with other neighbouring parts of the New Continent. In right of this discovery, England claimed a large portion of North America with the surrounding fisheries, but it was not until the reign of George II.-III.

that the vast Dominion of Canada, etc., was finally annexed as a British possession. The year following the success of Cabot, 1498, in the West—Vasco-da-Gama, a Portuguese explorer, discovered the passage round the Cape of Good Hope to India, and thus opened out the great future trade route to the East.

Under Henry VII., the Royal Navy was improved, and the second *Great Harry* was built, being so named after that monarch.

In addition to coin, plate, and bullion, horses were forbidden to be exported; and, by commercial treaties, English trade was strengthened with the Flemish merchants.

The impetus given by England and Spain to foreign discovery quickly spread to other countries, so that we find during the next ten years the following important discoveries made by eminent navigators :—

1. The Eastern Coast of America, by Americus-Vespucius, 1499.
2. Brazil, by the Portuguese, 1500.
3. Ascension Island and Sumatra, 1501.
4. St. Helena, 1502.
5. Ceylon, Madagascar.

HENRY VIII., 1509-47.—The first introduction of hops from Flanders, 1524, was made under Henry VIII. During this reign hemp, flax, and currants were imported for the first time. In 1543 the first merchant ship sailed to India, and as a further improvement of the Royal Navy, Woolwich Dockyard was established, the Trinity House founded, and a Naval Department established. Hume says :—

"The foreign commerce of England, during this age, was mostly confined to the Netherlands. The inhabitants of the Low Countries bought the English commodities, and distributed them into other parts of Europe."

EDWARD VI., 1547-53.—In Edward VI.'s reign the first

English ship entered the Russian port of Archangel, and other voyages of discovery were made in the Polar districts. This opened the way to a new trade with Russia and other Eastern powers; but commerce received a slight check in the repeal of the Charter of the Hanseatic Steelyard in 1552.

MARY, 1553-58.—Upon Mary's accession this charter was again granted to the merchants of the steelyard, and the new Russia Company was incorporated in 1554. The following year, Mercator produced his chart for navigation, as the globe unfolded to show the earth's surface at a glance.

ELIZABETH, 1558-1603.—Under Queen Elizabeth, monopolies hindered commerce and trade; but in 1600, the East India Company obtained a charter to carry on trade with the East Indies.

The expeditions to the north brought about the Whale Fisheries, which afterwards became a most important source of revenue, although many valuable lives were lost in the pursuit.

Among other commercial events of this period may be mentioned:—

1. The West Coast of African Trade, introduced by Sir John Hawkins in 1562.
2. The Royal Exchange in London founded by Sir Thomas Gresham in 1571.
3. The Hanseatic Steelyard closed upon the appeal of the London merchants.
4. Sir Walter Raleigh imported Tobacco and Potatoes.

The greatest geographical discovery of this age was the treble circumnavigation of the world by Sir Francis Drake, whose name appears as the chief among a brilliant company of English navigators, including Sir Martin Frobisher, Sir John Hawkins, Sir John Davis, Sir Humphrey Gilbert, and last, though not least, Sir Walter Raleigh, who discovered

Virginia in 1585, having chosen this name for the new Colony after Elizabeth, the *Virgin Queen.*

JAMES I. AND CHARLES I., 1603-49.—The Civil Wars of the Stuart period greatly advanced civilisation. Under James I., the East India Company renewed their charter in 1609. Virginia was re-colonised, and James Town, on the river James, was founded in 1607.

The charter for the Colonisation of North America was passed in 1609, and Plymouth, the first town of the New England States, was founded, in 1620, by a body of English Non-Conformists, who called themselves "The Pilgrim Fathers."

Australia, with the New Hebrides, were discovered in 1606, and during the next ten years, much attention was given to Arctic exploration by Hudson, Baffin, and others, who named their discoveries after themselves.

In 1619, our trade with the East Indies was regulated by an important commercial treaty with the Dutch.

THE COMMONWEALTH, 1649-60.—During the great Rebellion, many persons, both Republican and Royalist, founded new Colonies in North America and elsewhere.

The great naval wars between England and Holland during 1652-3, through the valour and energy of the British Admirals Blake, Penn, and Monk, proved that Britain had advanced above Holland as "Mistress of the Seas."

The Commonwealth, by reason of internal home troubles, left commerce very much alone, although several treaties and charters were passed.

CHARLES II., 1660-85.—After the Restoration, there was a great increase of British commercial trade, as shown by the incorporation of—

1. The Hudson's Bay Company.

2. The Colonisation of Carolina, 1676, and Pennsylvania in 1683.

3. The granting of Bombay to the East India Company, 1678.

It was during this reign (Charles II.) that the Board of Trade was established in 1670.

JAMES II., 1685-88.—From 1660 to 1688, Hume says:—" The shipping of England was more than doubled during these 28 years;" but, strange to say, so great was the change in the general decline of resources that Hallam writes:—" In 1696—*the very nadir of English prosperity*—it was hardly possible to pay the fleet from month to month, and a national bankruptcy seemed to be near at hand."

This shows a falling off of commercial trade, as compared with the glorious period before the Revolution.

WILLIAM AND MARY, 1689-1702.—In 1698, under William III., a rival East India Company was founded, but four years later the old and the new company united.

The nine years' war with France, from 1689 to 1697, greatly interfered with commerce and colonisation, until the grand alliance of England, Holland, and Germany in 1701 put matters upon a surer financial basis.

ANNE, 1702-14.—Under good Queen Anne, we have the war of the Spanish Succession by England, Holland, and Germany, against France and Spain, which lasted for eleven years from 1702-13. As a result of this war, the Treaty of Utrecht, 1713, gave to Great Britain, Hudson's Bay, Nova Scotia, Newfoundland, St. Christopher's, Gibraltar, and Minorca, among other commercial advantages.

GEORGE I., 1714-27.—To the Hanoverian Period belongs the chief growth of our Colonial Empire, although this Period was unfortunate at the commencement by the bursting of the South Sea Bubble in 1720, which gave a great shock to public credit.

GEORGE II., 1727-60.—Under George II., the Seven Years War, 1756-63, gave England the final possession of Canada, Cape Breton Island, Nova Scotia, Tobago, Dominica, St. Vincent, Grenada, and Senegal. While a considerable portion of India became subject to the British Crown by the victories of Clive, Hastings, and Wellesley.

GEORGE III., 1760-1820.—We have now to record the first great British loss of dominion: the United States, including many of our earliest Colonies, were lost by the war of American Independence, 1775.

The Colonists' Congress passed the Declaration of Independence against Great Britain. Thirteen States—Massachusetts, New Hampshire, Connecticut, Rhode Island, New York, New Jersey, Delaware, Maryland, Pennsylvania, Virginia, North Carolina, South Carolina, and Georgia were included as breaking away from the Mother Country.

In 1788, the Penal Settlement of Port Jackson, on Botany Bay, in New South Wales, was formed. The convicts after a time became settlers in their new home until transportation was discontinued in 1840.

The reign of George III. added greatly to our foreign possessions, in addition to the American and other French territories ceded by the Treaty of Paris in 1763. The Falkland Islands were settled in 1766; Sierra Leone and Norfolk Islands in 1789. The Seychelles were gained by conquest from the French in 1796. Ceylon was taken from the Dutch the same year, and Malta wrested from the French in 1800. Tasmania was settled in 1803. Cape Colony lost to the Dutch in 1806. Heligoland became a British possession, and was added in 1807. Mauritius in 1810, with Ascension Island and a further portion of India annexed in 1815.

GEORGE IV., 1820-30.—The first Free Trade measure passed was Huskisson's Reciprocity of Duties Bill, in 1823, under George IV. This reign also saw the duty reduced on the importation of silk; the laws extended for the import and export of wool; the Corn Laws modified, and foreign grain brought in at a fixed duty; the currency regulated; and the northern limits of North America laid down by Sir John Franklin and others.

WILLIAM IV., 1830-37.—The overland route to India was first used in 1834, and the Liverpool and Manchester Railway opened in 1830, followed by the London and North Western line to London.

VICTORIA, 1837.—The grandest period of British Commerce has been reserved for the present reign of Queen Victoria. In spite of the commercial panics of 1847, 1857, and 1866, so great advances have been made by the invention of the electric telegraph and telephone, the perfection of the British postal system, and the development of steamships and railways, that no other period has possessed such facilities for the encouragement of foreign and home commerce and trade. In a little time the advance was marked by millions sterling upon our export and import trade.

Again, the absence of foreign wars has enabled Britain, during a lengthened period of peace, to devote both capital and interest to the extension of her commerce.

Commercial Treaties have been signed with nearly every civilised country in the world, and the system of international trade has opened up markets for British manufactured goods in all quarters of the globe; while we in return, receive, by means of our excellent merchant navy, their raw produce, with food supplies of every kind.

Lastly, the marked extension of the British Dominions, since 1837, has provided new spheres of British trade to such a degree, that as above stated (pp. 10 and 12) we are now quite independent of the foreign trade of all other Powers, inasmuch as our possessions are at last able to supply every home need, whether animal, vegetable, or mineral productions, food supplies, or raw or manufactured goods.

"Queen Victoria's reign has been one long series of accessions to the Empire. Our Colonies are young, healthy, prosperous, and loyal: the magnificent Empire of India has been added to and consolidated; Africa has been explored, and is being colonised; and all over the whole globe the English are pushing their way; even the river Ob, so long deemed impracticable, has been opened to commerce by an Englishman. Steam has practically annihilated distance; and the old six months' voyage to India died the death when, on October 31, 1845, Lieutenant Waghorn practically demonstrated the feasibility of his 'overland route' to India. . . . . The cutting of the Suez Canal brought India and Australia, China and Japan, far nearer to us—you can now get to Bombay in 25 days; Melbourne in 45 days (going to Brindisi will knock off 8 days); and the Ocean Greyhounds will whisk you to New York in $5\frac{1}{2}$ days."—From "The Longest Reign in English History," by John Ashton, by permission of the author.—*English Illustrated Magazine.*

## TABLE OF BRITISH POSSESSIONS, WITH DATES, ETC.

| Col. | Date. | Name. | How Acquired. | Sovereign. | Area in Sq. Miles. | Population. | Seat of Government, etc. |
|---|---|---|---|---|---|---|---|
|  | 1497 to 1583 | Labrador, New Brunswick, Cape Breton, Nova Scotia, in North America, Newfoundland, discovered by Sir H. Gilbert, | Discovered by Cabot and others, | Henry VII.-VIII., Edward VI., Mary and Elizabeth | — | — | — |
| R. | 1584 | Virginia, discovered by Sir W. Raleigh, | Settlement, 1623, & Settlement as a colony in 1607, | Eliz. and James I. | 42,200 | 197,335 | S. John's. Declared Independent as one of the United States in 1776. |
|  | 1609 | Bermudas, |  | Eliz. and James I. | 18,000 | 15,743 | Hamilton. |
| C. | 1618 | Gambia and the Gold Coast, | Settlement, | James I. | 29,460 | 1,440,650 | Bathurst and Cape Coast Castle. |
|  | 1620 | Massachusetts, | " | " | — | — | Declared Independent as one of United States in 1776. |
| R. | 1623 | St. Kitts (West Indies), | " | " | — | — | Basseterre. |
|  | 1623 | New Hampshire, | " | " | — | — | Declared Independent in 1776 as one of the United States. |
| R. | 1624 | Barbadoes (West Indies), | " | Charles I. | 166 | 180,000 | Bridgetown. |
| R. | 1629 | Bahamas, etc., | " | " | 5,450 | 48,600 | Nassau. |
| R.R. | 1632 | Antigua and Montserrat, | " | " | 208 | 38,300 | S. John and Plymouth. |
|  | 1635 | Connecticut; 1634, Maryland; Rhode Island, 1636, | " | " | — | — | Declared Independent as United States in 1776. |
|  | 1650 | North Carolina, | " | The Commonwealth | — | — | " |
| R. | 1655 | Jamaica and Turk's Island, | Captured from Spaniards, Settlement, | " | 4,193 | 617,446 | Kingstown. |
| R. | 1650 | Anguilla (West Indies), | " | Charles II. | 35 | 309 | Roadtown. |
| R. | 1666 | Virgin Islands, | " | " | 57 | 4,639 | " |
|  | 1664 | Delaware; 1680 South Carolina; Pennsylvania, 1686, | Ceded by the Dutch Settlement, | " | — | — | Declared Independent as United States in 1776. |
|  | 1667 | Hudson Bay Territory, | Granted to a Company, | " | — | — | " |
| C. | 1670 | Honduras, | By Treaty with Spain, | " | 7,562 | 31,500 | Belize. |
| C. | 1673 | S. Helena, | Ceded by Dutch, | " | 47 | 5,000 | Jamestown. |
|  | 1674 | New York and New Jersey, | " | " | — | — | Declared Independent as United States in 1776. |
| C. | 1704 | Gibraltar, | Taken from Spaniards, | Queen Anne | 3 | 24,000 | Gibraltar. |
|  | 1753 | Georgia, | Settlement, | George II. | — | — | Declared Independent as United States in 1776. |
| R. | 1757 | Battle of Plassey. Rise of Indian Empire, |  | George II. |  |  |  |
|  | 1759 | Canada (Dominion), | Conquest, Taken from French, | " | 3,400,000 | 5,271,000 | Ottawa. |

## TABLE OF BRITISH POSSESSIONS, WITH DATES, ETC.—*Continued.*

| Col. | Date. | Name. | How Acquired. | Sovereign. | Area in Sq. Miles. | Population. | Seat of Government, etc. |
|---|---|---|---|---|---|---|---|
| — | 1763 | Canada (finally ceded), Cape Breton, Nova Scotia, Tobago, Grenada, S. Vincent, Dominica and Senegal, with other French possessions, | Cession by Treaty of Fontainebleau, | George III. | — | — | — |
| C. | 1763 | Florida, etc., | Ceded by Spain, | " | — | — | — |
| C. | 1766 | Falkland Isles, | " | " | 7,500 | 1,890 | Port Stanley. |
| C. | 1787 | Sierra Leone, | Settlement, | " | 3,000 | 75,000 | Freetown. |
| R. | 1787 | New South Wales; Norfolk Island, | " | " | 310,700 | 1,145,400 | Sydney. |
| C. | 1789 | Andaman Islands, | East India Co. to form a penal settlement for India, | " | — | — | — |
| C. | 1785 to 1819 | Straits Settlements, | | " | 1,472 | 506,000 | Singapore. |
| — | 1794 | Seychelles, Amirante, Rodrigues, and the Chagos Islands, | — | " | | | Port Victoria. |
| C. | 1796 | Ceylon, | Conquest from French, | " | 25,365 | 3,000,000 | Colombo. |
| C. | 1797 | Trinidad, | " from Dutch, | " | 1,754 | 206,000 | Trinidad. |
| R. | 1800 | Malta with Gozo and Comino, | " from Spanish, | " | 117 | 159,000 | Valeta. |
| R. | 1803 | Guiana, | " from French, | " | 109,000 | 270,000 | Georgetown. |
| R. | 1806-77 | Tasmania, | " from Dutch, | " | 26,215 | 137,000 | Hobartown. |
| | | Cape Colony with annexation, | Originally Conquest from Dutch, | " | 219,700 | 1,527,000 | Cape Town. |
| C. | 1806 | Auckland, Howe, etc., Islands, | Discovery, | " | 329 | Intended for Settlement. | |
| C. | 1807 | Heligoland, ceded to Germany, [1890, | Conquest from Danes, | " | | | Ceded to Germany in 1890. |
| C. | 1810 | Mauritius, | " from French, | " | 708 | 378,000 | Port Louis. |
| C. | 1815 | Ionian Islands, | Cession, | " | | | Ceded to Greece in 1864. |
| C. | 1815 | Ascension Island, | Annexation (Naval Admin.), | " | 35 | 160 | Georgetown. |
| I.E. | — | A considerable portion of India, | Conquest, | " | | | — |
| C. | 1818 | Tristan d'Acunha, | Annexation, | " | Small, | Uninhabited | |
| I.E. | 1824 | Singapore, | Purchase, | George IV. | (See Straits Sett.), now | Capital of Straits Settlement. | |
| | 1826 | Indian Provinces of Assam, Aracan and Tenasserim, etc., | Cession, | " | | | — |
| R. | 1829 | Western Australia, | Settlement, | " | 1,060,000 | 40,000 | Perth |

## TABLE OF BRITISH POSSESSIONS, WITH DATES, ETC.—*Continued.*

| Col. | Date. | Name. | How Acquired. | Sovereign. | Area in Sq. Miles. | Population. | Seat of Government, etc. |
|---|---|---|---|---|---|---|---|
| R. | 1835 | Victoria (Australia), Sep. from New S. Wales, 1851, | Colonized, | William IV. | 87,884 | 1,000,000 | Melbourne. |
| R. | 1836 | S. Australia, | Settlement, | " | 903,690 | 313,000 | Adelaide. |
| C. | 1839 | Aden, | Conquest from Sultan of Aden, | " | 68 | 40,000 | Aden. |
| R. | 1839 | New Zealand, | Proclaimed a B. Colony, | Victoria | 104,458 | 626,700 | Wellington. |
| C. | 1842 | Falkland Islands, | " | " | 6,500 | 2,000 | Port Stanley. |
| R. | 1843 | Natal, | " | " | 18,750 | 443,000 | Pietermaritzburg. |
| I.E. | 1843 | India: Sindh and other portions, | Annexation, | " | *Whole Indian Empire,* | | |
| I.E. | 1849 | " The Punjab, | " | " | *B. India,* 1,064,720 | 202,000,000 | } Calcutta. |
| I.E. | 1855 | " Nagpore, | " | " | *Prot. States,* | *Prot. States,* | |
| I.E. | 1856 | " Oudh, | " | " | 714,758 | 55,000,000 | |
| C. | 1846 | Labuan Island, | Cession, | " | (*See Borneo*) | 1881 & 1890 | |
| R. | 1849 | Vancouver Island, | Settlement, Hudson Bay Co., | " | (*See Dom. of Canada.*) | | Victoria). |
| C. | 1850 | Portions of Gold Coast, W. Africa, | Purchased from Danes, | " | (*See 1618,* 21 | *Gambia and* (*See Aden*), | *The Gold Coast*). |
| C. | 1854 | Kuris Muris Islands, | Cession, | " | | (*See Aden*), | |
| C. | 1857 | Perim, etc., | Occupation, | " | | | |
| B. | 1858 | British Columbia, | Made a B. Colony, | " | (*See Dom. of Canada*), | | Victoria on Vancouver Island. |
| R. | 1859 | Queensland (Australia), | Sep. from New South Wales, | " | 668,497 | 323,000 | Brisbane. |
| — | 1860 | Kowloon, | Annexed to Hong Kong by Tr'ty with Chinese, | " | (*See Hong Kong*), | | |
| C. | 1861 | Lagos Island, West Yoruba, | Cession from King, | " | 1,071 | 87,000 | |
| — | 1866 | British Kaffraria, | Annexation to Cape, | " | (*See Cape Colony*), | | |
| — | 1870 | Elmina and Dutch Guiana, | — | " | | | |
| — | 1871 | West Griqualand, | Annexed to Cape Colony, | " | (*See Cape Colony*), | | |
| Pro. | 1871 | Basutoland, Govt. Col., 1884, | Annexation, | " | 10,290 | 218,000 | Maseru. |
| C. | 1874 | Fiji Islands, | " | " | 7,754 | 126,000 | Suva. |
| C. | 1881 | Rotumah Islands, | " | " | 31,000 | 200,000 | Sandakau. |
| — | 1881 | N. British Borneo and Labuan, including Brunei and Sarawak, | By Charter N. Borneo Co., | " | 38,000 | 300,000 | Kutching. |
| — | — | Cyprus, | Occupied, | " | 3,584 | 209,291 | Nicosia. |
| — | 1886 | Upper Burmah & Shan States, | Annexation, | " | — | — | — |

TABLE OF BRITISH POSSESSIONS, WITH DATES, ETC.—*Continued.*

| Col. | Date. | Name. | How Acquired. | Sovereign. | Area in Sq. Miles. | Population. | Seat of Government, etc. |
|---|---|---|---|---|---|---|---|
| C. | 1884-8 | New Guinea (B), | Annexation, | Victoria | 86,487 | 135,000 | Port Moresby. |
| C. | 1886 | British Bechuanaland, | Protectorate, made a Crown Colony, now a part of Cape Colony, | ,, | 52,000 | 44,000 | Vryburg. |
| C. | 1886 | Kermadec Islands, | Occupied by Rear-Admiral Tryon, | ,, | 21 | Uninhabited | (*See New Zealand*.) |
|  | 1886 | Socotra, | Annexation, | ,, | 1,382 | 10,000 | Socotra. |
| P. | 1887 | Tongaland, | ,, | ,, | 5,200 | 30,000 | — |
| P. | 1887 | Zululand, | Conquest, | ,, | 9,900 | 150,000 | Ulundi. |
| P. | 1888 | British (N. & S.) Zambesia, including Matabeleland, Mashonaland, and N. Bechuanaland, | Granted by Charter to the B. South African Co., | ,, | 300,000 | 360,000 | Pretoria. |
|  | 1889 | Christmas, Fanning and Penrhyn Islands, | — | ,, | (*See Straits Settlements*), | — | — |
|  | 1889 | Hervey or Cook Islands, | Placed under Government of the Straits Settlements, | ,, |  |  | Singapore. |
| P. | 1889 | Nyasaland, | Protectorate Established | ,, | 42,700 | ? | — |
| P. | 1889 | Uganda, } | Ceded by Treaty with B. E. African Co., | ,, |  |  | — |
| P. | 1889 | Unyoro,  } |  | ,, | 70,000 | 5,000,000 | Mengo. |
| P. | 1890 | British E. Africa Co., Somali Protectorate, Zanzibar, and Pemba, | *Protectorate established*, | ,, | 985 | 377,986 | Mombasa. |
| P. | 1890 | Labuan, incorporated in N. Borneo (see above), | Borneo (see above), | ,, | — | — | — |
| P. | 1890 | Swaziland, | Convention (Eng. and Dutch Nations), | ,, | 8,000 | 60,000 | — |
| P. | 1891 | Niger and Oil Rivers (1885), | Protectorate formed by the Royal Niger Co., | ,, | 400,000 | 25,000,000 | Asaba. |
|  | 1893 | Natal obtained responsible Government (See 1843). |  |  |  |  |  |

# MAIL INTELLIGENCE AND POST AND CABLE RATES THROUGHOUT BRITISH POSSESSIONS.

| PLACE. | POST RATES. Letters. For a Letter per ½ oz. | POST RATES. Book-packets. For Newspapers or other printed matter per 2 ozs. | POST RATES. Parcels. | MAILS. Despatch from London. | MAILS. Homeward Mails due at Port of Arrival in United Kingdom. | MAILS. No. of Days in transit. | CABLE TELEGRAMS. Per Word. |
|---|---|---|---|---|---|---|---|
| ADEN | 2½d. | ½d. | Same as India (s. d.) | *Via*:—German Packet: M., Twice Monthly<br>Brindisi: E., every Friday | Twice Monthly<br>Every Tuesday | 11 | 3/9 E. |
| BAHAMAS | 2½d. | ½d. | Not exceeding 1 lb. - 0 10<br>For each additional pound or fraction of a pound up to 11 lb. 0 9 | E., every Wednesday; Aftn., every Saturday | Uncertain | 10 | 2/5 A.A., D.U.S. P.N.Y. W.U., C. |
| BARBADOS | 2½d. | ½d. | Not exceeding 1 lb. - 0 8<br>For each additional pound or fraction of a pound up to 11 lb. 0 8 | *Via*:—Southampton: M., Twice Monthly.<br>*U.S.A.*:—British Packet: E., every Wednesday; Aftn., every Saturday; uncertain from New York<br>German Packet: M., every Wednesday; and Weekly Mail; uncertain from New York<br>American Packet: M., every Saturday; uncertain from New York | Twice Monthly | 12 | 9/11 A.A. D.U.S. P.N.Y. W.U. C. |
| BERMUDAS | 2½d. | ½d. | Not exceeding 1 lb. - 0 9<br>For each additional pound or fraction of a pound up to 11 lb. 0 9 | *Via*:—New York: Aftn., Twice Monthly; and *supplementary*<br>Halifax: E., every Thursday; Aftn., every Saturday | Twice Monthly<br>Uncertain | 15 | 4/- *id.* |
| BRITISH GUIANA | 2½d. | ½d. | Not exceeding 1 lb. - 0 10<br>For each additional pound or fraction of a pound up to 11 lb. 0 8 | By British Packet: M., Twice Monthly<br>By French Pkt.: E., 7, and *supplementary* M., 8 each month | Twice Monthly<br>25 each month | 13¾ | 12/2 *id.*<br>9/2 E., D.S. |
| BRITISH HONDURAS | 2½d. | ½d. | Not exceeding 1 lb. - 0 8<br>For each additional pound or fraction of a pound up to 11 lb. 0 8 | *Via New York*:—British Packet: E., every Wed., and *supplementary* Aftn., every Sat.<br>German Packet: Same as Barbados }<br>American Packet: M., every Sat. } | Every Sunday<br>Uncertain | 16 | 1/3 (by post from New Orleans). |
| BRITISH INDIA | 2½d. | ½d. | Not exceeding 1 lb. - 1 0<br>For each additional pound or fraction of a pound up to 11 lb. 0 8 | *Via*:—Brindisi: E., every Friday | Every Tuesday | Bombay 16¼<br>Calcutta 19¼<br>Madras 18¾ | 4/- E. I.E.<br>(Burmah 4/2.) |
| BRITISH NEW GUINEA | 2½d. | ½d. | Same as Queensland | Same as Queensland | Same as Queensland | | |
| BRIT. NORTH BORNEO | 2½d. | ½d. | Not exceeding 1 lb. - 0 11<br>For each additional pound or fraction of a pound up to 11 lb. 0 8 | *Via*:—Brindisi / French Pkt. } Same as Hong Kong | Same as Hong Kong | — | 5/9 (by post from Singapore). |
| CANADA | 2½d. | ½d. | Not exceeding 1 lb. - 0 8<br>For each additional pound or fraction of a pound up to 11 lb. 0 6 | By Canadian Packet: E., every Thursday<br>*Via U.S.A.*:—British Packet: E., every Wed. Aftn., every Sat. | Every Tuesday<br>Sunday & Thursday | Halifax 9<br>Montreal 9<br>Ottawa 9½<br>Quebec 9 | 1/- A.A., P.N.Y., W.U., D.U.S. C.<br>B.C. & Vanc'ver, 1/6 |

# MAIL INTELLIGENCE AND POST AND CABLE RATES THROUGHOUT BRITISH POSSESSIONS—*Continued.*

| PLACE. | POST RATES. | | | | MAILS. | | | CABLE TELEGRAMS. |
|---|---|---|---|---|---|---|---|---|
| | Letters. For a Letter per ½ oz. | Book-packets. | For Newspapers or other printed matter per 2 oz. | Parcels. | Despatch from London. | Homeward Mails due at Port of Arrival in United Kingdom. | No. of Days in transit. | Per Word. |
| | | | | s. d. | | | | |
| CANADA—*con.* | 2½d. | ½d. | | | German Packet: Same as Barbados American Packet: M., every Saturday | Same as Barbados | Vanc'ver 15 Winnip'g 13 | Manitoba, 1/6 N.W. Territory, 1/6 |
| CAPE COLONY | 2d. | ½d. | | Not exceeding 1 lb. - 0 9 For each additional pound or fraction of a pound up to 11 lb. 0 9 | M., every Saturday | Thursday Every Monday | 19 | Cape Town, 5/- Other places, 5/2 E., D.S. |
| CEYLON | 2½d. | ½d. | | Not exceeding 1 lb. - 0 9 For each additional pound or fraction of a pound up to 11 lb. 0 6 | *Via:*—Brindisi: E., Twice Monthly Naples: E., French Packet: E., *supplementary* following mornings German Packet: M., Twice Monthly | Twice Monthly | 18 | 4/1 E. I.E. |
| FALKLAND ISLANDS | 2½d. | ½d. | | Not exceeding 1 lb. - 0 9 For each additional pound or fraction of a pound up to 11 lb. 0 8 | *Via:*—Tilbury: E., At Intervals Liverpool: E., *supplementary via* Lisbon | Monthly Mails | 31 | 4/6 (by post from Monte Video). |
| FIJI ISLANDS | 2½d. | ½d. | | Not exceeding 2 lb. - 1 0 For each additional pound or fraction of a pound up to 11 lb. 0 8 | *Via:*—Vancouver: E., Monthly Mails; *supplementary* Italy: Same as New South Wales S. Francisco: Aftn., Monthly Mails | Same as New South Wales | 3 | 4/11 (by post from New South Wales). |
| GIBRALTAR | 2½d. | ½d. | | Not exceeding 1 lb. - 0 8 For each additional pound or fraction of a pound up to 11 lb. 0 4 | *Via France:*—Morning and Evening | Daily | 4½ | /-4½ E. D.S. |
| GOLD COAST HONG KONG | 2½d. 2½d. | ½d. ½d. | | Same as Sierra Leone Not exceeding 1 lb. - 0 10 For each additional pound or fraction of a pound up to 11 lb. 0 6 | E., Every Friday *Via:*—Brindisi: E., Twice Monthly French Packet: E., *supplementary* German Packet: M., Monthly Mails Vancouver: E., | Every Tuesday Twice Monthly Monthly Mails | 22 *Via:*— Brindisi 32 Vancouver 40 | 7/- G.N. I.E. |
| JAMAICA | 2½d. | ½d. | | Not exceeding 1 lb. - 0 9 For each additional pound or fraction of a pound up to 11 lb. 0 9 | San Francisco: Aftn., Twice Monthly, with additional Mails *Via:*—Southampton U.S.A. | Uncertain Same as Barbados | 16 | 5/10 (same as Barbados). |
| LEEWARD ISLANDS | 2½d. | ½d. | | Not exceeding 1 lb. - 0 7 For each additional pound or fraction of a pound up to 11 lb. 0 7 | Same as Barbados | Same as Barbados | Antigua 14½ D'mica13½ St. Kitts 15½ | Antigua, 9/10 Dominica, 9/2 (same as Barbados) |

## MAIL INTELLIGENCE AND POST AND CABLE RATES THROUGHOUT BRITISH POSSESSIONS—*Continued.*

| PLACE. | POST RATES. | | | MAILS. | | | CABLE TELEGRAMS. |
|---|---|---|---|---|---|---|---|
| | Letters For a Letter per ½ oz. | Book-packets | Parcels (s. d.) | Despatch from London. | Homeward Mails due at Port of Arrival in United Kingdom. | No. of Days in transit. | Per Word. |
| MALTA | 2½d. | ½d. | Not exceeding 1 lb. — 0 8<br>For each additional pound or fraction of a pound up to 11 lb. 0 4 | *Via :*—Italy : M., Daily | Daily | 4 | 6d. E. |
| MASHONALAND | 2½d. | ½d. | Not exceeding 1 lb. — 2 9<br>(Including Matabeleland)<br>For each additional pound or fraction of a pound up to 7 lb. 2 9 | M., every Saturday | Every Monday | — | 5/5 |
| MAURITIUS | 2½d. | ½d. | Not exceeding 3 lb. — 3 2<br>Exceeding 3 lb. but not exceeding 7 lb. — 3 9<br>Exceeding 7 lb. but not exceeding 11 lb. — 4 4 | *Via :*—Marseilles : E., 8, 23 each month ; *supplementary* following mornings | 1, 10 each month | 25 | /9 E.E.<br>F. |
| | | | Not exceeding 3 lb. — 2 0<br>Exceeding 3 lb. but not exceeding 7 lb. — 3 0<br>Exceeding 7 lb. but not exceeding 11 lb. — 4 0 | *Via :*—Ceylon : E., Monthly Mails ; *supplementary* following Morning | Uncertain | | |
| NATAL | 2½d. | ½d. | Not exceeding 1 lb. — 0 9<br>For each additional pound or fraction of a pound up to 11 lb. 0 9 | M., every Saturday | Every Monday | 22 | Durban 5 E.<br>D.S.<br>Other places 5/2<br>1/- (same as Canada). |
| NEWFOUNDLAND | 2½d. | ½d. | Not exceeding 1 lb. — 0 9<br>For each additional pound or fraction of a pound up to 11 lb. 0 6 | E., Twice Monthly | Dates not fixed | 9 | |
| NEW SOUTH WALES | 2½d. | ½d. | Not exceeding 2 lb. — 1 0<br>For each additional pound or fraction of a pound up to 11 lb. 0 6 | *Via :*—Brindisi : E., Twice Monthly<br>Naples : E., Monthly Mails<br>Vancouver : E., Monthly Mails *supplementary* E.<br>San Francisco: Aftn., Monthly Mails French Packet : E., *supplementary* following mornings<br>German Packet : M.,<br>Same as New South Wales. | Every Tuesday *via* Brindisi & Naples alternately<br>Uncertain<br>Monthly Mails | 36 | 4/11 E.<br>I.E. |
| NEW ZEALAND | 2½d. | ½d. | Same as New South Wales | | Same as New South Wales | Wellington 35<br>Auck'd (*via* S. Franc'o) | 5/2 E.<br>I.E. |
| QUEENSLAND | 2½d. | ½d. | Same as New South Wales | *Via :*—Brindisi and Torres Straits : E., Monthly Mails (subsequent dates not fixed) | Dates not fixed | [33] | |

## MAIL INTELLIGENCE AND POST AND CABLE RATES THROUGHOUT BRITISH POSSESSIONS—*Continued*.

| PLACE. | POST RATES. | | | MAILS. | | | CABLE TELEGRAMS. |
|---|---|---|---|---|---|---|---|
| | Letters. For a Letter per ½ oz. | Book-packets. For Newspapers or other printed matter per 2 ozs. | Parcels. | Despatch from London. | Homeward Mails due at Port of Arrival in United Kingdom. | No. of Days in transit. | Per Word. |
| QUEENSLAND—*continued* | 2½d. | ½d. | *s. d.* | Brindisi or Naples: E., every Friday <br> Vancouver <br> San Francisco } Same as New South Wales <br> French Packet <br> M., Monthly Mails | Every Tuesday via Brindisi or Naples alternately. <br> Same as New South Wales | 39 | 9/- E. <br> I.E. |
| ST. HELENA | 2½d. | ½d. | Same as Barbados | | Monthly Mails | 17 | 5/- (by post from Cape Colony). |
| SIERRA LEONE | 2½d. | ½d. | Not exceeding 1 lb. - 0 9 <br> For each additional pound or fraction of a pound up to 11 lb. 0 9 <br> Same as New South Wales | By British Packet: E., every Friday and Monthly Mails | Every Tuesday | 14 | 6/9 E. <br> D.S. |
| S. AUSTRALIA | 2½d. | ½d. | Not exceeding 1 lb. - 0 9 <br> For each additional pound or fraction of a pound up to 11 lb. 0 9 | Same as Hong Kong | Same as New South Wales | 34 | 4/9 E. <br> I.E. |
| STRAITS SETTLEMENTS (SINGAPORE) | 2½d. | ½d. | Not exceeding 1 lb. - 0 9 <br> For each additional pound or fraction of a pound up to 11 lb. 0 9 | Same as Hong Kong | Same as Hong Kong | Singapore 26 <br> Penang 24 | 5/9 } I.E. <br> 5/0 } E. <br> 5/5 } I.E. |
| TASMANIA | 2½d. | ½d. | Not exceeding 2 lb. - 1 0 <br> For each additional pound or fraction of a pound up to 11 lb. 0 6 | Same as New South Wales | Same as New South Wales | 37 | |
| TRINIDAD | 2½d. | ½d. | Same as Barbados | *Via*:—Southampton { Same as Barbados <br> U.S.A. <br> *Via*:—French Packet: E., 7, 24, supplementary M., 8, 25 each month | Same as Barbados. | 13¾ | 10/5 (same as Barbados). |
| VICTORIA | 2½d. | ½d. | Same as New South Wales | Same as New South Wales | 17, 25 each month <br> Same as New South Wales | 35 | 4/10 E. <br> I.E. |
| W. AUSTRALIA | 2½d. | ½d. | Same as New South Wales | *Via*:—Brindisi } Same as New South Wales <br> Naples | Same as New South Wales | 32 | 4/9 E. <br> I.E. |
| WINDWARD ISLANDS | 2½d. | ½d. | Same as Barbados | Same as Barbados | Same as Barbados | Grenada 13¾ <br> St. Vinc't 12¾ <br> S. Lucia 12¾ | 9/11 A.A. <br> 9/6 D.U.S. <br> 9/2 P.N.Y. <br> W.U. <br> C. |

CABLE TELEGRAPH COMPANIES—E., Eastern; I.E., Indo-European; A.A., Anglo-American; D.U.S., Direct United States; P.N.Y., Paris and New York; W.U., Western Union; C., Commercial; G.N., Great Northern; D.S., Direct Spanish; F., via France.

## PASSENGER STEAMSHIP LINES TO THE COLONIES AND INDIA.

| Name of Colonies, etc. | Steamship Lines. | Ports of Departure. | Duration of Voyage. Days. | Ports of Arrival. | Reference to other Pages for further details. |
|---|---|---|---|---|---|
| Aden | Peninsular and Oriental | (i) London | 18 | Aden | For Dates of Departure and Arrival see the *Imperial Institute Monthly Journal*, 6d. |
|  | North German Lloyd | (iii) Southampton | 19 | Aden |  |
|  | Messageries Maritimes | (vi) Marseilles | 10 | Aden |  |
|  | German E. Africa Line | Hamburg | 26 | Aden |  |
| Antigua | Royal Mail S. P. | Southampton | 14 | St. Johns |  |
| Bahamas | Ward Line | New York | 3 | Nassau |  |
| Barbados | Royal Mail S. P. | Southampton | 12 | Bridgetown |  |
|  | Harrison Line | Liverpool | 15 | Barbados |  |
| Bermudas | Quebec Steamship | New York | 2 | Hamilton |  |
| British Burma | Bibby Line | (v) Liverpool | 30 | Rangoon |  |
| British E. Africa | Messageries Maritimes | (vi) Marseilles | 18 | Zanzibar |  |
|  | German E. Africa Line | Hamburg | 36 | Zanzibar |  |
| British Guiana | Royal Mail S. P. | Southampton | 14 | Georgetown |  |
| British Honduras | Special Steamer | New Orleans, U.S.A. (once a week) | — | Belize |  |
| British New Guinea |  | Cooktown (Queensland), every four weeks | — | Port Moresby |  |
| Canada | Allan Line | Liverpool | 8 to 9 | Quebec and Montreal / St. John (Newfoundland) and Halifax |  |
|  | do | Liverpool | 8 to 9 | Halifax, N.S. and St. John, NB. |  |
|  | Furness Line | London | 9 to 12 | Quebec and Montreal |  |
|  | Dominion Line | Liverpool | 8 to 9 | Quebec and Montreal |  |
|  | Beaver Line | Liverpool | 9 to 10 | Quebec and Montreal |  |
| Cape Colony | Union Line | Southampton | 15 to 23 | Cape Town |  |
|  | Castle Mail Packet | (ii) London | 16 to 23 | Cape Town |  |
|  | N. Zealand Shipping Co. | London | 22 | Cape Town |  |
|  | Shaw, Savill & Albion Co. | London | 22 | Cape Town |  |
|  | Aberdeen Line | London | 23 | Cape Town |  |
|  | Clan Line | Liverpool | 25 | Cape Town |  |
|  | British & Colonial S.N.C. | London | 25 | Cape Town |  |
| Ceylon | Peninsular and Oriental | (i) London | 25 | Colombo |  |
|  | North German Lloyd | (iii) Southampton | 25 | Colombo |  |
|  | Messageries Maritimes | (vi) Marseilles | 15 to 17 | Colombo |  |
|  | Orient Line | (iv) London | 25 | Colombo |  |

## PASSENGER STEAMSHIP LINES TO THE COLONIES AND INDIA—*Continued.*

| Name of Colonies, etc. | Steamship Lines. | Ports of Departure. | Duration of Voyage. Days. | Ports of Arrival. | Reference to other pages for further details. |
|---|---|---|---|---|---|
| Ceylon—*Continued* | Bibby Line | (v) Liverpool | 25 | Colombo | For Dates of Departure and Arrival see the *Imperial Institute Monthly Journal*, 6d. |
|  | Clan Line | Liverpool | 27 | Colombo |  |
| Cyprus | Messageries Maritimes | Marseilles | 13 | Larnaca |  |
| Falkland Islands | Kosmos Steamers | Punta Arenas (Straits of Magellan) | 2 | Stanley |  |
| Fiji Islands | N. Zealand Shipping Co. | London | 53 | Suva |  |
| Gambia, The | British & African S.N. Co. | Liverpool | 12 | Bathurst |  |
|  | African S.S. | Liverpool | — | Bathurst |  |
| Gibraltar | Peninsular and Oriental | London | 4 | Gibraltar |  |
|  | Orient Line | (ie) London | 5 | Gibraltar |  |
| Grenada | Royal Mail S. P. | Southampton | 13 | St. George's |  |
| Hong Kong | Peninsular and Oriental | London | 39 | Hong Kong |  |
|  | Canadian Pacific S. L. | Vancouver | 22 | Hong Kong |  |
|  | North German Lloyd | (iii) Southampton | 36 | Hong Kong |  |
|  | Messageries Maritimes | Marseilles | 27 to 30 | Hong Kong |  |
| India | Peninsular and Oriental | (i) London | 24 | Bombay |  |
|  | do | do. | 32 | Calcutta |  |
|  | Harrison Line | Liverpool | 30 | Calcutta |  |
|  | Anchor Line | Liverpool | — | Bombay and Kurrachee |  |
|  | do | Liverpool | — | Calcutta |  |
|  | Hall Line | Liverpool | 33 | Kurrachee |  |
|  | do | Liverpool | 35 | Bombay |  |
|  | Messageries Maritimes | (iv) Marseilles | 16 | Bombay |  |
|  | Clan Line | Liverpool | 25 | Bombay |  |
|  | do | Liverpool | 30 | Madras and Calcutta |  |
|  | City Line | Liverpool | 30 | Calcutta |  |
|  | do | Liverpool | 26 | Bombay |  |
| Jamaica | Royal Mail S. P. | Southampton | 16 | Kingston |  |
| Lagos | British African S. N. Co. | Liverpool | 21 | Lagos |  |
|  | African Steamship Co. | Liverpool | 21 | Lagos |  |
| Leeward Islands (*see* Antigua). |  |  |  |  |  |
| Malta | Peninsular and Oriental | London | 8 | Vuletta |  |

## PASSENGER STEAMSHIP LINES TO THE COLONIES AND INDIA—Continued.

| Name of Colonies, etc. | Steamship Lines. | Ports of Departure. | Duration of Voyage. Days. | Ports of Arrival. | Reference to other Pages for further details. |
|---|---|---|---|---|---|
| Mauritius | Messageries Maritimes | Marseilles | 29 & 24 | Port Louis | For Dates of Departure and Arrival see the *Imperial Institute Monthly Journal*, 6d. |
| Natal | Castle Line | (ii) London | 44 | Port Louis | |
| | do | (ii) London | 20 to 28 | Port Natal | |
| | Union Line | Southampton | 20 to 28 | Port Natal | |
| | British & Colonial S. N. C. | London | 41 | Port Natal | |
| | German E. Africa Line | Hamburg | 62 | Durban | |
| | Aberdeen Direct Line | London | 27 | Durban | |
| New South Wales | Peninsular and Oriental | (i) London | 47 | Sydney | |
| | Orient Line | (iv) London | 45 | Sydney | |
| | Shaw, Savill & Albion Co. | London | 45 | Sydney | |
| | North German Lloyd | (vi) Southampton | 43 | Sydney | |
| | Messageries Maritimes | (vi) Marseilles | 34 | Sydney | |
| | Canadian-Austral | Vancouver | 24 | Sydney | |
| | Aberdeen Line | London | 47 | Sydney | |
| | Union S. S. of N. Zealand | San Francisco | 26 | Sydney | |
| | American & Austr'l'n Line | San Francisco | 26 | Sydney | |
| New Zealand | New Zealand Shipping | London | 44 | Wellington | |
| | Shaw, Savill & Albion Co. | London | 45 | Auckland | |
| | Union S. S. of N. Zealand | San Francisco | 21 | Auckland | |
| | American & Austr'l'n Line | San Francisco | 21 | Auckland | |
| Queensland | Aberdeen Line | London | — | Brisbane | |
| | Queensland Royal Mail | London | 56 | Brisbane | |
| Sierra Leone | African Steamship | Liverpool | 12 to 15 | Freetown | |
| | British & African S.N. Co. | Liverpool | 12 to 15 | Freetown | |
| South Australia | Peninsular and Oriental | (i) London | 42 | Adelaide | |
| | Orient Line | (ii) London | 39 | Adelaide | |
| | North German Lloyd | (iii) Southampton | 40 | Adelaide | |
| | Messageries Maritimes | (iv) Marseilles | 29 | Adelaide | |
| | Aberdeen Line | London | 44 | Adelaide | |
| | N. Zealand Shipping Co. | London | 44 | Adelaide | |
| | Shaw, Savill & Albion Co. | London | 46 | Adelaide | |
| | Bethell, Gwyn & Co. | London (monthly) | 48 | (Port Darwin) | |

## PASSENGER STEAMSHIP LINES TO THE COLONIES AND INDIA—*Continued.*

| Name of Colonies, etc. | Steamship Lines. | Ports of Departure. | Duration of Voyage. Days. | Ports of Arrival. | Reference to other pages for further details. |
|---|---|---|---|---|---|
| Straits Settlements | Peninsular and Oriental | London | 31 / 33 | Penang / Singapore | For Dates of Departure and Arrival see the *Imperial Institute Monthly Journal*, 6d. |
| Tasmania | Messageries Maritimes | (vi) Marseilles | 20 & 23 | Singapore | |
| | N. Zealand Shipping Co. | London | 40 | Hobart | |
| | Shaw, Savill & Albion Co. | London | 40 | Hobart | |
| Trinidad | Royal Mail S. P. | Southampton | 14 | Port of Spain | |
| | Harrison Line. | Liverpool | 17 | Trinidad | |
| Victoria | Peninsular and Oriental | (i) London | 44 | Melbourne | |
| | Orient Line | (iv) London | 41 | Melbourne | |
| | Aberdeen Line | London | 42 | Melbourne | |
| | Messageries Maritimes | (vi) Marseilles | 31 | Melbourne | |
| | N. Zealand Shipping Co. | London | 42 | Melbourne | |
| | Shaw, Savill & Albion Co. | London | 42 to 44 | Melbourne | |
| Western Australia | Peninsular and Oriental | (i) London | 39 | King George's Sound | |
| | Orient Line | (iv) London | 36 | Albany | |
| | Messageries Maritimes | (vi) Marseilles | 26 | King George's Sound | |
| | North German Lloyd | Southampton | 36 | Albany | |
| | Bethell, Gwyn & Co. | London | 42 | Fremantle | |
| | Bethell, Gwyn & Co. | Liverpool (every fortnight) | 55 | Fremantle (via Singapore) | |
| | North German Lloyd | Southampton | 36 | Albany | |
| Windward Islands | (see Grenada) | | | | |

(i) Passengers by the Overland Route (*via* Brindisi) may leave London on the Friday evening in the following week. (ii) Leaving Southampton following day. (iii) Passengers may join the ship 8 days later at Genoa, and 10 days later at Naples. (iv) Passengers by the Overland Route (*via* Naples) may leave London on the Friday evening in the week following these dates. (v) Leaving Marseilles 7 days later. (vi) Passengers can reach Marseilles in 24 hours from London.

# TABLE OF DISTANCES

BETWEEN THE VARIOUS PORTS

ACCORDING TO THE

ROUTES TAKEN BY THE STEAMERS

OF THE

**Peninsular and Oriental Steam Navigation Company.**

122, LEADENHALL STREET, E.C.

*(By special permission of the P. & O.S.N.C.)*

Malta to Port Said direct .. 935 miles.

| Port | From London by sea, direct. | From London by sea, via Naples. | From London by sea, via Marseilles. | London (if via Plymouth add 90) | Plymouth | Gibraltar | Marseilles | Malta | Naples | Trieste | Venice | Ancona | Brindisi | Alexandria | Port Said | Ismailia | Aden | Bombay | Colombo | Madras | Calcutta (calling at Madras) | Calcutta (omitting Madras) | Penang | Singapore | Hong Kong | Shanghai | Nagasaki | Hiogo | Yokohama | King Geo.'s Sound | Adelaide | Melbourne |
|---|---|---|---|---|---|---|---|---|---|---|---|---|---|---|---|---|---|---|---|---|---|---|---|---|---|---|---|---|---|---|---|---|
| Plymouth | | | | 295 | | | | | | | | | | | | | | | | | | | | | | | | | | | | |
| Gibraltar | | | | 1299 | 1054 | | | | | | | | | | | | | | | | | | | | | | | | | | | |
| Marseilles | | | | 1993 | 1748 | 694 | | | | | | | | | | | | | | | | | | | | | | | | | | |
| Malta | | | | 2280 | 2035 | 981 | | | | | | | | | | | | | | | | | | | | | | | | | | |
| Naples | | | | 2272 | 2027 | 873 | 468 | | | | | | | | | | | | | | | | | | | | | | | | | |
| | | | | Via Brindisi | Via Brindisi | Via Brindisi | | Via Brindisi | | | | | | | | | | | | | | | | | | | | | | | | |
| Trieste | | | | 3100 | 2855 | 1801 | | 820 | | | | | | | | | | | | | | | | | | | | | | | | |
| Venice | | | | 3035 | 2790 | 1736 | | 755 | | 65 | | | | | | | | | | | | | | | | | | | | | | |
| Ancona | | | | 2910 | 2665 | 1611 | | 630 | | 190 | 125 | | | | | | | | | | | | | | | | | | | | | |
| Brindisi | | | | 2640 | 2395 | 1341 | | 360 | | 460 | 395 | 270 | | | | | | | | | | | | | | | | | | | | |
| Alexandria | | | | 3465 | 3220 | 2166 | | 1185 | | 1285 | 1220 | 1095 | 825 | | | | | | | | | | | | | | | | | | | |
| Port Said | 3215 | 3382 | 3501 | 3570 | 3325 | 2271 | 1508 | 1290 | 1110 | 1390 | 1325 | 1200 | 530 | 155 | | | | | | | | | | | | | | | | | | |
| Ismailia | 3258 | 3425 | 3544 | 3613 | 3368 | 2314 | 1551 | 1333 | 1153 | 1433 | 1368 | 1243 | 973 | 198 | 43 | | | | | | | | | | | | | | | | | |
| Aden | 4610 | 4777 | 4896 | 4965 | 4720 | 3666 | 2903 | 2685 | 2505 | 2785 | 2720 | 2595 | 2325 | 1550 | 1395 | 1352 | | | | | | | | | | | | | | | | |
| Bombay | 6274 | 6441 | 6560 | 6629 | 6384 | 5330 | 4567 | 4349 | 4169 | 4449 | 4384 | 4259 | 3989 | 3214 | 3059 | 3016 | 1664 | | | | | | | | | | | | | | | |
| Colombo | 6703 | 6870 | 6989 | 7058 | 6813 | 5759 | 4996 | 4778 | 4598 | 4878 | 4813 | 4688 | 4418 | 3643 | 3488 | 3445 | 2093 | 875 | | | | | | | | | | | | | | |
| Madras | 7313 | 7480 | 7599 | 7668 | 7423 | 6369 | 5606 | 5388 | 5208 | 5488 | 5423 | 5298 | 5028 | 4253 | 4098 | 4055 | 2703 | 1485 | 610 | | | | | | | | | | | | | |
| Calcutta (calling at Madras) | 8083 | 8250 | 8369 | 8438 | 8193 | 7139 | 6376 | 6158 | 5978 | 6258 | 6193 | 6068 | 5798 | 5023 | 4868 | 4825 | 3473 | 2255 | 1380 | 770 | | | | | | | | | | | | |
| Calcutta (omitting Madras) | 7967 | 8134 | 8253 | 8322 | 8077 | 7023 | 6260 | 6042 | 5862 | 6142 | 6077 | 5952 | 5682 | 4907 | 4752 | 4709 | 3357 | 2139 | 1264 | | | | | | | | | | | | | |
| | | | | | | | | | | | | | | | | | | | | Via Colombo | Via Colombo | Via Colombo | | | | | | | | | | |
| Penang | 7981 | 8148 | 8267 | 8336 | 8091 | 7037 | 6274 | 6056 | 5876 | 6156 | 6091 | 5966 | 5696 | 4921 | 4766 | 4723 | 3371 | 2153 | 1278 | 1888 | 2658 | 2542 | | | | | | | | | | |
| Singapore | 8362 | 8529 | 8648 | 8717 | 8472 | 7418 | 6655 | 6437 | 6257 | 6537 | 6472 | 6347 | 6077 | 5302 | 5147 | 5104 | 3752 | 2534 | 1659 | 2269 | 3039 | 2923 | 381 | | | | | | | | | |
| Hong Kong | 9799 | 9966 | 10085 | 10154 | 9909 | 8855 | 8092 | 7874 | 7694 | 7974 | 7909 | 7784 | 7514 | 6739 | 6584 | 6541 | 5189 | 3971 | 3096 | 3706 | 4476 | 4360 | 1818 | 1437 | | | | | | | | |
| Shanghai | 10669 | 10836 | 10955 | 11024 | 10779 | 9725 | 8962 | 8744 | 8564 | 8844 | 8779 | 8654 | 8384 | 7609 | 7454 | 7411 | 6059 | 4841 | 3966 | 4576 | 5346 | 5230 | 2688 | 2307 | 870 | | | | | | | |
| Nagasaki | 10866 | 11033 | 11152 | 11221 | 10976 | 9922 | 9159 | 8941 | 8761 | 9041 | 8976 | 8851 | 8581 | 7806 | 7651 | 7608 | 6256 | 5038 | 4163 | 4773 | 5543 | 5427 | 2885 | 2504 | 1067 | | | | | | | |
| Hiogo | 11255 | 11422 | 11541 | 11610 | 11365 | 10311 | 9548 | 9330 | 9150 | 9430 | 9365 | 9240 | 8970 | 8195 | 8040 | 7997 | 6645 | 5427 | 4552 | 5162 | 5932 | 5816 | 3274 | 2893 | 1456 | | 389 | | | | | |
| Yokohama | 11801 | 11768 | 11897 | 11956 | 11711 | 10657 | 9894 | 9676 | 9496 | 9776 | 9711 | 9586 | 9316 | 8541 | 8386 | 8343 | 6991 | 5773 | 4898 | 5508 | 6278 | 6162 | 3620 | 3239 | 1802 | | 735 | 346 | | | | |
| | | | | | | | | | | | | | | | | | | | | | | | Via Colombo | Via Colombo | Via Colombo | Via Colombo | Via Colombo | Via Colombo | Via Colombo | | | |
| King Geo.'s Sound | 10093 | 10260 | 10379 | 10448 | 10203 | 9149 | 8398 | 8168 | 7988 | 8268 | 8203 | 8078 | 7808 | 7033 | 6878 | 6835 | 5483 | 4265 | 3390 | 4000 | 4770 | 4654 | 4668 | 5049 | 6486 | 7356 | 7553 | 7942 | 8288 | | | |
| Adelaide | 11100 | 11267 | 11386 | 11455 | 11210 | 10156 | 9393 | 9175 | 8995 | 9275 | 9210 | 9085 | 8815 | 8040 | 7885 | 7842 | 6490 | 5272 | 4397 | 5007 | 5777 | 5661 | 5675 | 6056 | 7493 | 8363 | 8560 | 8949 | 9295 | 1007 | | |
| Melbourne | 11585 | 11752 | 11871 | 11940 | 11695 | 10641 | 9878 | 9660 | 9480 | 9760 | 9695 | 9570 | 9300 | 8525 | 8370 | 8327 | 6975 | 5757 | 4882 | 5492 | 6262 | 6146 | 6160 | 6541 | 7978 | 8848 | 9045 | 9434 | 9780 | 1492 | 485 | |
| Sydney | 12145 | 12312 | 12431 | 12500 | 12255 | 11201 | 10438 | 10220 | 10040 | 10320 | 10255 | 10130 | 9860 | 9085 | 8930 | 8887 | 7535 | 6317 | 5442 | 6052 | 6822 | 6706 | 6720 | 7101 | 8538 | 9408 | 9605 | 9994 | 10340 | 2052 | 1045 | 560 |

ETHNOLOGY—ORIGIN OF THE BRITISH PEOPLE—In the absence of reliable historical records from the earliest ages, we are alone enabled to find a clue to the past among the archæological remains of a powerful race, together with the modern light thrown upon ancient inscriptions, tumuli, etc. See Prof. Rey's "*Celtic Britain.*"

True, we have the fable of Pytheas, who is supposed to have visited Britain during the Fourth Century, B.C.; with Julius Cæsar's romantic description of the inhabitants of Britain, previous to the Christian era; yet these may scarcely be regarded as reliable sources. Next follows Tacitus, who clearly describes two or more distinct races as dwellers in Britain, *e.g.*, "interior and coast lands;" while Gildas, a British monk, in his weird song, tells of the forlorn state of Britain after the departure of the Romans.

The Venerable Bede, who wrote two centuries later, unfortunately used conjecture rather than facts; and the Saxon Chronicle, some two centuries afterwards, cannot be altogether trusted. Then we meet with a remarkable gap until the Twelfth Century, when Geoffry of Monmouth wrote his strange history of the English race, which is more peculiar than correct.

Professor Burrows, in his recent work, "Commentaries on the History of England,"[1] states, "The people of Great Britain are not only composed of more various elements than any other in Europe, but those elements have been more gradually compounded and ultimately more completely fused. That circumstance, perhaps, considering what races formed the compound, is at the root of the position which they and their offshoots hold."

The great Aryan waves gave to Europe the following

---

[1] "Commentaries on the History of England," by Professor Burrows. W. Blackwood & Sons, 1893.

races:—The Celtic in the west, the Teutonic in the centre, and the Slavonic in the east.

These Aryan races further drove before them, in their progress from east to west, an earlier race called the Turanians, among whom were the Ivernians, who inhabited Britain, together with the Cave men, the remnant of a still earlier race. Some of the Ivernians were driven as far west as Ireland, hence the name "Erin" or "Ernia."

Now these Celtic peoples were composed of two distinct branches, *viz.* :—

> 1. The Gaels, or Mountain Men, who were fierce warriors.
> 2. The Brythons, or Men of the Plains, who were lovers of peace and agriculture.

Undoubtedly it was these two branches of Celtic inhabitants which the Romans found dwelling in Great Britain, B.C. 54-55.

The Gaels undoubtedly were nearly related to the Gaels or Celts who inhabited Gaul. (*See* Cæsar "De Bello Gallico.") They appeared to have understood the uses of metals, and though they wore but little clothing, and probably stained their bodies with vegetable dyes, *e.g.*, woad, which made them appear fierce savages, yet in times of peace they dwelt in huts, and were semi-civilised, although much engaged in the chase.

The Roman Invasions of Britain, from Cæsar, 54 B.C., to Agricola, 78 A.D., changed everything, and the war-like Celts or Gaels were driven to the utmost portions of the Island —Scotland, Wales, and Cornwall—where they remained, still as bitter enemies to Rome, under the names of Picts, or painted men of the North (Scotland); the Scots of Ireland; and the Cymry, or Strangers of Wales; while the Brythons, or more peaceful Celts, accepted the yoke of Rome and learned civilisation, agriculture, law, and government. The walls of Agricola and Hadrian were erected to prevent the war-like Picts from plundering the more northern portion of Roman Britain.

When the Roman armies were withdrawn from Britain, the Brythons were left well-nigh powerless to resist any foreign invaders; hence the success of the Teutons or English, who came in shoals from the western mainland of Europe until they gained possession of Britain. Mr. J. R. Green, in his excellent "History of the English People," describes these Teutonic invaders as under:—

1. Engle, or English folk, who dwelt on the banks of the rivers Elbe and Weser.
2. Jutes, from Jutland, who were found to the north of the English.
3. Saxons, dwelling to the south of the English, and occupying a wide tract stretching from the Elbe to the Rhine.

These three Teuton tribes combined, and became the English race. He says, "The blood-bond gave both its military and social form to old English society. Kinsmen fought side by side in the hour of battle. . . . So they dwelled side by side on the soil . . . . and each 'wick,' or 'ham,' or 'stead,' or 'tun' took its name from the kinsmen who dwelt in it" (p. 3). The same author in another volume, "The Making of England," divides their history into four periods:—

1. The Conquest of the Saxon Shore, *e.g.*, the Jutes, under Hengist and Horsa, in the centre; and north and south of these, the East and South Saxons; and finally the Angles.
2. The Conquest of Angles from the Forth to the Thames, with that of the West Saxons, from the Thames along the South Coast of Britain.

3. The Heptarchy, or Government of the Invaders.
4. The Triarchy, which, later still, merged into one kingdom and ruler, under Egbert.

In this way *England* was made.

A later period tells the story of the Invasion by the Norsemen, or Fingaels (*Fairmen*), who, sometime in the Eighth Century, had settled in the Scottish Islands, the Isle of Man, and the Eastern Coast of Ireland.

Next came the Danes or Dubhgaels (*Darkmen*). These two united were known as Ostmen (*Eastmen*), and they ravaged the French Coast, and invaded England, giving the English but little rest from warfare. Their object appears to have been more plunder and destruction than settlement, and it rested with Alfred the Great to restore order, and to quell the power of these fierce sea-warriors.

The season of bloodshed and disorder ends with the Danish sovereignty, and the Celtic races of Wales (Wealas) displayed their hatred of the English by leaguing with the Norsemen against them.

A number of minor incidents, partly religious and partly historical, brought about the later conquest by the Normans, under the Duke William, their leader, which, though it ushered in a horde of strangers, as foreign retainers of the new king, William the Conqueror, did not annihilate the habits or manners of the English race, other than the planting of a new system of royal service, called the Feudal System, by which all land was declared to belong to the king, and the rights of his subjects to hold estates was vested in service, etc.

THE ENGLISH LANGUAGE.—Under the Normans, the language of the poor in England was unchanged, while the Court and Church adopted the more fashionable French-Latin tongue. Hence it is that the history of the English language, now so widely known through the civilized world, is plainly and simply the history of the English people. It is a fusing together of many tongues, and her literature in this way has become greatly enriched by the gradual welding together of so many different peoples, minds, and languages.

Dr. Angus, in his excellent manual, *Handbook of the English Tongue* (p. 4), says:—"The English, though a composite language, is derived mainly from the Anglo-Saxon. The classic languages, Greek and Latin, and their modern representatives, the French, Italian, and Spanish, have contributed largely to produce the English language; but Anglo-Saxon is the chief source. To it may be traced both the *matter* of our tongue, the words that compose it, and many of the *forms* which these words assume." There are, roughly speaking, about 40,000[1] words in ordinary everyday use among the English people. Of this number, it is generally estimated that five-eighths are Saxon; two-eighths or one-fourth are Latin, either direct or through the French; and one-eighth miscellaneous in origin, and varying greatly in importance. Of these last, the Keltic stands first. Then follows a numberless class, including the Norse or Danish, Greek, and Hebrew, with contributions from nearly every known tongue, by reason of Britain's continuous intercourse with foreign nations. After these root words, we have a large number of naturalized and trade terms taken from persons and places, etc.; but these may hardly be considered as strictly belonging to the English Language in the same historical sense as the former classes.

---

[1] If we include Scientific and Terms of Art, the numbers rise to 80,000 words.

# PART II.

## THE BRITISH ISLANDS.

INTRODUCTION.—In the Atlantic Ocean, lying off the western shores of the Continent of Europe, there may be seen a small and irregular cluster of islands, about 2000 in number, of which not quite one-fifth are inhabited, and forming the most important Archipelago in the world. It is known by the name of the British Isles.

This remarkable group of islands belongs to the Continent of Europe, from which they are separated by the North Sea or German Ocean on the East, and on the South by the English Channel and the Straits of Dover, which at its narrowest part is but twenty-one miles in breadth. They are situated in a central position of the great land and water Hemispheres, which naturally gives them unrivalled facilities for commerce.

Great Britain, the largest island in Europe, and *the seventh*[1] *in size among the islands of the world*, is the chief or queen of this group, and the sister island lying off its western coast, and separated from it by the Irish Sea, and St. George's Channel, which ranks next to it in size, is called Ireland.

There is a marked contrast in the coast-line of these islands on the east and south compared with the

---

[1] A comparison of the Islands of the World gives the following in order of size :—Australia, New Guinea, Borneo, Sumatra, Niphon or Hondo, Madagascar, and Great Britain.

IMPERIAL BRITAIN. MAP II.

west and north. These latter shores are fully exposed to the Atlantic Ocean, and, consequently, the coast is wonderfully broken and irregular, being clothed as it were with a fringe of smaller islands, varying in size from mere barren rocks, rising abruptly from the water, to the larger islands of the Western Group, called the Hebrides, situated off the coast of Scotland, or the Island of Achill, lying off the western shores of Ireland.

CONNECTION WITH THE CONTINENT.—Many thousands of years ago, the British Islands formed a part of the mainland of Europe. This is no mere conjecture; but it may be proved by a complete chain of evidence, such as:—

1. The shallowness of the Ocean between England and France.
2. The corresponding nature of the rocks upon the opposite shores, *e.g.*, the soft chalk hills of Northern France are continued in the Downs of Kent; the harder granite rocks of Brittany occur in a continuous range in Cornwall.
3. The formation of the rocks, and the particular shape of the remaining portions of land in the North of Scotland and the outlying islands of the Orkney and Shetland groups, prove a connecting link with the Continent on the shores of Norway.

Professor Meiklejohn, in his *Comparative Geography of the British Islands*, states:—"The Submarine Plateau, of which the British Isles are prominent or outstanding parts, is a vast continuation of the European Continent, and stretches from the corner of the Bay of Biscay to the north of the Shetland Isles. It drops, in a long steep cliff, to the deeper depths of the Atlantic Ocean, a little to the West of Ireland" (p. 33).

CLIMATE.—The great Gulf Stream, or "Atlantic River of Warm Water in the Sea," greatly moderates the extreme cold of winter in the British Islands beyond places, both in the Eastern and Western Hemispheres, having the same position as regards latitude. These are much colder, and the winter season more severely prolonged than with us. Again, the influence of the sea breezes upon all parts of the British Isles tends to lower the summer heat. On the whole, then, these islands may be described as possessing a most variable climate yet of equable temperature, the average degrees registered being from 45° to 52°. The rainfall is naturally excessive from their position in the Atlantic Ocean. The average is 30 inches, and the heaviest fall is along the Western Coasts.

POSITION.—The principal island, called GREAT BRITAIN, is somewhat irregular in shape. It is situated between parallels of latitude 49° and 61° North of the Equator, and longitude 2° East and 8° West of Greenwich. It includes the two kingdoms of England and Scotland, and the principality of Wales.

IRELAND is situated about 60 miles to the west of Great Britain, lying in the Atlantic Ocean between parallels of north latitude 51° 26' and 55° 23', and west longitude 5° 20' and 10° 26'.

EXTENT.—(a.) GREAT BRITAIN.—The extreme length, measured from Dunnet Head in the north to Start Point in Devonshire, is 600 miles, and in breadth it varies from 280 miles between Lowestoft and St. David's Head, to about 35 miles between the Forth and the Clyde. The area, 88,340 square miles, may be sub-divided thus:— England, 51,000 square miles; Wales, 7,363 square miles; Scotland, 30,000 square miles.

(b.) IRELAND.—This island is more compact in shape than Great Britain. Its length, from Fair Head in the northeast to Mizen Head in the south-west, is about 300 miles, and its greatest breadth, from Howth Head to Slyne Head, is 200 miles. Its area is 32,520 square miles, or, roughly speaking, about one-third the size of Great Britain.

(*c.*) The total area of the smaller coast islands is about 260 square miles, so that the total area of the British Isles is estimated at 120,883 square miles, or equal in extent to about one-thirtieth of that of Europe.

The chief islands and groups on the coasts are :—

SCOTLAND. 3,700 sq. miles in area.
- On the North Coast.
  - The Orkneys—67 islands, including Pomona, Hoy, North and South Ronaldshay, Westray, etc.
  - The Shetlands — 100 islands, including Mainland, Yell, Unst, etc.
- On the West Coast.
  - The Hebrides—(Outer and Inner groups) a large number, including Lewis, Skye, Mull, Jura, Islay, N. and S. Uist, etc.
  - Islands of the Clyde—The principal being Arran, Bute, Great and Little Cumbray.
- On the East Coast.
  - Few and unimportant, except for Lighthouse Stations, as Bass Rock, Bell Rock, May Isle, and Inchkeith.

ENGLAND.
- On the East Coast.
  - Holy Island, the Farne Islands, and Coquet. Sheppey and Thanet are only Islands in name, and part of the County of Kent.
- On the South Coast.
  - Isle of Wight, Lundy, the Scilly Isles, 145 in number (6 inhabited).
- On the West Coast.
  - Anglesey, Holyhead, Bardsey, Walney, with the Isle of Man, etc.

IRELAND. All small.
- On the North Coast—Rathlin and Tory.
- On the South Coast—Clear, Spike, Saltee Islands, etc.
- On the East Coast—Dalkey, Ireland's Eye, Lambay.
- On the West Coast—N. Aran, Achill, Clare, Valentia.

POPULATION.—The Population of the British Isles in 1891 was as follows :—

GREAT BRITAIN.
- England, 27,501,362
- Wales, - 1,501,163   } 29,002,525
- Scotland, 4,025,647— 4,025,647   } 33,028,172
- Ireland, 4,704,750

37,732,922

The Census of 1891 gave the following interesting statistics of the occupation of the inhabitants of the British Isles :—

1. 
   - 45 per cent. of the people were employed.
   - 55 per cent. of the people were unemployed, including wives and children, etc.
2. Of the 45 per cent. employed :—

   100
   - 54 per cent. were in towns engaged in trade and manufacture.
   - 15 per cent. were in the country engaged in agriculture and fishing.
   - 14 per cent. were in domestic and other service.
   - 9 per cent. were in commerce.
   - 8 per cent. were professional persons.

EXPENDITURE.—*The annual expenditure* or cost of the Government of the United Kingdom was £103,360,000 in 1897. This large sum includes the interest on money borrowed by the Government, popularly called "The National Debt," to the amount of £25,000,000 ; the expenses of maintenance for the Army and Navy, which may be estimated at another £36,000,000 ; the postal and telegraph services, together with elementary education, and the Courts of Law and Justice, etc., etc.

REVENUE.—The sum annually voted by Parliament to meet this expenditure, and known as the Budget of the Chancellor of the Exchequer, is raised by means of Customs Duties on the imported goods ; Excise Duties on luxuries, such as beer, spirits, etc., produced at home; taxes on incomes, houses, property, and land ; stamp duties on all legal documents and money payments, with the receipts of the postal and telegraph services of the country. In 1897, £103,949,885.

GOVERNMENT.—The form of Government is a limited hereditary monarchy, which consists of the Sovereign as head and chief, aided by the two Houses of Parliament—the Lords and the Commons—without whose joint approval no measure may become law, although the Executive have

Houses of Parliament, London.

large powers of discretion. These powers are vested in the Cabinet or Crown Ministers for the time being, who are responsible to both the Sovereign and the people during their period of office.

"The Cabinet," says Mr. Gladstone, "is the threefold hinge that connects together for action the British Constitution of King or Queen, Lords and Commons. Every one of its members acts in these capacities: as Administrator of a Department of State, as member of its Legislative Chamber, and as a confidential adviser of the Crown."— *Gleanings of Past Years.*

"The House of Lords, or the Upper House, consists of (*exclusive of* 14 *Minors*) 6 Princes of the Blood, 2 Archbishops, 22 Dukes, 22 Marquises, 121 Earls, 30 Viscounts, 24 Bishops, 387 Barons, 16 Scottish Representative Peers elected for each Parliament, and 28 Irish Representative Peers elected for life (2 Irish Representative Peers are also included as Peers of England), in all, 658."—*Whitaker's Almanack*, 1898.

The House of Commons consists of 670 Members of Parliament:—England, 465; Wales, 30; Scotland, 72; Ireland, 103; who are elected by the people.

Under our present Queen Victoria, whom may God preserve, the British Parliament has passed through 20 Ministries, as follows:—

ADMINISTRATIONS OR MINISTRIES DURING QUEEN VICTORIA'S REIGN.

| Year | Minister | No. | Year | Minister | No. |
|---|---|---|---|---|---|
| 1835. | Viscount Melbourne | 2nd. | 1868. | William E. Gladstone | 1st. |
| 1841. | Sir Robert Peel | 2nd. | 1874. | { Benjamin Disraeli / Earl of Beaconsfield } | 2nd. |
| 1846. | Lord John Russell | 1st. | | | |
| 1852. | Earl of Derby | 1st. | 1880. | William E. Gladstone | 2nd. |
| 1852. | Earl of Aberdeen | 1st. | 1885. | Marquis of Salisbury | 1st. |
| 1855. | Lord Palmerston | 1st. | 1886. | William E. Gladstone | 3rd. |
| 1858. | Earl of Derby | 2nd. | 1886. | Marquis of Salisbury | 2nd. |
| 1859. | Lord Palmerston | 2nd. | 1892. | William E. Gladstone | 4th. |
| 1865. | Earl Russell | 2nd. | 1894. | Lord Rosebery | 1st. |
| 1866. | Earl of Derby | 3rd. | 1895. | Marquis of Salisbury | 3rd. |
| 1868. | Benjamin Disraeli | 1st. | | | |

THE BRITISH ISLANDS. 55

The present Parliament is also the fourteenth of Her Most Gracious Majesty's reign.

The Executive Power, or Cabinet of Ministers, is given below:—

THE STATE:—CHIEF OFFICERS WITH STIPENDS ATTACHED TO THE OFFICE.

ENGLAND.

| | |
|---|---|
| * Prime Minister. | |
| * Chancellor of the Exchequer | £5,000. |
| * Lord High Chancellor | 10,000. |
| * Lord Privy Seal | 2,000. |
| * Lord President of the Council | 2,000. |
| * Secretary of State for Home Department | 5,000. |
| * ,, ,, Foreign Affairs | 5,000. |
| * ,, ,, Colonies | 5,000. |
| * ,, ,, War | 5,000. |
| * ,, ,, India | 5,000. |
| * First Lord of the Admiralty | 4,500. |
| * President of the Board of Trade | 2,000. |
| * President of Local Government Board | 2,000. |
| President of Board of Agriculture | 2,000. |
| * Chancellor of the Duchy of Lancaster | 2,000. |
| * Postmaster-General | 2,500. |
| General Commanding-in-Chief | 6,632. |
| Paymaster-General | Unpaid. |
| * Chief Commissioner of Works | 2,000. |
| * Vice-President of Council for Education | 2,000. |
| Attorney-General | 7,000. |
| Solicitor-General | 6,000. |
| * First Lord of the Treasury | 5,000. |
| Judge Advocate General | By Fees. |

HER MAJESTY'S HOUSEHOLD.

| | |
|---|---|
| Lord Steward | £2,000. |
| Lord Chamberlain | 2,000. |
| Master of the Horse | 2,500. |
| Master of the Buckhounds | 1,500. |
| Treasurer of the Household | 904. |
| Comptroller of the Household | 904. |

SCOTLAND.

| | |
|---|---|
| * Secretary for Scotland and Keeper of the Great Seal | £2,000. |
| Lord Advocate | 5,000. |
| Solicitor-General | 2,000. |

## IRELAND.

| | |
|---|---|
| Lord-Lieutenant | £20,000. |
| Lord Chancellor | 8,000. |
| *Chief Secretary and Keeper of the Privy Seal | 4,425. |
| Attorney-General for Ireland | 5,000. |
| Solicitor-General for Ireland | 2,000. |

* The asterisk marks the Cabinet Ministers.

ARMY AND NAVY.—The British Army at home is decidedly a small one, if taken in comparison with the greater armies of Europe, but the Navy is the largest and most powerful in the world. Yet, if we include the Colonial forces and foreign troops under the British flag, we represent the third largest Standing Army in the world, China and Russia alone being greater in numerical strength.

Britain has gained for herself the title of "Mistress of the Seas" solely through the immense power and strength of her Navy; and it is the ambition of our Naval Authorities not only to fully maintain this high standard of power in the future, but to increase, and improve, our naval defences, and ships of war, that we shall alone be able to stand against an attack made by the United Navies of the World.

*The following table will show the strength of the British Army and Navy with that of foreign countries:—*

| Country. | Area Square Miles. | Population. | Standing Army. | Navy Warships. |
|---|---|---|---|---|
| British Empire | 9,000,000 | 327,000,000 | 715,683 | 632 |
| United States | 2,935,004 | 62,622,250 | 27,038 | 79 |
| Russia | 8,450,081 | 108,787,235 | 800,000 | 247 |
| Germany | 208,670 | 49,428,470 | 584,734 | 191 |
| France | 204,146 | 38,218,903 | 550,429 | 353 |
| Austro-Hungary | 204,219 | 41,359,202 | 391,675 | 133 |
| Italy | 110,623 | 30,947,307 | 279,982 | 200 |
| Spain | 194,744 | 17,545,160 | 120,000 | 126 |
| Norway & Sweden | 295,182 | 6,785,898 | 57,553 | 111 |
| Ottoman Empire | 1,710,000 | 39,500,000 | 180,000 | 102 |
| China | 4,468,750 | 300,000,000 | 1,200,000 | 154 |
| Japan | 162,655 | 41,390,000 | 273,268 | 117 |

*N.B.*—1. The Standing Army figures are those quoted in time of peace, but the war standard of most of the countries is considerably higher.

2. Again, the numbers quoted above are for Imperial Britain, or including the vast territories of Britain throughout the world. The home Army, not including Militia, Cavalry, Volunteers, or Army Reserve, is only 160,000 men.

The British Empire is distinctly a maritime power, so that it is but of little importance if her home Army falls below the huge armies of continental powers, so long as her Navy maintains the highest place to guard her shores and vast foreign possessions.

THE ARMY.—The total strength of the British Army numbers 160,000 men, including officers and privates. Then we have the Army Reserve, numbering 80,100; the Militia another 140,000 men; the Volunteers, 263,000; and the Cavalry Yeomanry, 12,000. So that, roughly estimated, the entire British Army is about 655,000 men, and these numbers do not include the great Native Indian Army, and the Colonial Militia and Volunteer Forces ready to protect our foreign possessions in all parts of the world. It has been said:—

"War has been revolutionised. Rifled small arms, breech-loading and with magazines, rifled cannon carrying many miles, with gunpowder getting effete, owing to newer and more powerful explosives, range-finders, heliographs, field-telegraphs, and balloons all belong to this reign; while the famous 'Wooden Walls of Old England,' of the Georgian era, would be knocked into matchwood in a very few minutes by the guns of, or torpedoes fired from, an armour-plated steamship."—From "The Longest Reign in English History," by kind permission of the author, Mr. John Ashton. (*English Illustrated Magazine.*)

ARMY BOARD.—Upon the retirement of H.R.H. the Duke of Cambridge, Nov. 1st, 1895, from the command of the

British Army, the Government established an Army Board of five members in place of the one man in command. Each of these five members is respectively responsible for his own department to the Secretary of State for War, who is the representative of the Government.

The Army Board consists of the Commander-in-Chief (Viscount Wolseley, for five years); the Adjutant-General; the Quarter-Master General; the Inspector-General of Fortifications; and the Inspector-General of Ordnance.

ARMY STATIONS.—The chief Army Stations at home include Aldershot, Belfast, Birmingham (*Small Arms Factory*); Brixton (*Military Prison*); Chatham, Chelsea (*Duke of York's School*); Chester, Colchester, Cork, Curragh, Devonport, Dover, Dublin, Edinburgh, Enfield Lock (*Small Arms Factory*); Hounslow, Hythe (*School of Musketry*); London (*Horse Guards, numerous Barracks, and the Tower*); Netley (*Army Medical School*); Portsmouth, Shoeburyness (*School of Gunnery*); Shorncliffe, Waltham Abbey (*Royal Gunpowder Factory*); Woolwich and York. The Army Estimates amount annually to £18,000,000 sterling.

THE NAVY.—The total strength of the British Navy is nearly 100,000 officers, seamen, boys, coastguards and marines. It is imperative upon Great Britain, with her vast Colonies and foreign possessions, year by year to increase and improve her vessels of war, so that no estimate of her fighting power will stand good for any length of time, and the numbers given below may have materially changed in a few months' time, as new warships are continually being launched.

The British Fleet now numbers 61 battleships; 41 first-class cruisers; 60 second-class cruisers; 54 third-class cruisers; with 18 port defence ships, and 199 torpedo boats. There are also 95 new rapid torpedo boat destroyers, which mark off a new era in maritime warfare and its weapons.

In addition to the above, there are now building 5 first-class battleships; 4 first-class cruisers; 16 second-class cruisers; 7 third-class cruisers; and 9 torpedo boat destroyers.

*Portsmouth.*

These numbers do not include gunboats, etc. The Navy Estimates amounted in 1897 to £22,780,473 sterling.

NAVAL STATIONS.—The principal Dockyards for the

Royal Navy at home are at Chatham, Devonport, Pembroke, Portsmouth, Sheerness, and Woolwich.

*Naval and Victualling Yards and Stations* have been established at Deptford, Gosport, Haulbowline, Plymouth, at home; and abroad, at Ascension Island, Bermuda, Cape of Good Hope, Esquimalt, Gibraltar, Halifax in Nova Scotia, Hong Kong, Jamaica, Malta, and Sydney (Australia). The Naval Hospitals are at Dartmouth, Haslar (*Gosport*), Plymouth, Portsmouth, Walmer.

There are Naval Prisons at Bodmin and Lewes, and Schools and Training Institutions, in addition to the several Training Ships, have been established at Greenwich College, Naval School, Eltham, etc.

INTERNAL COMMUNICATION.—This may be considered under the different heads of (1) Railways; (2) Post and Telegraph; (3) Canals and Navigable Rivers; (4) Roads.

I. RAILWAYS.—The Railways of the British Isles are one of its grand features as describing its internal trade, wealth, and industry. A Railway Map of England will suffice to show at a glance what a perfect network the principal railway systems and their branches have cast over the whole country, and this remarkable growth dates from the first railway constituted in 1832 (The Liverpool and Manchester), but 62 years ago. Though the same increase of "The Iron Road" has not yet extended to the Sister Kingdoms of Ireland or Scotland, yet they are well supplied in comparison with the amount of trade and population to be found there.

Next to Belgium, Great Britain shows the most perfect system of railway accommodation among the European powers. Its railways measure 21,000 miles, and new lines are being projected each year. This gives about 17 miles of railway to each 100 square miles in area, so that few parts of England and Wales are more than 10 miles from a

# IMPERIAL BRITAIN. MAP III.

railway station which connects them, however distant, with the Metropolis, the coal fields, and the manufacturing centres of trade. The chief railway systems of Great Britain radiate from London, as the main centre of wealth, pleasure, trade, and commerce. There are other local systems which are not directly connected with the Metropolis except by the more important trunk lines of other systems. Such are the Scottish Railways; the Cambrian Railways of Wales; and several systems in the North of England; *viz.*, the Lancashire and Yorkshire Railway; the North Eastern Railway; and the Cheshire Lines.

The Board of Trade have recently sanctioned Light Railways, some of which we may hope to see constructed shortly, for the conveyance of agricultural produce, goods and passengers, in those districts unprovided at present with railway communication. Truly may it be said:—

"Our civil engineers have performed feats which had no counterpart in former times. They have surveyed and laid a perfect network of railways all over England, overcoming every mechanical difficulty; they have made the bridges which span the Menai Straits, the Forth, Tay, and Tower bridges, tunnels innumerable through hills and mountains, five under the Thames, and the Mersey and the Severn tunnels. In architecture we have vastly improved in this reign, not only because the architects are better educated, but their patrons are so as well, and are far better able to judge of the fitness of style than they were."—From "The Longest Reign in English History," by kind permission of the author, Mr. John Ashton. (*English Illustrated Magazine.*)

ENGLISH RAILWAYS RADIATING FROM THE METROPOLIS:—

1.—*The London and North-Western Railway* stands first on account of its great services for passengers and goods to America (*via* Liverpool), Scotland, Wales, and

Ireland (*via* Holyhead). It is also the richest of our railway systems. Its London terminus is Euston station, from which every hour numerous trains are leaving for Carlisle, its connecting point with the Caledonian Railway of Scotland, Liverpool, Manchester, Crewe, Stafford, and the Potteries, Birmingham, Wolverhampton, Rugby, Coventry, and Northampton, etc., or Holyhead for the Irish Steam Packet.

2.—*The Great Western Railway* is the longest system in England, its length being 2,500 miles. Its London terminus is Paddington Station, and it forms the main route for passengers and traffic to the Western, Central, and South-Western districts of England and Wales. Its trunk lines run through Reading, Swindon, Bath, Bristol, Exeter, Plymouth, to Penzance in Cornwall; but there are many important branches connecting Oxford, Warwick, Birmingham, Wolverhampton, Chester, Shrewsbury, Gloucester, and the lines of South Wales with the Metropolis.

3.—*The Midland Railway*, so called because it connects London with the Midland Counties of England, and thus unites the largest number of manufacturing and other towns within its area, has St. Pancras Station for its London terminus. The chief towns situated upon its system are Bedford, Kettering, Leicester, Derby, Sheffield, Nottingham, Leeds, Birmingham, Worcester, Cheltenham, Gloucester, Manchester, and Liverpool, by means of its numerous branches.

4.—*The Great Northern Railway*, as its name implies, is the main line to Scotland. After York, which is, strictly speaking, the end, this route is continued by means of the North-Eastern Railway as far as Berwick-on-Tweed, where again the Eastern Coast trunk of the North British Railway connects the Metropolis with Edinburgh and other northern towns. This system combined is popularly called *the East Coast Route to Scotland*, to distinguish it from *the West Coast Route*, which is a combination of the London and North-Western and Caledonian Railways. The Great Northern, with its colleagues, the North-Eastern and the North British Railways, attain the highest speed of any of the British railways. The Flying Scotsman, which completes the entire journey from London to Edinburgh in $8\frac{1}{2}$ hours, a distance of 395 miles, is the fastest train in the world. The London terminus of the Great Northern Railway is King's Cross.

5.—*The Great Eastern Railway*, with its London terminus, Liverpool Street, is a dual line. It consists of two main trunks running through the Eastern Counties, with numerous smaller branches. One trunk runs from London to Harwich, and conveys passengers and goods to and from the Continent; the other main line connects London with Yarmouth, Norwich, Ely, and Cambridge, etc. There is also the Ipswich branch. Milk, fish, and agricultural produce are conveyed to the Metropolis at exceedingly low rates by this railway.

6.—*The Manchester, Sheffield, and Lincolnshire Railway Company* are constructing a new main line to the Metropolis with a view to convey passengers, and bring their mineral and heavy goods traffic, direct to London upon their own system. By this means, Manchester, Sheffield, and other large northern towns will gain another important communication with London, as at present the M. S. and L. Railway is a cross country system, running from east to west, *i.e.*, from Liverpool and Manchester, through Sheffield to Grimsby, on the Lincolnshire coast.

The railways south of the Thames do not compare favourably with those running in the opposite direction. This is probably owing to the shorter distance traversed, the loss of the mineral and other traffic, and the small populations of the towns upon the routes, which are not, as a rule, centres of manufacture—yet these four railways possess the advantages of the principal continental traffic.

7.—The most important of the southern lines is *The London and South-Western Railway*, which has its London terminus at Waterloo Station. This railway runs direct from London to Devonport, through Basingstoke, Salisbury, and Exeter, while with its branches it connects Portsmouth, Southampton, and Weymouth, the two latter ports having a direct communication, by a daily service of steam packets, with the Channel Islands.

Since the recent dock strikes on the banks of the Thames, there is a tendency to increase the commercial traffic with Southampton, and this, with the passenger and mail service, falls into the hands of the London and South-Western Railway Company.

8.—*The South-Eastern Railway*, with its double London termini, Charing Cross and Cannon Street, has direct mail and passenger service with the Continent of Europe *via* Folkestone and Boulogne; Dover and Calais; Port Victoria and Flushing, etc. The chief places of importance along its route are Tunbridge, Tunbridge Wells, Ashford, Canterbury, Dover, Hastings, Ramsgate, and Margate.

9.—*The London, Brighton, and South Coast Railway* also possesses a double London termini at London Bridge and Victoria Stations. This railway has an important continental service *via* Newhaven and Dieppe. It is also in direct communication with the fashionable seaside towns of the South Coast, which are each year visited by a large number of visitors. The main trunks are two, which divide near Croydon, one proceeding direct to Brighton, Hastings, and Eastbourne, passing through Redhill, Three Bridges, etc., and the other running through Horsham and Chichester for Portsmouth and the Isle of Wight Railways.

10.—*The London, Chatham and Dover Railway* has a double termini at St. Paul's and Victoria Stations. This railway possesses a considerable passenger and goods traffic with the Continent, *via* Dover and Calais, and Queenboro' Pier and Flushing. The home traffic touches in many points the same districts as the South-Eastern Railway.

11.—*The London, Tilbury, and Southend Railway* has its London terminus at Fenchurch Street. It has lines running along the north side of the Thames as far as Shoeburyness. This company takes a considerable number of passengers to Tilbury Docks for the Orient, and Peninsular and Oriental, steamships to India, Australia, etc.

12.—*The North London Railway* is one of the suburban railways which encircle the Metropolis, either as an underground, or overground, system. This line extends from Broad Street to Richmond. It has a considerable passenger traffic.

13.—*The West London Extension* is another suburban railway connecting Kensington with Clapham Junction, where it meets the London and South-Western, and the London, Brighton and South Coast systems.

14.—*The East London*, a third suburban line, connects the Great Eastern Railway with the Southern lines, the London, Brighton and South Coast, and the South-Eastern Railways, by way of the Thames Tunnel.

15.—*The Metropolitan Railway* extends as far as Aylesbury in Buckinghamshire, *via* Willesden, Harrow, and Rickmansworth, although its principal service of trains is confined to the suburban districts, which it connects with the City and the other London district railways.

16.—*The District Railway* consists of an Inner and an Outer Circle, with branches in connection, that is, the trains continue running in the same direction, and the "up" or "down" trains are thus marked for the convenience of passengers.

Other railway systems, either projected or in course of construction, are:—

1.—*The Lancashire, Derbyshire, and East Coast*, connecting Lincoln with the West Coast.

2.—*Electric Railways* :—

>   a. The City and South London Electric Railway runs underground from the Monument to Stockwell at present.
>   b. The Waterloo and City Railway, an electric underground line to connect the London and South-Western with the City.
>   c. The Central London Railway, running from Liverpool Street to Shepherd's Bush.

The chief railway systems in Great Britain which do not touch the Metropolis are:—

1.—*The North-Eastern Railway*, which connects the Great Northern Main Line at York with the East Coast Lines of Scotland at Berwick-upon-Tweed.

2.—*The Caledonian Railway*, which joins the London and North-Western railway system at Carlisle, and runs in a north-easterly direction to Edinburgh, Glasgow (by connecting branches), Stirling, Perth, and Aberdeen.

3.—*The Glasgow and South-Western Railway* connects the Midland Railway also at Carlisle, with Dumfries, Paisley, Ayr, and Glasgow.

4.—*The North British Railway* is a double connecting link with the English Railways at Carlisle, where it joins the Midland system at Berwick-upon-Tweed with the North-Eastern system. This railway runs principally from Edinburgh by various routes through the Lowlands.

5.—*The Highland and Great Northern of Scotland, with the West Highland Railways*, have opened up new districts for tourists and goods in these parts, where the scenery is proverbially beautiful.

6.—*The Lancashire and Yorkshire Railway.*
7.—*The Cambrian Railways.*
8.—*The Cheshire Lines.*
9.—*The Isle of Wight Railways*, and some other minor lines.

More than nine hundred millions of passengers, exclusive of season ticket holders, were conveyed by the British Railways in 1896.

The principal Irish Railways have their centres at Dublin and Belfast. United they possess about 3,178 miles of line. They are:—

1.—*The Great Southern and Western*, from Dublin to Cork, and Queenstown, where the American mails are taken.
2.—*The Midland Great Western*, from Dublin to Galway.
3.—*The Dublin, Wicklow, and Wexford*, from Dublin to Wexford.
4.—*The Great Northern*, from Dublin to Belfast.
5.—*The Belfast and Northern Counties*, from Belfast to Londonderry.
6.—*The Waterford and Limerick,* joining these ports.

*N.B.*—A considerable portion of the West of Ireland knows no railway communication.

II. POSTAL AND TELEGRAPHIC COMMUNICATION.—The most perfect system of Postal and Telegraphic Communication exists in all parts of the British Empire. These are now in the hands of the Government, hence their efficiency, and regularity of transit, are well-nigh perfect.

The head offices are at S. Martin's-le-Grand in the City of London, where continuous communication exists with every part of the world by means of the submarine cables which connect Great Britain with both the Old and the New World.

Nearly 100,000 persons are employed in the Postal and Telegraphic Service in the British Isles. Eighteen hundred millions of letters, besides an innumerable quantity of post-cards, book-packets, and newspapers, are delivered each year. This gives an average of 45·6 letters to each person in population, being nearly at the rate of one each week. The New Parcels Post carries some fifty-seven million parcels annually. Another branch of the Post Office system is the Postal and Money Order Department, which is largely used to the enormous amount of twenty-five millions per annum; then its Post Office Savings Bank has a capital of more than seventy-six millions sterling.

*The Telegraph Department* sends each year some eighty million messages along its 36,000 miles of telegraph lines; and in addition, the National Telephone Company, which is not at present under Government, passes about two million messages per week.

" We must not forget that to the reign of Queen Victoria we owe the uniform postage rate of one penny per letter.

" It was early in 1837 that Mr. (afterwards Sir) Rowland Hill broached his plan of a uniform penny postage; but as a tentative measure, a uniform rate of fourpence was imposed in 1839. By this means the machinery of the Penny Post was inaugurated, and letters were carried at that price on January 10th, 1840.

" At first the postage was paid as before, but on May 1st the Mulready envelope, so well known to collectors, was issued; but it was the subject of so much ridicule, as to necessitate the destruction of nearly all the vast number prepared for issue. Then other stamped envelopes were made, and finally, in 1841, adhesive stamps were issued. Book-post came in 1855. Money orders, inaugurated in 1792, first became general in 1840, when the tariff was reduced. Halfpenny postcards were first issued on October

1st, 1870, and the Parcel Post came into operation on August 1st, 1883. The Post Office Savings Bank began in 1861, and work commenced on the Post Office Telegraphs on February 5th, 1869."—From "The Longest Reign in English History," by John Ashton, by kind permission of the Author. (*English Illustrated Magazine.*)

III. CANALS AND NAVIGABLE RIVERS.—The internal water-ways of Great Britain have decreased in importance as the iron roads have increased, yet a considerable trade is still maintained by means of our water traffic.

Some 4,000 miles of canals spread their lines as connecting links between our colliery, and other mining districts, with the more important centres of trade and manufacture.

Many of our rivers are navigable, and therefore available for barge and steamboat traffic at all seasons of the year.

The grandest canal in the United Kingdom is the Manchester Ship Canal, which connects the River Mersey, at Eastham, with the City of Manchester, thus making this inland town, a port, and commercial city. It is 37 miles long, and wide enough to allow sea-going vessels up to 7,000 tons burden to pass through it. This magnificent piece of engineering skill took more than six years to construct, at a cost of more than £15,000,000 sterling.

The Scotch and Irish Canals are of less importance than those of England.

The chief canals in England are:—(1) Lancashire; (2) Leeds and Liverpool; (3) Grand Trunk; (4) Grand Junction; (5) Oxford; (6) Trent and Mersey; (7) Kennet and Avon; (8) The Shropshire Union. There are other smaller ones.

In Scotland we find:—(1) The Forth and Clyde; (2) The Caledonian; (3) The Crinan; (4) The Union. These are the principal ones in Scotland.

In Ireland, The Grand, and The Royal Government Canals are the most important; but there are several others connected with the trade centres, such as Belfast, etc.

IV. ROADS.—It is somewhat surprising to find that the roads of the United Kingdom have not been taken up by the Government, instead of being left as they are at present to the control and management of local bodies, such as the County Council, and District Highway Boards. By the Government making the roads and highways of Great Britain and Ireland a national matter, an immense burden would be lifted from the now overtaxed landowner and agriculturist, and by a universal tax spread upon all classes alike, for all use the roads in common, a much fairer system of rates would be levied, and uniformity with excellence would prevail throughout the country.

*N.B.*—Since the abolition of the toll gates upon our turnpike, or highway roads, with the exception of the parliamentary grants voted for a few years after the Act, the whole burden of repairs and maintenance has fallen upon the land; whereas the landowners do not use the roads in proportion one-third so much as the manufacturing and trading classes of population do, who escape scot-free in this particular.

The highroads of England alone would, if stretched out continuously in one line, encircle the surface of the globe, being 25,000 miles in length; and the cross roads and bye-lanes would, in addition, pass round it four times, being 100,000 miles in length.

Both in Scotland and in Ireland there are excellent turnpike roads.

EXTERNAL COMMUNICATION.—This is a wide subject, almost demanding more space than we can give to it in a passing notice here. A volume rather than a chapter would be needed to treat fully of this magnificent work, as it embraces not only travel, but commerce, trade, and the entire defence and protection of our numerous and vast foreign possessions. If at any future period the external communication should become either broken, or weakened, in any particular, the wealth, power, and greatness of Great Britain would fall with it. It is important, therefore, that our external communication should not be limited, or curtailed. The supremacy of the sea is our golden key to the markets of the world, and our best, in Men, Matter, and Money, must not be grudged to maintain this, whatever may be said, or written, to the contrary.

Again, our central position, in both the Land and the Water Hemispheres of the world's surface, opens out for us grand facilities for commercial relations with every nation, however distant from us; while the sea, which is our servant to aid us in maintaining our magnificent position in commerce and trade, is also our safeguard, and defence, from any attack from the enemy so long as our ships of war and coast defences are of the first order.

Under the heads of Postal and Telegraph Communication and Foreign Trade (imports and exports) details are given (*see* p. 72), so that it remains but to speak of England's commerce here as the main secret of her greatness and power.

COMMERCE.—The old theory, that the sea separates countries and people, has been entirely refuted, for it has become, by reason of extended navigation, the great, and only means, of uniting them. Thus it is that Britain's vast possessions and wealth arise from her unique position as a sea power. Being in command of the great ocean highways, Britain is ever extending her multitudinous lines of navigation eastward, westward, northward, and southward. Her merchant navy, which is the best and largest in the world, being staffed with nearly 300,000 officers and men, carry foreign and home goods and produce as imports and exports to the enormous amount of £1,050,000,000 sterling. The granaries and markets of the world are thus placed within her reach for the sale and purchase of every conceivable kind of raw material, or manufactured article; thus it is that foreigners regard us as a nation of shopkeepers, or traders. One-fourth of the entire trade of Great Britain is confined to her own possessions abroad, *viz.*, India and the Colonies.

According to Lloyd's Register of British and Foreign Shipping, showing the total number of vessels (steamships and sailing) of 100 tons register and upwards, to be 30,368 vessels with a tonnage of 25,107,632; the British Empire claims 11,536 vessels with a tonnage of 13,242,639. It will thus be seen at a glance that nearly two-fifths of the whole merchant service of the world belongs to us, and that our vessels carry more than half the produce of the world's markets.

IMPORTS AND EXPORTS.—It naturally follows that if the United Kingdom is the first commercial country in the world, her imports and exports must be both valuable and varied.

The combined trade value of these imports and exports exceeds £640,000,000 sterling per annum. Of this enormous amount, nine-tenths belong to England and Wales, and the remaining tenth rests with Scotland, and Ireland, to the proportion of 7 to 3.

Again, nearly one-fourth of the goods imported into this country comes from our own possessions, while in exchange we send them about one-third of our exports.

The principal imports are food supplies and raw materials.

The principal exports are woollen and other manufactured goods, clothing, coal, metals, articles, and general wares.

Our corn supplies come chiefly from Russia, the United States, Australia, and Canada.

Our timber supplies come from the Baltic and Canadian forests, although fancy woods, etc., are imported from all parts of the world.

Our wool comes from Australia and New Zealand, etc. Our cotton from the United States, Egypt, India, etc. Our hides and skins from India, South Africa, South America, the United States, and the Continent. Our flax and hemp from Russia, Ireland, Italy, and India. Our tea

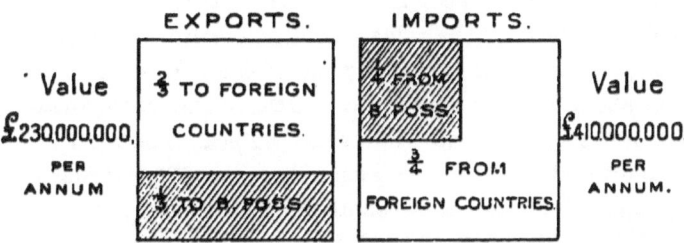

from India, China, Ceylon. Our coffee from India, Ceylon, Central and South America. Our wines from the Continent, Australia, and the Cape.

FISHERIES.—The Board of Trade has power, under the Sea Fisheries Regulation Act, passed in 1888, to form coast districts within the territorial waters of England and Wales. The chief coast fishery districts are :—

(1) The Northumbrian Coast; (2) The North-Eastern, from Durham to Lincolnshire; (3) The Eastern, from Donna Nook (Lincolnshire), including The Wash with Norfolk and Suffolk ; (4) Kent and Essex, including the Estuary of the Thames; (5) The Sussex or South-Eastern Coast ; (6) The Southern, Hampshire and Dorset; (7) The Devonshire Coast; (8) The Cornish Coast; (9) Glamorgan, from Nash

Point to Worms Head; (10) Milford Haven from Worms Head to Cemmaes Head; (11) The Western, from Cemmaes Head to Carnarvonshire; (12) The Lancashire Coast. Scotland and Ireland have each a separate Fisheries Board. Nearly every kind of sea-fish abounds, but certain districts are noted for particular kinds, *e.g.*, the Norfolk Coast for herrings and crabs, etc.; the Cornish Coast for pilchards; the cod fisheries of North and Eastern Scotland. Mackerel are also plentiful upon the South and East Coasts at certain seasons.

It will be gathered from the above-named division of the coast districts that sea-fishing is an important industry with the British people. The Eastern Coast of Great Britain is perhaps the richest field of labour, as the North Sea is noted for its excellent yield of fish. It is estimated that about 255,000 tons, or five-sixths of the whole amount taken each year, comes from these waters. The total yield of the English and Welsh Fisheries equals 330,000 tons per annum; Scotland adds another 300,000 tons; and Ireland from 30,000 to 40,000 tons each year, so that the British sea-fisheries are valued at nearly £8,000,000 per annum.

To give some idea of the extent of labour employed to produce this vast amount each year, we find that 126,000 men are regularly employed in the work, and that nearly 35,000 boats, varying in size from the huge steam trawler to the tiny smack, are engaged throughout the greater portion of the year at this perilous employment.

The chief markets for sea-fish in England are London (Billingsgate, the largest in the world), Hull, Grimsby, Yarmouth, and Harwich; but fish are conveyed both by sea and land to every part of the country, and it forms no small part of the food supply of both the rich and the poor.

Besides the home consumption of fish, we export some

40,000 barrels of pilchards each year to the ports of the Mediterranean from the Cornish Coast. These alone are valued at £3,000,000 per annum.

The freshwater fishing is confined to the rivers and lakes of the British Isles. Many of the lakes and rivers, as well as the smaller streams, teem with salmon, salmon-trout, grayling, pike, perch, tench, dace, chub, eels, etc., so that angling is a most common pastime throughout the country.

The following description of our fishermen by H.R.H. the Duke of Saxe Coburg and Gotha, or, as he is better known to us by his more homely title, "Duke of Edinburgh," will be of marked interest here :—

*Our Fishermen.*—How few there are who consider that, if, from any cause, the thousands of fish now swarming in the sea were to swim away to the depths of the ocean beyond the range of man's power to take them, to-morrow over half-a-million of our fellow-subjects would be without the means of buying their bread!

In this half million, I include only the fishermen and their wives and children, and do not reckon the buyers, curers, coopers, carters, boat-builders, net-makers, and dealers in the towns.

It is of the fishermen I wish to speak.

They must toil hard and long to gain enough to supply their wants, and risk dangers and hardships known only to those who have spent a long time upon the sea.

In winter cold, and summer heat, almost every port and bay sends out daily to the fishing-grounds its fleet of boats, manned by their eager crews, prepared almost to face any danger to gain its treasures from the deep.

From the earliest times the people of our coasts have made the sea yield them food. This calling has produced a race of men—strong, used to hardships, patient and hardworking, brave, active, and ready to meet danger.

Our first commerce must have been conducted by our fishermen, who also manned our fighting ships. The fisheries of the west of England were the nurseries, or training places, of the sailors who enabled Drake to sail round the world, and, as he said, to "singe the King of Spain's beard," on more than one memorable occasion.—*H.R.H. Duke of Edinburgh.*

RISE OF LITERATURE DURING THE REIGN OF QUEEN VICTORIA.—Steam printing, and the withdrawal of the "Paper Tax" of 1862, have greatly aided the production of cheap literature, which is one of the greatest glories of Queen Victoria's reign. The brilliant and ever increasing body of British authors, both grave and gay, have done, and are still doing, noble work, which will live on and tend to enrich this great Empire and its language, spreading, as it does, to every region of the globe. No nation, past or present, has such a great and varied *glory-roll* of authors, both living and dead.

"The Newspaper Press has resembled everything else in this reign—it has developed in an extraordinary manner. No exact information as to the numbers of periodical literature can ever be obtained, for some papers have but an ephemeral existence; but the following is the latest list of newspapers I can obtain:—

| | | | | | | |
|---|---|---|---|---|---|---|
| England | { London, 456 <br> { Provinces, 1,342 | ... | ... | ... | 1,798 |
| Wales | ... | ... | ... | ... | ... | 98 |
| Scotland | ... | ... | ... | ... | ... | 217 |
| Ireland | ... | ... | ... | ... | ... | 168 |
| British Isles | ... | ... | ... | ... | ... | 23 |
| | Total ... | | ... | .. | ... | 2,304 |

"The magazines now in course of publication, including the quarterly reviews, number 2,081, of which more than

487 are of a decidedly religious character."—From "The Longest Reign in English History," by kind permission of the author, Mr. John Ashton. (*English Illustrated Magazine.*)

RELIGION.—In Great Britain the greatest freedom, and protection, in religious worship is extended to all classes; but there are two State Churches—the Established Episcopal Church of England, in England and Wales, and the Established Presbyterian Church of Scotland, with numerous other branches.

The National Religion, therefore, of the British Isles may be described as :—

*A.* The National Church of England, in England and Wales.

*B.* Presbyterianism of various kinds, including the Church of Scotland, the Free Church of Scotland, and the United Presbyterian Church, with the Auld Lights' Community, or Original Secession Church in Scotland.

*C.* Roman Catholics in Ireland, with the Church of Ireland (Episcopal); being a daughter of the Church of England.

*A.*—1. *The National Episcopal Church of England* is governed by 2 Archbishops—Canterbury and York; and 32 Bishops[1]—London, Durham, Winchester, Norwich, Gloucester and Bristol, Hereford, Bath and Wells, Chichester, *St. David's*, Liverpool, Newcastle, *Llandaff*, Oxford, Southwell, Ripon, Lincoln, Exeter, Salisbury, Ely, Manchester, Wakefield, Chester, *St. Asaph*, *Bangor*, St. Albans, Worcester, Rochester, Peterborough, Truro, Lichfield, Carlisle, and Sodor and Man.

To assist the Bishops there are 26 Suffragan and Coadjutor Bishops engaged in diocesan work; also 30

---

[1] The Bishoprics of the English Church in Wales are indicated by italics.

Deans, 89 Archdeacons, 132 Residentary Canons, 810 Rural Deans, and about 14,300 Beneficed Clergy, with nearly 10,000 Unbeneficed, who are engaged as curates, schoolmasters, or in secretarial work, etc., to the various Church Societies.

The 2 Archbishops and 24 of the Bishops have seats in the House of Lords to protect, and arrange, the laws relating to the Church and its institutions.

2. *The Episcopal Church in Scotland*, being a daughter of the Church of England, in addition has 7 Bishops—Brechin (*Primus*), St. Andrews, Moray and Ross, Aberdeen, Argyle and the Isles, Edinburgh, Glasgow, with 182 Beneficed Clergy and 150 Unbeneficed in 1895.

3. *The Church of Ireland*, a second daughter of the English Church, has 2 Archbishops—Armagh (Primate) and Dublin; and 11 Bishops—Meath, Limerick, Derry, Cashel, Cork, Ossory, Killaloe, Kilmore, Down, Clogher, Tuam. *N.B.—Some of these Bishops have a double and others a treble title, e.g., as Down, Connor, and Dromore, but only the first is given here.*

The total number of Beneficed Clergy in Ireland is 1,232, and Unbeneficed Clergy about 360. *N.B.*—It must not be taken that the above figures represent the entire working body of the Church of England, for the enormous growth in our Colonies, and Foreign Possessions, is now represented by another 82 Indian, Colonial, or Missionary Bishops, and a large and influential body of English and Native Clergy working under them.

B. *The Church of Scotland* (*Presbyterian*) abolished the Order of Prelates, or Bishops, at the Reformation, and its present constitution was arranged. Its government is strictly Presbyterian, *i.e.*, it recognises the equal episcopacy of all presbyters. Each congregation is ruled by a Session, or board of elders, of which the parish minister is the President. The Session in turn is governed by the Presbytery, or board of ministers, with one elected elder for each congregation within the district. Next follows the Synod, or representatives from the Presbyteries of each Province; and above all is the General Assembly, or Supreme Court, which meets annually, in May, in Edinburgh. There are some 1,700 ministers, and nearly 10,000 elders in the Church of Scotland proper; and 1,100 ministers in the Free Church of Scotland, which broke away from the former in 1843 under the leadership of Dr. Chalmers. The United Presbyterian Church and "Auld Lights" connection are smaller and less important bodies.

*Other Religious Bodies.*—The Registrar General's list shows a mixed company of Nonconformists of every shade of religion, thought, and practice. Some 300 different sects are there enumerated as holding their own separate places of worship and teaching.

Our Services are well cared for with regard to religious ministration; both the Navy and the Army have their special chaplains, which are paid by the Government.

The Merchant Service receives marked attention also by means of the various sea and waterside missions of the Church of England, which carry on a great and good work among all classes of sailors and dock labourers, etc., at our principal ports.

And lastly, the foreign sailors who visit our ports have been, in many instances, provided with churches and mission rooms, where they may be gathered together for worship in their own mother tongue, *e.g.*, the Danish and Swedish Churches for sailors.

*C.* There is no State Church in Ireland. The National Religion is Roman Catholic, which is governed by 4 Archbishops and 23 Bishops. What is popularly called the Irish Church (see above) is really the Church of England in Ireland, which is both Protestant, and Episcopal. This Church was disestablished in 1871.

The Preamble and Declaration of Authority in matters legal and civil sets forth :—" The Church of Ireland, deriving its authority from Christ, Who is Head over all things to the Church, doth declare that a General Synod of the Church of Ireland, consisting of the Archbishops and Bishops, and of representatives of the Clergy and Laity, shall have chief legislative power therein, and such administrative power as may be necessary for the Church and consistent with its Episcopal constitution."

EDUCATION.—Every class in the British Isles is well provided for under the head of education.

*A*. The ancient Universities of Oxford and Cambridge amply provide for the education of the more wealthy classes, in addition to the great Public Schools of Eton, Harrow, Winchester, Rugby, Westminster, etc., etc.

*B*. The smaller Universities of London, Dublin, Durham, St. Andrews, Glasgow, Edinburgh, etc., together with a large number of Public and Endowed Schools, meet the general needs of the middle classes.

*C*. The poor and working classes have Elementary Education now provided free in all State-aided Schools, if so required. Elementary Education is compulsory in theory, if not in practice, throughout the United Kingdom.

The Elementary Schools are of two kinds :—(1) Voluntary Schools, belonging to the Church of England, the Wesleyan, or Roman Catholics, which are maintained by private subscription; and (2) Board Schools, which are supported by the rates.

*D*. Secondary Education, Science and Art, and Technical Instruction, have received much attention of late years from the Government, and in addition there are Naval and Military Schools, Medical and Engineering Schools, with

Agricultural and Science Colleges; also, Training Colleges for Teachers, and Theological and Missionary Colleges for the Clergy.

The following statistics show at a glance the chief features of Elementary Education, as provided for in our Voluntary and Board School systems in England and Wales:—

CHIEF ELEMENTARY EDUCATION ACTS SINCE 1870.

1. 1870—33 and 34 Vic., c. 75, W. E. Forster.
2. 1873—36 and 37 Vic., c. 86, W. E. Forster.
3. 1876—39 and 40 Vic., c. 79, Lord Sandon.
4. 1880—43 and 44 Vic., c. 23, Mr. A. J. Mundella.
5. 1889—52 and 53 Vic., c. 40, Welsh Intermediate Education.
6. 1889—Technical Instruction Act.
7. 1891—54 and 55 Vic., c. 26, Sir W. Hart Dyke, Bart. (*Free Education*).
8. 1896—59 Vic., c. 172, Further Provisions for Education, England and Wales, Sir John Gorst (*Dropped*).
9. 1897—60 Vict., c. 5, Voluntary Schools Act, Mr. A. J. Balfour.

GROWTH OF THE GOVERNMENT GRANT FOR ELEMENTARY EDUCATION.

| | |
|---|---|
| 1833—£20,000. | 1880—£2,497,216. |
| 1843—£50,000. | 1890—£3,678,540. |
| 1851—£151,000. | 1891—£4,106,657. |
| 1860—£798,167. | 1892—£5,965,516. |
| 1870—£903,978. | 1893—£6,500,000. |

1896—(Including Science and Art) about £7,000,000.

GOVERNMENT INSPECTION STATISTICS, YEAR ENDING AUGUST 31, 1896.

| Voluntary Contributions. | Kind of School. | Accommodation. | No. on Registers. | Average Attendance. |
|---|---|---|---|---|
| £643,386 0 0 | Church Schools ... | 2,780,939 | 2,297,659 | 1,871,653 |
| 88,541 0 0 | British ,, ... | 351,807 | 286,455 | 232,762 |
| 21,593 0 0 | Wesleyan ,, ... | 184,570 | 157,477 | 125,998 |
| 97,448 0 0 | R. Catholic ,, ... | 371,647 | 294,627 | 235,505 |
| By Rates. | Board ,, ... | 2,433,411 | 2,386,771 | 1,956,992 |
| £850,968 0 0 | Grand Totals....... | 6,122,374 | 5,422,989 | 4,422,911 |

VOLUNTARY EXPENDITURE ON CHURCH SCHOOLS AND TRAINING COLLEGES.

From 1811 to 1870—£15,149,938 0 0
Since 1870— 23,840,080 0 0
Total—£38,990,018 0 0

CHURCH SCHOOLS.

|  | 1870. | 1896. | Increase. |
|---|---|---|---|
| Accommodation......... | 1,365,084 | 2,730,939 | 1,365,855 |
| Average Attendance.. | 844,334 | 1,871,653 | 1,027,319 |

NUMBER OF ELEMENTARY SCHOOLS INSPECTED BY H.M. INSPECTORS IN ENGLAND AND WALES—19,756.

From "The Clergyman's Ready Reference Diary," 1897, by the Author. (Messrs. Bemrose & Sons, 23 Old Bailey, E.C.)

THE ROYAL FAMILY OF ENGLAND.

The Queen. (Alexandrina) Victoria, Queen of the United Kingdom of Great Britain and Ireland, Empress of India, only child of Edward, Duke of Kent; *born* May 24th, 1819; succeeded to the throne on the decease of her uncle, King William IV., June 20th, 1837; Proclaimed June 21st, 1837; Crowned June 28th, 1838; *married* February 10th, 1840, H.R.H. Albert, Prince of Saxe-Coburg and Gotha, *born* August 26th, 1819, *died* December 14th, 1861.

*Issue:*—Victoria Adelaide Mary Louisa, *Princess Royal,* born November 21st, 1840; *married* January 25th, 1858, to H.R.H. the Crown Prince of Germany (who *died* June 15th, 1888), and has had issue four sons and four daughters.

Albert Edward, Prince of Wales, K.G., *born* November 9th, 1841; *married* March 10th, 1863, to H.R.H. the Princess Alexandra of Denmark, *born* December 1st, 1844, and has had issue three sons—Prince Albert Victor, *born* January 8th, 1864, (*died* January 14th, 1892); George Frederick Ernest Albert, *born* June 3rd, 1865, *married* Princess Victoria Mary Louise Pauline Claudine Agnes of Teck, July 6th, 1893, issue two sons—*Edward Albert Christian George Andrew Patrick David, born* June 23rd, 1894, and Albert F.A.G., *born* December 14th, 1895; Alexander, *born* April 6th, 1871 (*died* April 7th, 1871); and three daughters, Louisa Victoria Alexandra Dagmar, *born* February 20th, 1867, *married* July 27th, 1889, to Alexander W. George, Marquis of Macduff and Duke of Fife, issue two daughters; Victoria Alexandra Olga Mary, *born* July 6th, 1868, and Maude Charlotte Mary Victoria *born* November 26th, 1869, *married* Prince Charles of Denmark July 22nd, 1896.

Alice Maud Mary, *born* April 25th, 1843 (*died* December 14th, 1878); *married* July 1st, 1862, to H.R.H. Prince Louis of Hesse (*died* March 13th, 1892). Issue now living —one son and four daughters.

Alfred Ernest Albert, Duke of Edinburgh, *born* August 6th, 1844; *married* January 9th, 1874, to the Grand Duchess Marie of Russia, and has issue one son and four daughters.

Helena Augusta Victoria, *born* May 25th, 1846; *married* July 5th, 1866, to H.R.H. Prince Frederick Christian Charles Augustus of Schleswig-Holstein-Sonderburg-Augustenburg. Issue living—one son and two daughters.

Louise Caroline Alberta, *born* March 18th, 1848; *married* March 21st, 1871, to the Marquis of Lorne.

Arthur William Patrick Albert, Duke of Connaught and Strathearn, *born* May 1st, 1850; *married* Princess Louise Margaret of Prussia, March 13th, 1879, and has issue two daughters and one son.

Leopold George Duncan Albert, Duke of Albany, *born*

April 7th, 1853; *married* Princess Helena of Waldeck, April 27th, 1882; *died* March 29th, 1884. Issue—a daughter and son.

Beatrice Mary Victoria Feodore, *born* April 14th, 1857; *married* H.R.H. Prince Henry of Battenberg, July 23rd, 1885 (*died* January 20th, 1896). Issue—three sons and a daughter.

OTHER ROYAL PRINCES AND PRINCESSES.

Ernest, Duke of Cumberland, *born* September 21st, 1845.

George, Duke of Cambridge, *born* March 26th, 1819.

Augusta G., Duchess of Mecklenburg-Strelitz, *born* July 19th, 1822.

ROYAL PALACES, CASTLES, ETC.

1. *Ancient.*—Windsor Castle, Tower of London, Westminster Hall and Palace, Winchester, Savoy Palace, Woodstock or Blenheim Palace, Greenwich Palace, St. James' Palace, Whitehall, Hampton Court Palace, etc.

2. *Modern.*—Kensington Palace, Somerset House, Kew Palace, Buckingham Palace, Osborne, Balmoral, Marlborough House, Sandringham, etc.

BRITISH PATRON SAINTS AND NATIONAL SYMBOLS, ETC.

1. England........S. George........Lion, Rose, S. George's Cross
2. Scotland........S. Andrew......Thistle
3. Ireland.........S. Patrick......Shamrock
4. Wales...........S. David........Leek

### NAVAL BATTLES SINCE THE NORMAN CONQUEST.

| | | | | |
|---|---|---|---|---|
| 1. Damme | 1213 | 13. Cape Passaro | 1718 |
| 2. Dover | 1217 | 14. Cape Finisterre | 1747 |
| 3. St. Mahé | 1293 | 15. Minorca | 1756 |
| 4. Sluys | 1340 | 16. Doggerbank | 1781 |
| 5. The Spanish Armada | 1588 | 17. Guadeloupe | 1782 |
| 6. North Downs | 1652 | 18. Brest | 1794 |
| 7. I. Goodwin Sands | 1653 | 19. St. Vincent | 1797 |
| 8. Portland and Texel | 1653 | 20. Nile | 1798 |
| 9. II. Goodwin Sands and N. Foreland | 1666 | 21. Baltic | 1801 |
| | | 22. Trafalgar | 1805 |
| 10. Southwold Bay | 1672 | 23. Navarino | 1827 |
| 11. Beachy Head | 1690 | 24. Bomarsund | 1854 |
| 12. La Hogue | 1692 | | |

Windsor Castle.

## PRINCIPAL WARS.

| Date. | Wars. | Contending Parties. | Remarks. |
|---|---|---|---|
| B.C. 55 to A.D. 410 | Roman Conquest | Romans and Britons | Romans conquer Britain |
| A.D. 450 | Saxon Invasion | Saxons and Britons | Saxons conquer Britain |
| ,, 787 | Danish Invasion | Danes and Saxons | Danes made Settlements |
| ,, 827 | Egbert and Heptarchy | Egbert became First | King of England |
| ,, 871-896 | Alfred the Great | Alfred and the Danes | The Danes defeated |
| ,, 1013 | Danish Invasion | Sweyn and Ethelred the Unready | Danish Victory and Settlement |
| ,, 1066 | Norman Conquest | Duke William & Harold | William I. crowned King |
| ,, 1093 | Scotland | Malcolm III. and Percy | Malcolm slain |
| ,, 1136 | Scotland | David I. and Stephen | ) To win the Crown for the Em- |
| ,, 1139-1151 | Civil War of Succession | Matilda and Stephen | } press Matilda |
| ,, 1169-1171 | Conquest of Ireland | Strongbow, Henry II. and Irish | Irish Princes give homage |
| ,, 1180 | Third Crusade | Richard I. and Saladin | To regain Holy Land |
| ,, 1216 | I. Baron's War | John and the Barons | To claim Natural Rights |
| ,, 1265-1269 | II. Baron's War | Henry III. and Barons | Refusal of King to comply with Barons |
| ,, 1276-1282 | Invasion of Wales | Edward I. and Welsh | Non-submission of Llewellyn |
| ,, 1297-1304 | Scottish Wars | English and Scotch | Competition for the Crown of Scotland |
| ,, 1312-1322 | III. Baronial War | Edward II. and Barons | Foolish government of Edward |
| ,, 1337-1360 | French War | Edward III. and French | Competition for Crown of France |
| ,, 1415-1421 | ,, | Henry V. and French | Loss of French Possessions |
| ,, 1455-1485 | Wars of the Roses | York and Lancaster | Contending Claimants for Throne |
| ,, 1588 | Spanish Armada | Elizabeth and Spain | English plundered Spanish Possessions |
| ,, 1642-1651 | Civil War | King and Parliament | King deposed and beheaded |
| ,, 1652-1674 | Dutch Wars | English and Dutch | Jealousy of Dutch of English [Power |
| ,, 1702-1713 | Spanish Succession | English, French, and Allies | Death of Charles II. of Spain |
| ,, 1756-1763 | Seven Years' War | English, French, and Allies | Jealousy of French in America and India |
| ,, 1775-1783 | American Independence | English and Americans | Opposition of Americans to Taxes |
| ,, 1793-1802 | French War | English and French | Execution of Louis XVI. Opening Scheldt [Engl'd. |
| ,, 1803-1815 | French and Peninsula | ,, | Napoleon's wish to subjugate |
| ,, 1824-1826 | Burmese War | English and Burmese | Burmese trespassed in Bengal |
| ,, 1837-1841 | Canadian War | English and Canadian Rebels | Wish of Canadians to form a Republic |
| ,, 1840 | Chinese War | English and Chinese | Opium Trade |
| ,, 1845-1849 | Sikh War | English and Sikhs | Rebellion of the Sikhs |
| ,, 1854-1856 | Crimean War | Eng., French, & Russia | Protection of Turkey |
| ,, 1856-1859 | Indian Mutiny | English and Sepoys | Mutiny of Sepoys in India |
| ,, 1868 | Abyssinian War | English and King Theodore | Imprisonment of English in Abyssinia [territory |
| ,, 1873 | Ashanti War | English and King Koffee | King Koffee plundered English |
| ,, 1878-1880 | Afghan War | English and Shere Ali | Cabul occupied & Candahar taken |
| ,, 1879 | Zulu War | Cetewayo and English | Cetewayo taken prisoner |
| ,, 1880-1881 | Boer War | English and Dutch | English Parliament recalled troops at moment of victory |
| ,, 1882 | Egyptian War | English & Arabi Pasha | Arabi Exiled. British occupation of Egypt |
| ,, 1881-1885 | Soudan War | Ah Mahdi and English | Gordon and Col. Burnaby slain |
| ,, 1885 | Burmese War | King Theebaw & English | Burmah Annexed to India, 1886 |
| ,, 1894 | First Matabele War | English and Matabele Chiefs | Rising quelled, Lobengula defeated, & Cap. Buluwayo taken |
| ,, 1895 | Chitral Expedition | English and Native Tribes | British Authority Established, and Road from Peshawar to Chitral opened up |
| ,, 1895 | Ashanti Campaign | English and Ashantis | No fighting. Capital Coomassie taken and King imprisoned. |
| ,, 1896 | Dr. Jameson's Raid | S. African Republic and British S. Africa Co. | Dr. Jameson defeated and imprisoned |
| ,, 1896 | Second Matabele War | Eng. & Matabele Chiefs | Rising quelled as in 1893-4 |
| ,, 1896 | Dongola Expedition | English and Dervishes | Dervishes defeated and district |
| ,, 1897 | Afridis War | English and Natives | To punish Afridis [liberated |
| ,, 1898 | II. Soudan War | English and Dervishes | Dervishes defeated and Chief Mahmoud taken |

[1] LANGUAGES OF THE BRITISH ISLES.—The several languages spoken in the British Islands are:—

1. *English.*—"And how hear we every man in our own tongue wherein we were born?" Acts ii. 8.

2. *Welsh.*—"A pha fodd yr ydym ni yn eu clywed hwynt bob un yn ein hiaith ein hun yn yr hony'n ganed ni?"

3. *Gaelic.*—"Agus cionnus a ta sinne 'gan cluinntinn gach aon 'nar cànain féin, anns an d'rugadh sinn?"

4. *Irish.*—"Agus cionnos do cluin ṙ nne ᵹaċ áon oᵹuinn a teanᵹuiḋ ḟéin ann aṙ ṗuᵹaḋ ṙinn?"

5. *Manx.*—"As kys dy vel shin clashtyn dy chovilley ghoinney loayrt ayns chengey ny mayrey ain hene?"

GENERAL HISTORY.—Previous to the Roman Invasion of Britain by Julius Cæsar (B.C. 55 and 54) the history of these islands is veiled in obscurity, and very little really trustworthy information has been found (*see* p. 43).

B.C. 55—The Romans held possession of Britain for 460 years, from B.C. 55 to A.D. 410.

A.D. 446—The Saxons and Danish hordes followed and remained masters of the country from A.D. 446 until the Norman Conquest by William I., 1066.

597—S. Augustine's Mission of Christianity to Britain.

---

[1] Taken from a small pamphlet issued by the British and Foreign Bible Society illustrating specimens of the different languages into which the Bible has been translated.

827—Egbert of Wessex destroyed Heptarchy, and became sole monarch.

1066—Battle of Hastings (Telham Hill Battle) or Senlae.

1096—The First Crusade.

1171—Ireland annexed. Henry II. became the First Lord of Ireland.

1208-14—Six Years' Interdict, English King John and people, by Pope Innocent III.

1215—Magna Charta.

1265—House of Commons instituted.

1276-1282—Conquest of Wales by Edward I. (Edward II. proclaimed 1st Prince of Wales.)

1296—Edward I. invades Scotland.

1328—Independence of Scotland proclaimed.

1534—Act of Supremacy passed separating the English Church from Government of Pope.

1536—Wales united with England.

1547—English Reformation commenced.

1588—Spanish Armada defeated.

1603—English and Scottish Crowns united by James I. England (James VI. Scotland).

1607—Colonial Empire of Britain Commences.

1611—Authorised Version of the English Bible issued.

1643—Solemn League and Covenant.

1649—Charles I. executed.

1649-1660—The Commonwealth. (Oliver Cromwell in power.)

1651—Navigation Act passed.

1665—Great Plague of London.

1666—Great Fire of London.

1693—National Debt instituted.

1716—Septennial (Parliamentary Act passed).

1776—American Colonies lost. Declaration of Independence of United States.

1800—Ireland united under the British Crown.

1806—Slave trade abolished in British possessions.

1831-2—First Reform Bill.

1837—Victoria proclaimed Queen of Great Britain.

1841—Prince of Wales born.

1851—First International Exhibition (Hyde Park).

1858—India transferred to British Crown.

1861—Death of Prince Consort.

1867—Confederation of Canada.

1869—Irish Church disestablished.

1873—The First London Board School built and opened.

1875-6—Prince of Wales visits India.

1876—Queen Victoria assumed the title of Empress of India.

1886—Burmese Empire annexed to Britain.

1887—Queen Victoria proclaimed her Jubilee (50 years' reign).

1889—The British South Africa Co. granted a Charter.

1890—The Forth Bridge opened.

1894—The Tower Bridge opened.

1894—The Manchester Ship Canal completed.

1897—Queen Victoria reigned 60 years (Diamond Jubilee).

## TRADE STATISTICAL NOTES.

Reprinted by special permission from *The Imperial Institute Journal*, vol. ii., No. 22, October, 1896, p. 378.

**United Kingdom.**—Value of Total Imports from, and of Total Exports to, the principal Foreign Countries and British Possessions for the five years, 1891-95.

*The Exports in this Table include British and Foreign and Colonial Produce.*

| Countries. | | 1891. | 1892. | 1893. | 1894. | 1895. |
|---|---|---|---|---|---|---|
| FOREIGN. | | £ | £ | £ | £ | £ |
| Russia—Northern Ports | Imports | 12,442,112 | 9,737,873 | 10,332,702 | 12,078,482 | 13,211,128 |
| | Exports | 6,903,102 | 7,671,102 | 8,963,795 | 10,114,981 | 9,370,619 |
| Russia—Southern Ports | Imports | 11,668,139 | 5,385,304 | 8,241,863 | 11,520,266 | 11,525,791 |
| | Exports | 1,290,030 | 1,205,797 | 1,399,876 | 1,427,076 | 1,315,714 |
| Sweden and Norway | Imports | 11,873,280 | 11,806,679 | 11,986,844 | 11,987,783 | 12,615,083 |
| | Exports | 6,586,438 | 6,279,921 | 6,125,028 | 6,558,937 | 6,568,779 |
| Denmark Proper and Iceland | Imports | 7,936,787 | 8,041,062 | 8,936,835 | 9,543,706 | 9,799,328 |
| | Exports | 3,032,612 | 3,038,520 | 2,971,569 | 3,038,055 | 3,135,122 |
| Germany | Imports | 27,031,743 | 25,726,738 | 26,364,849 | 26,874,470 | 26,992,559 |
| | Exports | 29,944,361 | 29,641,814 | 27,954,494 | 29,217,328 | 32,736,651 |
| Holland | Imports | 27,301,657 | 28,820,921 | 28,851,490 | 27,606,397 | 28,419,477 |
| | Exports | 14,988,930 | 15,630,922 | 15,746,028 | 13,879,096 | 11,272,258 |
| Belgium | Imports | 17,253,265 | 17,013,967 | 16,848,979 | 17,052,404 | 17,545,636 |
| | Exports | 13,272,472 | 12,613,305 | 13,016,450 | 13,041,091 | 11,934,653 |
| France | Imports | 44,777,460 | 43,519,130 | 43,658,090 | 43,450,074 | 47,470,581 |
| | Exports | 24,336,676 | 21,337,350 | 19,795,500 | 19,751,062 | 20,324,998 |
| Portugal | Imports | 2,952,965 | 3,440,822 | 2,377,892 | 2,390,065 | 2,491,926 |
| | Exports | 2,349,254 | 1,772,759 | 2,179,289 | 1,809,352 | 1,865,973 |
| Spain | Imports | 10,523,875 | 10,916,636 | 10,353,932 | 10,547,195 | 11,314,518 |
| | Exports | 5,527,061 | 5,212,271 | 4,182,672 | 4,407,103 | 4,052,806 |
| Italy | Imports | 3,419,281 | 3,284,486 | 2,948,336 | 3,129,173 | 3,132,720 |
| | Exports | 6,853,048 | 6,308,361 | 5,077,652 | 6,189,953 | 6,211,337 |
| Austrian Territories | Imports | 1,464,106 | 1,237,634 | 1,627,036 | 1,385,762 | 1,221,783 |
| | Exports | 1,607,191 | 1,525,453 | 1,547,969 | 1,918,127 | 2,149,552 |
| Turkey | Imports | 5,442,881 | 5,551,798 | 4,978,721 | 4,899,815 | 5,751,537 |
| | Exports | 7,098,474 | 6,680,645 | 6,191,272 | 6,914,747 | 5,632,932 |
| Egypt | Imports | 10,658,288 | 10,525,230 | 8,845,426 | 9,284,801 | 9,524,507 |
| | Exports | 3,875,064 | 3,316,364 | 3,434,149 | 4,065,814 | 3,414,556 |
| United States | Imports | 104,409,050 | 108,186,317 | 91,783,847 | 89,607,392 | 86,548,860 |
| | Exports | 41,066,147 | 41,412,006 | 35,715,274 | 30,775,460 | 44,067,703 |
| Brazil | Imports | 4,249,909 | 3,511,941 | 4,036,102 | 3,940,069 | 3,614,155 |
| | Exports | 8,605,293 | 8,218,050 | 8,067,768 | 7,826,566 | 7,643,789 |
| Argentine Republic | Imports | 3,451,228 | 4,540,358 | 4,836,682 | 6,168,624 | 9,084,497 |
| | Exports | 4,366,028 | 5,808,279 | 5,658,230 | 4,633,315 | 5,490,548 |
| Chili | Imports | 3,710,356 | 3,871,399 | 3,797,429 | 3,711,544 | 3,436,142 |
| | Exports | 2,205,969 | 4,029,338 | 2,613,901 | 2,389,532 | 3,454,332 |
| China (exclusive of Hong Kong and Macao) | Imports | 4,713,508 | 3,583,248 | 3,894,258 | 3,543,362 | 3,343,865 |
| | Exports | 6,525,662 | 5,836,597 | 4,699,336 | 4,592,140 | 5,363,536 |
| Japan | Imports | 1,152,585 | 804,003 | 1,046,598 | 958,541 | 1,143,382 |
| | Exports | 3,060,893 | 3,281,644 | 3,731,644 | 3,918,743 | 4,772,829 |
| Total of all Foreign countries | Imports | 335,976,546 | 326,027,578 | 312,918,724 | 314,432,644 | 321,159,448 |
| | Exports | 215,775,599 | 210,428,625 | 198,554,958 | 195,199,909 | 209,760,256 |

## TRADE STATISTICAL NOTES, ETC.—*Continued*.

| Countries. | | 1891. | 1892. | 1893. | 1894. | 1895. |
|---|---|---|---|---|---|---|
| BRITISH POSSESSIONS. | | £ | £ | £ | £ | £ |
| North American Colonies | Imports | 12,606,415 | 14,566,464 | 13,343,596 | 12,907,646 | 13,400,570 |
| | Exports | 8,209,942 | 8,529,522 | 8,561,140 | 7,381,088 | 6,594,003 |
| West India Islands and Guiana | Imports | 2,443,758 | 2,893,817 | 2,513,261 | 2,791,586 | 2,628,784 |
| | Exports | 3,345,005 | 3,295,847 | 3,636,001 | 3,372,591 | 3,037,647 |
| Australasia | Imports | 31,261,571 | 30,542,630 | 29,874,362 | 31,859,210 | 33,362,797 |
| | Exports | 28,256,120 | 21,523,228 | 16.981,004 | 17,968,076 | 19,347,664 |
| British India | Imports | 32,234,398 | 30,513,106 | 26,223,949 | 27,648,857 | 26,431,315 |
| | Exports | 32,549,207 | 29,047,287 | 29,931,554 | 30,114,943 | 25,487,089 |
| The Straits Settlements | Imports | 5,356,865 | 4,868,289 | 4,518,387 | 4,584,783 | 4,645,446 |
| | Exports | 2,589,262 | 2,205,419 | 1,848,722 | 2,398,922 | 2,032,820 |
| Ceylon, | Imports | 4,168,998 | 3,945,209 | 4,252,794 | 4,101,275 | 4,524,843 |
| | Exports | 1,061,374 | 989,586 | 946,672 | 988,875 | 1,017,639 |
| Natal | Imports | 1,183,428 | 867,954 | 750,405 | 688,055 | 716,745 |
| | Exports | 2,493,088 | 2,066,422 | 1,463,403 | 1,526,534 | 1,731,581 |
| Cape of Good Hope | *Imports | 5,071,000 | 4,595,324 | 4,799,748 | 4,301,521 | 4,709,259 |
| | Exports | 6,145,449 | 6,528,412 | 7,892,388 | 7,511,310 | 9,731,994 |
| Total of *all* British Possessions | *Imports | 99,464,718 | 97,766,304 | 91,769,454 | 93,912,166 | 95,570,210 |
| | Exports | 93,338,119 | 81,211,541 | 78,583,312 | 78,585,958 | 76,072,151 |
| Total of *all* Foreign Countries and British Possessions | *Imports | 435,441,264 | 423,793,882 | 404,688,178 | 408,344,810 | 416,689,658 |
| | Exports | 309,113,718 | 291,640,166 | 277,138,270 | 273,785,867 | 285,832,407 |
| *Value of Diamonds imported from the Cape of Good Hope, not included in the above totals. | | 4,077,608 | 3,805,183 | 3,069,384 | 2,987,953 | 4,754,085 |

## AGRICULTURAL RETURNS OF GREAT BRITAIN, 1896.

Preliminary Statement for 1896, compiled from the Returns collected on the 4th June; and comparisons with previous Years.

| Crops and Live Stock. | 1896. | 1895. | 1894. | 1893. |
|---|---|---|---|---|
| | *Acres.* | *Acres.* | *Acres.* | *Acres.* |
| Wheat | 1,693,957 | 1,417,483 | 1,927,902 | 1,897,524 |
| Barley | 2,104,764 | 2,166,279 | 2,095,771 | 2,075,097 |
| Oats | 3,095,488 | 3,296,063 | 3,253,401 | 3,171,756 |
| Potatoes | 563,741 | 541,217 | 504,454 | 527,821 |
| Hay from clover & rotation grasses | 2,171,966 | 2,303,431 | 2,121,904 | 2,047,008 |
| Hay from permanent pasture | 4,638,722 | 4,760,889 | 4,852,442 | 4,270,480 |
| Hops | 54,249 | 53,940 | 59,535 | 57,564 |
| | *No.* | *No.* | *No.* | *No.* |
| Cows & Heifers in Milk or in Calf | 2,511,675 | 2,485,820 | 2,460,086 | 2,554,624 |
| Other Cattle :—2 Years & above | 1,365,057 | 1,431,525 | 1,516,072 | 1,580,242 |
| ,, 1 Year & under 2 | 1,306,313 | 1,190,368 | 1,217,145 | 1,354,523 |
| ,, Under 1 Year | 1,310,537 | 1,246,623 | 1,153,210 | 1,211,287 |
| Total of Cattle | 6,493,582 | 6,354,336 | 6,347,113 | 6,700,676 |
| Ewes kept for Breeding | 9,925,587 | 9,663,129 | 9,668,002 | 10,128,676 |
| Other Sheep :—1 Year & above | 6,427,982 | 6,334,386 | 6,342,730 | 6,911,063 |
| ,, Under 1 Year | 10,351,760 | 9,794,680 | 9,850,768 | 10,240,595 |
| Total of Sheep | 26,705,329 | 25,792,195 | 25,801,500 | 27,280,334 |
| Sows kept for Breeding | 393,729 | 415,210 | 351,119 | 308,722 |
| Other Pigs | 2,485,072 | 2,469,221 | 2,038,907 | 1,804,808 |
| Total of Pigs | 2,878,801 | 2,884,431 | 2,390,026 | 2,113,530 |

## AGRICULTURAL RETURNS OF GREAT BRITAIN—Continued.
### Comparisons with 1895 and 1894.

| Crops and Live Stock. | Increase. | | | | Decrease. | | | |
|---|---|---|---|---|---|---|---|---|
| | Over 1895. | | Over 1894. | | Under 1895. | | Under 1894. | |
| | Acres. | Per Cent. | Acres. | Per Cent. | Acres. | Per Cent. | Acres. | Per Cent. |
| Wheat | 276,474 | 19·5 | .. | .. | .. | . | 234,005 | 12·1 |
| Barley, | .. | .. | 8,993 | 0·4 | 61,515 | 2·8 | .. | .. |
| Oats | .. | .. | .. | .. | 200,575 | 6·1 | 157,913 | 4·9 |
| Potatoes | 22,524 | 4·2 | 59,287 | 11·8 | .. | .. | .. | .. |
| Hay from clover | .. | .. | 50,062 | 2·4 | 131,465 | 5·7 | .. | .. |
| Hay from pasture | .. | .. | .. | .. | 122,167 | 2·6 | 213,720 | 4·4 |
| Hops | .. | .. | .. | .. | 4,691 | 8·0 | 5,286 | 8·9 |
| | No. | Per Cent. | No. | Per Cent. | No. | Per Cent. | No. | Per Cent |
| Cows | 25,855 | 1·0 | 51,589 | 2·1 | .. | .. | .. | .. |
| Other cattle, 2 & above | .. | .. | .. | .. | 66,468 | 4·6 | 151,615 | 10·0 |
| ,, 1 & under 2 | 115,945 | 9·7 | 89,168 | 7·3 | .. | .. | .. | .. |
| ,, Under 1 | 63,914 | 5·1 | 157,327 | 13·6 | .. | .. | .. | .. |
| Total Cattle | 139,246 | 2·2 | 146,469 | 2·3 | .. | .. | .. | .. |
| Ewes | 262,458 | 2·7 | 257,585 | 2·7 | .. | .. | .. | .. |
| Other sheep, 1 & above | 93,596 | 1·5 | 85,252 | 1·3 | .. | .. | .. | .. |
| ,, Under 1 | 557,080 | 5·7 | 500,992 | 5·1 | .. | .. | .. | .. |
| Total Sheep | 913,134 | 3·5 | 843,829 | 3·3 | .. | .. | .. | .. |
| Sows | .. | .. | 42,610 | 12·1 | 21,481 | 5·2 | .. | .. |
| Other Pigs | 15,851 | 0·6 | 446,165 | 21·9 | .. | .. | .. | .. |
| Total Pigs | .. | .. | 488,775 | 20·5 | 5,030 | 0·2 | .. | .. |

(Reprinted from the *Journal of the Board of Agriculture* for September, 1896, for the information of Occupiers of Land.)

Board of Agriculture,
September, 1896.

N.B.—To prove the advanced state of cultivation in the British Isles, a recent survey has classed the total area of land as follows:—
1. \* Permanent pastures and grazing land, 58 per cent.
2. Arable or cultivated farm and garden land, 36 per cent.
3. Woods and common land, 6 per cent.

\* Increasing each year.

## TABLE SHOWING CHIEF FEATURES IN THE BRITISH ISLANDS.

| Country. | Area Square miles. | Population. | Highest Mountain. | Longest River. | Largest Lake. | Chief Island. | Capital and Population. |
|---|---|---|---|---|---|---|---|
| ENGLAND | 51,000 | 27,501,362 | Scafell, 3,166 feet | Severn, 240 miles | Windermere, 3 square miles | Isle of Man, 281 square miles | London, 4,232,118 |
| SCOTLAND | 30,000 | 4,025,647 | Ben Nevis, 4,373 feet | Tay, 110 miles | Loch Lomond 45 square miles | Lewis, 980 square miles | Edinburgh, 333,268 |
| WALES | 7,363 | 1,501,163 | Snowdon, 3,571 feet | Severn 240 miles | Bala Lake, 2½ square miles | Anglesea, 271 square miles | Merthyr Tydfil, 58,080 |
| IRELAND | 32,520 | 4,704,750 | Carrantuel, 3,414 feet | Shannon 224 miles | Lough Neagh 153 square miles | Achill Island, 80½ square miles | Dublin, 311,209 |
| Total | 120,883 | 37,732,922 | — | — | — | — | — |

IMPERIAL BRITAIN. MAP IV.

# PART III.

## ENGLAND AND WALES.

EXTENT.—The irregular triangle, not unlike the letter A in shape, forming the largest, and most southern portion, of the British Isles, is called England and Wales.

The extreme length, from Berwick-upon-Tweed in the North, to Start Point in the South of Devonshire, is about 400 miles; and its breadth varies from 300 miles in the South, from Dover to Land's End, to only 60 miles in the North, from the Solway Firth to the River Tyne.

AREA.—The total area, if we include the adjacent islands, is 58,186 square miles, England alone being 50,823 square miles, and Wales 7,363 square miles. By comparison we find this small country is equal in area to $\frac{1}{80}$ part of Europe, or it represents but $\frac{1}{900}$ of the area of the world.

POSITION.—England and Wales is really a peninsula, surrounded on three sides by the sea, *viz.*, on the East, West, and South, and joined with Scotland on the North. It lies between parallels of latitude 50° and 56° North of the Equator, and between longitude 2° East and 6° West of Greenwich.

BOUNDARIES.—*North* by Scotland; *East* by North Sea or German Ocean; *South* by English Channel, and the Straits of Dover; and *West* by Irish Sea, St. George's Channel, and the Bristol Channel.

COAST LINE.—The coast line is considerable, the total length being 2,765 miles. Excellent harbour accommodation abounds, and every part of it is fringed and studded with signs of commerce and coast industry, from the crowded seaports, where our ships carry on their continuous trade of passengers, and merchandise, to and from other lands, to the quiet fishing villages, where the tiny craft quietly put forth to take the harvest of the deep for the food of the inhabitants.

England and Wales have one mile of coast for every 21 square miles of area. Twenty-nine of the counties touch the sea-board, so that every part of the country is most easily accessible to the coast. These facts, with the prevalence of high tides, which enable the largest vessels to enter our ports, and the many river mouths, or estuaries, offering the best facilities for docks and harbours, have tended to bring our commercial interests to the present high standard of value.

The coast scenery is, also, both varied, and beautiful for the most part. The smooth chalk cliffs of the Eastern and Southern shores are a most pleasing feature, and contrast, in a marked way, with the bolder, and more broken, rocky parts of the Western Coast. With but few exceptions, small boats may put in to nearly every part, the shores being chiefly of sand, pebbles, and broken shells, although clay and marl are to be met with. Sea-bathing can be indulged in with safety in many parts, as the water is shallow, and the shores slope gradually, while the beach is firm and even.

The more rugged and wilder portions of the coast are to be met with in Cumberland, Wales, and Cornwall on the Western side. Here the coast is somewhat dangerous, owing to the existence of numerous rocks and headlands jutting abruptly out of the deep water, while the sea is less calm, and more subject to storm exposure.

*A*. THE EASTERN COAST.—This coast is remarkably even, whether we view it from the land or from the sea. Passing from North to South, we lose the bold, rocky, coast line, with Flamborough Head on the Yorkshire coast, and from this point until we reach the North Foreland in Kent, there are to be seen only a succession of flat marsh lands, or occasional sand hills or levels, with here and there, as on the Norfolk coast, a range of low cliffs formed by the neighbouring chalk hills.

The gain and loss on this Eastern Coast of England is somewhat remarkable. Whereas the sea is rapidly encroaching along a portion of the Yorkshire coast, so that considerable tracts have been lost; a little further south, on the Lincolnshire coast, the land appears to be gaining on the sea.

*The chief Capes and Headlands on the East Coast are six in number :—*

1. Flamborough Head in Yorkshire, the highest point on this coast, in olden days used as a Beacon Station, hence its name.
2. Spurn Head, or Point, also in Yorkshire, jutting out and forming the mouth of the Humber.
3. Hunstanton Point in Norfolk, the extreme point of the East Anglican heights.
4. Lowestoft Ness, or Nose, in Suffolk, the most easterly point in the British Isles.
5. The Naze (another form of Nose), and Foulness in Essex.
6. The North Foreland in Kent, which is noted as the beginning of the *White Cliffs of Albion's Isle.*

*The chief Openings or Inlets are six in number :—*

1. Tynemouth, noted for its shipbuilding and colliery trade.
2. Mouth of the Tees, an important outlet for coals and iron, etc.
3. The Humber Estuary, with its ports of Hull and Grimsby.

4. The Wash, between Lincolnshire and Norfolk. It is shallow and full of dangerous sandbanks.
5. Mouth of the Rivers Stour, and Orwell, between Suffolk and Essex.
6. The Estuary of the Thames, forming the great waterway to London, the Metropolis of the world's trade and commerce.

*B.* THE SOUTHERN COAST.—At the eastern part the striking chalk cliffs are continued as noted on the Eastern Coast. Here the shores are most even, and less indented than the Western part, which partakes in great measure of the bolder scenery of the Western Coast of Britain.

*The chief Capes and Headlands are eight in number :—*

1. The South Foreland, again terminating in White Chalk Hills of Kent.
2. Dungeness, probably the nose, or point of danger, also in Kent.
3. Beachy Head } in Sussex.
4. Selsea Bill
5. St. Alban's Head } on the Dorset coast.
6. Portland Bill
7. Start Point, sometimes called the *tail* of Devonshire.
8. The Lizard, the most southerly point of the British Isles.

There are also St. Catherine's Point, and the Needles, in the Isle of Wight.

*The chief Openings or Inlets are seven in number :—*

1. Portsmouth Harbour, an important naval station and dockyard.
2. Southampton Water, one of our chief openings for commerce.
3. Weymouth Bay, protected by Portland breakwater.

ENGLAND AND WALES. 99

4. Torbay, in Devonshire.
5. Plymouth Sound, also a naval station and excellent harbour.
6. Falmouth Harbour, in Cornwall.
7. Mount's Bay, so called from St. Michael's Mount here.

*C*. THE WESTERN COAST.—We now meet with grander scenery, a bolder and more irregular outline of coast, having much deeper indentations than on the Eastern and Southern Coasts. This is due to the exposure of this Western Coast to the storms of the Atlantic Ocean.

*The chief Capes and Headlands are ten in number :—*
1. Land's End, in Cornwall, the most westerly point of England.
2. Hartland Point, in Devonshire.
3. Morte Point, opposite to Lundy Island, also in Devonshire.
4. Worm's Head, in Glamorganshire.
5. St. David's Head, in Pembrokeshire, is the most westerly part of Wales.
6. Braich-y-Pwll, the extreme south-western point of Caernarvonshire.
7. Great Orme's Head is 673 feet high, making it the highest point on the coast of England and Wales.
8. Point of Aire, in Flintshire.
9. Formby Point, in Lancashire.
10. St. Bees' Head, in Cumberland. Here the cliffs are a red sandstone.

*The chief Openings or Inlets are fourteen in number :—*
1. Barnstaple Bay
2. Mouth of the Severn
3. Swansea Bay
4. Caermarthen Bay

} in the Bristol Channel, where high tides are prevalent.

5. Milford Haven is one of the grandest natural harbours in the world.
6. St. Bride's Bay, in Pembrokeshire.
7. Cardigan Bay, the largest in Wales.
8. Tremadoc Bay, the most northern part of Cardigan Bay.
9. Caernarvon Bay, of small size.
10, 11, 12. Mouths of the Dee, Mersey, and Ribble. Unfortunately, there are sandbanks which hinder large ships from entering except at high tides.
13. Morecambe Bay is both sandy and shallow.
14. Solway Firth, dividing England and Scotland.

Before leaving the sea coast, which has been most appropriately called the battleground between sea and land, on account of the gain and loss which continually takes place, and so ever changes the line of boundary, we must mention the Straits, and Islands, which surround it on every side.

STRAITS.—The Straits of Dover are the first of importance, separating England from France, on the mainland of Europe, and joining the North Sea with the English Channel. In the narrowest point, between Dover and Calais, the breadth is but 21 miles, and the depth does not exceed 200 feet. Many dangers are experienced here to vessels entering the English Channel, by reason of the meeting of cross currents from the wider expanse of waters at either end, and the shifting sandbanks, known as the Goodwin Sands, which impede navigation at the entrance. To do away with these difficulties two schemes have been promulgated. The English plan is to bore a submarine tunnel from England to France, which would be a somewhat costly and difficult enterprise; and the French scheme is to bridge the Channel across by constructing enormous piers of sufficient strength to carry a railway over it. This will never be accomplished, as it not only bristles with difficulties of construction and maintenance, but it would add tenfold to the dangers of navigation during sea storms. Well-nigh every conceivable style of steamer has been tested on this short passage, the most novel being the *Calais-Douvres*, or twin steamship, which literally consists of two small steamers rivetted firmly together to prevent the rolling motion, and give comfort and confidence to passengers crossing the Channel. There are several daily passages carried on by the Southern Railway Companies of England. (*See* pp. 64-5.)

The other two Straits are narrow water passages lying between the mainland of England and Wales and two of the principal islands. Thus on the Southern Coast we have the Solent and Spithead, dividing Hampshire from the Isle of Wight. This Strait offers great protection to vessels of all kinds as a sheltering roadstead during stormy weather.

On the Western Coast, the Menai Straits, lying between Anglesea Island and Caernarvonshire, are 14 miles long, and vary in width from 260 yards to 2 miles. The island has a double connection with the mainland, in the two finely constructed bridges, commonly known as (1) Stephenson's Tubular Railway Bridge, and (2) Telford's Suspension Chain Bridge, 560 feet long. The scenery here is very beautiful.

ROADSTEADS.—Here may be mentioned also the principal roadsteads, or natural harbours of refuge, situated along the shores of England and Wales. They are sheltering places for our shipping during the all too sudden and frequent storms which overtake them.

The chief are The Downs, or Smooth Channel, lying between the shores of Kent and the Goodwin Sands. This is the largest natural harbour in the world. It will accommodate hundreds of vessels during a storm. Yarmouth

Roads is also formed by a number of sandbanks lying off the coast of Norfolk. This roadstead is a great protection to the coasting vessels which pass from London to Aberdeen, Dundee, Leith, Hull, etc.

Other roadsteads on the southern shores of England are, Plymouth Sound, and the channel known as Portland Roads.

ISLANDS.—If we compare the Navigation Charts of the Admiralty with the ordinary map of England and Wales, we shall well-nigh be disposed to query the truth they represent of the numerous islands, rocks, shoals, and sandbanks, thickly studded with danger signals in the form of lighthouses, lightships, and floating buoys, which apparently surround every part of our coasts. Such charts are a necessity to safe navigation, and even with these valuable aids which all vessels carry to direct their course, each year brings a long list of shipwrecks, and coast casualties, in which there is recorded a heavy loss of valuable lives and property.

For general purposes we must, however, pass over these minute details, which strictly belong to navigation rather than to descriptive geography, and restrict ourselves to a survey of the well-known islands lying off our coasts.

On the Eastern Coast we have no large islands, and but few smaller ones to mention here.

The principal islands in order of position we meet with in travelling from North to South are:—

I. Those of the Northumbrian Coast, including—

1. *Lindisfarne*, or *Holy Island*, which by ancient law belongs to the county of Durham, although it is situated $1\frac{1}{2}$ miles off the coast of Northumberland, is about 9 miles in circuit, with an area of nearly 1,000 acres. This island, with the cluster of the Farne Islands, some seven miles distant, constitutes a parish. The inhabitants are mostly fishermen. Occasionally at low water mark, Lindisfarne

may be reached by a dangerous though possible winding track across the sands; but quicksands abound here, and a guide is a necessity. This island received its title of Holy from the ancient Abbey, and Bishopric, founded here towards the end of the seventh century. By reason of the marauding Danes, who visited these parts to plunder and kill, the monks and their bishop removed to Durham, A.D. 900, hence its present connection with that See and County. The population, in 1891, was under 1,000.

2. *The Farne, or Ferne, Islands* are a cluster of 17 rocky islets lying off the Northumbrian Coast, on a line with Bamborough Head. The largest of the group is barely a mile in circumference, and the surface is generally barren. Two lighthouses mark out the dangerous channels and hidden rocks of this coast. These islands have been long noted as the scene of fearful wrecks; yet of these the loss of the *Forfarshire* is still the most noted, by reason of the courage and skill of the lighthouse-keeper and his noble daughter, Grace Darling, who toiled alone to save the crew and passengers from drowning during a fearful storm in 1838.

3. *Coquet Isle* is an important lighthouse station, situated at the mouth of the River Coquet in Northumberland. It is about a mile in circumference. There are two lighthouses here, the keepers of which are the only inhabitants during a portion of the year; at other times a few fishermen visit the huts provided for their accommodation there.

4. *N.B.—Spern Island*, off the Yorkshire Coast, is only an island at high tide.

II. *The Islands of Thanet and Sheppey*, on the southern shore of the Estuary of the Thames, and forming part of the County of Kent, are islands only in name.

1. *Sheppey* is the largest and most important. It is about eleven miles in length, by eight in breadth, and its

surface is a low, flat, marshy pasturage. It is formed by the mouths of the Rivers Thames and Medway, together with the Swale Strait, which now has become a mere narrow drainage channel to carry off the flood waters. The chief town is Sheerness.

2. *Thanet* is more of a district of Kent than an island, although it is surrounded by the River Stour, which forms two branches, or mouths, at Sarrwall before entering the sea. It is ten miles long, by eight broad. Although the surface presents a barren appearance, yet vegetation is good, and early crops are always produced. Margate and Ramsgate are the two chief towns.

On the Southern Coast, the *Isle of Wight* is the only one of importance. It has been described as "the garden of England," or "England in miniature;" and by reason of its natural attractions of position, climate, and scenery, besides being one of the royal residences of our great and good Queen, it has naturally become one of the most fashionable watering-places in the British Isles. The island is $22\frac{1}{2}$ miles long from east to west, and $13\frac{1}{2}$ miles broad from north to south. Its coast line is about 56 miles, and its area 136 square miles. It is included in the diocese of Winchester for ecclesiastical, and in the county of Hampshire for civil purposes, from which it is separated by the Solent and Spithead.

The interior is beautifully diversified, and the soil most fertile. A range of chalk hills forms a pleasant feature in the landscape, stretching through the centre of the island from east to west. One point, St. Catherine's Hill, is 800 feet high, and there are several rivulets, called the Medina, Yar, Wootton, Newton, and others, which flow on to the coast through lovely woods, or rich park-like lands, making the inland scenery attractive in nearly every part.

The coast scenery is also charming, and there is great

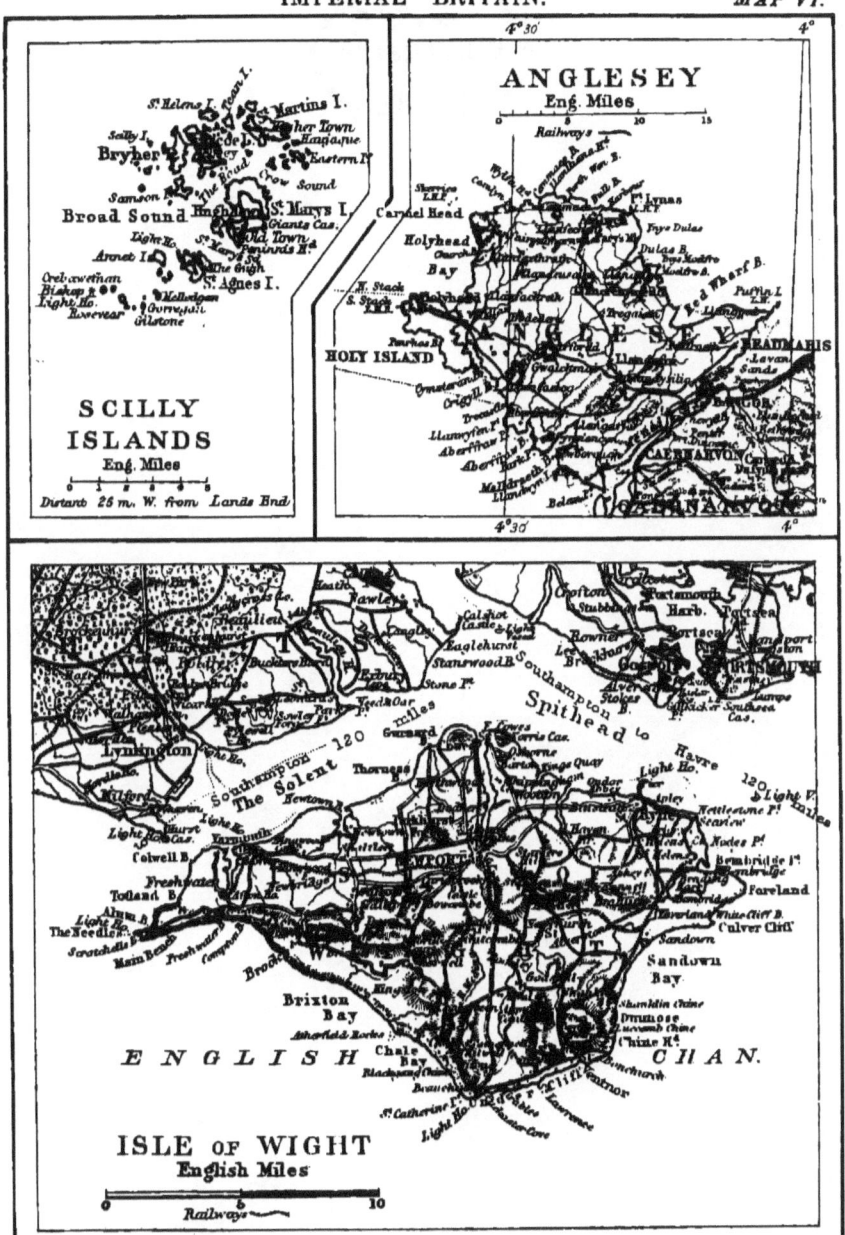

variety seen in the bold rugged coasts of the neighbourhood of the Needles, when compared with the shallow shelving sands of Sandown, etc.

The chief towns are Newport (the capital, in the centre of the island), Ryde, East and West Cowes, Yarmouth, Ventnor, Shanklin, Sandown, Freshwater, Brading, and St. Helens.

The royal residence of Osborne stands a little to the east of Cowes, where it commands an excellent view of Spithead and Portsmouth Harbour.

*History.*—But little is known of the island or its inhabitants before the Roman invasion of Britain, 55 B.C. In A.D. 686, Cadwalla gave as a present to Archbishop Wilfrid of York one-fourth of the island. Later on William the Conqueror bestowed the whole island as an estate upon his kinsman, William Fitz-Osborne. In 1293 Edward I. purchased it as a Crown possession. Charles I. was imprisoned here in Carisbrooke Castle in 1648. The Princess Beatrice of Battenberg, Her Majesty's youngest daughter, is now the governor of the island, since the death of her husband, Prince Henry, in 1895.

*Portland Isle*, in Dorsetshire, is a penal settlement for convicts, who are chiefly employed in the famous stone quarries there.

On the Western Coast the chief islands are :—

1. *The Scilly Isles*, wrongly called by the ancients "Cassiterides," or the Tin Islands, are a picturesque cluster of about 45 islands, and 100 smaller ones, some of which are mere granite rocks, lying about 30 miles south-west of Land's End, and included for ecclesiastical and civil purposes within the county of Cornwall. The united area is nine square miles. On a clear day these islands may be seen from Land's End. Only six of the larger islands are inhabited, the chief being St. Mary's,

which is 10 miles in circumference. Its capital is Hughtown. The other inhabited islands are Fresco, St. Martin, St. Agnes, Samson, and St. Helen. Steam packets ply frequently between Penzance in Cornwall and Hughtown. As the coasts of these islands are somewhat dangerous, several lighthouses have been erected on the rocks, the chief being St. Mary's Pier Lighthouse, Bishop's Rock Lighthouse, and a floating lighthouse on Seven Stones.

The soil of these islands is most fertile, and the inhabitants being industrious, large quantities of early fruit, flowers, and vegetables, are grown for the London markets.

The Prince and Princess of Wales visited the Scilly Isles in 1865.

2. *Lundy Isle* is situated some 10 miles to the north-west of Hartland Point in North Devon, at the entrance to the Bristol Channel. It is a lofty granite rock, only accessible on the eastern side, while its northern coast, where stands the Constable Rock Lighthouse, is very high and precipitous.

This rocky islet is about three miles long and one broad. Its area is 2,000 acres.

The inhabitants, which are under 100, are engaged in agriculture and the rearing of cattle, sheep, pigs, and poultry.

Lundy Island, throughout the Middle Ages, was the home of pirates. Morisco dwelt here in the twelfth century. During the reign of William and Mary, the French seized possession of the island, but shortly afterwards they gave it up.

Lying off the Welsh Coast are several islands of minor importance. Among these may be mentioned:—

   1. *Tuskar Rock, Flatholme* and *Steepholme*, off Glamorganshire, in the Bristol Channel.

2. *Caldy, Skokham, Skomer, Ramsey, St. Margaret's,* and *Bishop* and *Clerk's Rocks,* off the coast of Pembroke.
3. *St. Tudwal's Island* in Tremadoc Bay.
4. *Bardsey Island,* lying off the Braich-y-Pwll in Carnarvonshire. There are others, merely used as lighthouse stations, which are occasionally visited by the coast fishermen.
5. *Anglesea,* with *Holyhead,* situated off the north-western coast of Carnarvonshire.

*Anglesea,* or *Mona,* is an island and county of North Wales, situated in the Irish Sea, and separated from the mainland by the Menai Strait, over which are two remarkable bridges—the Stephenson Tubular Railway Bridge and the Telford Suspension Bridge. (*See* Straits, p. 101.)

The island is 24 miles long and 17 miles broad, and its area is 271 square miles. Coal is found on the Island.

The surface is undulating and the scenery diversified. There are several small streams, and the soil is fertile, yielding a large quantity of corn, potatoes, and other vegetables. Excellent pasturage abounds.

The island consists of seventy-four parishes, and its chief towns are Beaumaris (capital), Holyhead, on Holy Isle, Amlwch, Llangefni, and Llanerchymedd. Many Druidical remains are to be met with in different parts of the island, the surface of which was once covered with forests, wherein the Druids held their services. The circular stone temples may yet be seen there.

It was here that the Romans massacred the several religious orders of Druidism during one of their great festivals, because they incited the Britons to revolt against their conquerors.

The small island of Holyhead,[1] so named after the Cape,

---

[1] *See* Illustration, page 259, "South Stack Lighthouse."

is really a small island seaport town, included under Anglesea. The harbour here is a safe one; and there is an excellent pier and landing-stage, from which the Irish passengers, travelling by the London and North-Western Railway, embark for Dublin. This being the chief station of the Irish steam packets, the letters and mails are despatched through Holyhead.

*The Isle of Man*, situated in the Irish Sea, midway between England, Ireland, and Scotland, and *The Channel Islands*, lying off the French Coast, being classed as dependencies of Great Britain, have been placed among the British possessions in Europe, rather than as parts of the British Isles.

COAST DEFENCE AND SAFEGUARDS.—No country in the world is provided with the same means of coast defence against a foreign foe, and safeguards for life from either wrecks or boat accidents, as the British Isles.

*A*. In addition to the Channel Squadron of warships, the coasts are under a strict surveillance of armed cruisers, and other smaller vessels, in every part. Training ships are moored at the mouths of several of the larger rivers, and a continuous chain of coastguard service has been established, as land watchmen and guardians over our mercantile interests.

*B*. The principal methods of saving life resorted to are:—

1. Lighthouses and lightships.
2. Floating buoys.
3. Lifeboat stations. These are principally under the care of the Royal National Lifeboat Institution, which was founded in 1824. This excellent Society has 303 lifeboats engaged in service around the coasts of Great Britain, and others

are being added each year by the munificence of private donors, or by public subscription. "During the past 40 years the self-righting boats have been launched more than 7,400 times on service, and have saved upwards of 16,000 lives. The total number of lives saved since the Institution was founded is 38,992."—From *Hazell's Annual*, 1896.

CINQUE PORTS.—The Cinque Ports are seven in number, although, as the name implies, there were originally but five towns, or ports, claiming this ancient title. All are situated in Kent and Sussex, on the South Coast of England, *viz.*, Dover, Hastings, Hythe, Romney, and Sandwich, to which have been added, Rye and Winchelsea. William the Conqueror granted certain rights and privileges to these Cinque Ports, conditionally to their maintaining and providing certain ships of war for the king's use. The Chief Officer is called the Lord Warden of the Cinque Ports; but the duties are now not observed. The Marquis of Salisbury is the present Lord Warden of the Cinque Ports.

SURFACE.—It is a little difficult to fully gauge the great variety of surface which is presented in the limited area of this country from a general study of the map, unless it be a raised one, showing the diversified nature and varied situations of mountain range and valley, of isolated peak and low-lying plains, of forest and meadow, of wild tracts and highly cultivated lands; yet a careful survey presents all these changes of surface.

Generally speaking, the surface of England is an undulating plain, with here and there bolder ranges of verdure-clothed hills of aqueous formation, and occasionally broken somewhat abruptly by either steep rugged mountain ranges or groups. Few parts of England and Wales are really flat, yet nearly two-thirds of the whole surface may be considered to be a plain, so much so, that Professor Geikie, in his "Geography of the British Isles," says [1]:—

"It is important to realise how low and level a great part of the country really is. If the island were sunk 500 feet below its present level, England would be reduced to a scattered group of islands, the largest of which would extend from near Derby to Hexham. Wales would form a second island of about the same size; the uplands of Eastern Yorkshire would make a third; and a scattered archipelago would run from Cornwall eastwards to Kent, northwards to Shropshire, and north-eastwards to Lincolnshire. If the depression were only to the extent of 250 feet, the sea would spread over all the low grounds from the Tees to the Thames, and from Westmoreland to Shropshire."

MOUNTAINS.—This somewhat quaint description of the surface of England and Wales graphically points out the position of the mountain ranges and highlands, and arranges for us the mountainous districts of England and Wales under three heads or systems:—

1. The Northern System, consisting of the Cheviot Hills, the Pennine Chain, and the Cumbrian Group.
2. The Cambrian or Western System, which includes all the mountains of Wales.
3. The Devonian or Southern System, consisting of the hills of Cornwall, Devon, and Somersetshire.

I. In describing the Northern System of mountains and hills, we must commence with the:—

1. *Cheviot Hills*, an historical range of pastoral mountains, running in a south-westerly direction between England and Scotland, and forming, with the River Tweed,

---

[1] "Geography of the British Isles." (*Macmillan.*)

the boundary of the two countries. The Cheviots separate the western part of Northumberland from the county of Roxburgh, and though their average height varies from 1,000 to 2,000 feet, yet the highest point, known as The Cheviot, is 2,636 feet. The rich, sloping pastures of these hillsides afford excellent grass for the well-known breed of sheep called "the Cheviots." Throughout the Middle Ages, the rival border lords, Percy and Douglas, often met in battle here. Each regarded these hills as his hunting grounds; and beneath the range, where now the Newcastle and Carlisle Railway runs, the Romans at an earlier period raised the Wall of Hadrian to keep back their warlike and most troublesome neighbours, the Picts. The northern branch of the River Tyne takes its rise in the Cheviots. The boundary river, the Tweed, flows from the Lowther Hills in Scotland, and not from the Cheviots.

2. Almost at right angles to the Cheviot Hills runs the *Pennine Range*, which is really the backbone of this country. This is the longest and most important range in England, as its extends from the Cheviots, on the borders of Scotland, as far as the Peak in Derbyshire, nearly 200 miles in length.

Strictly speaking, the Pennine Range is an elevated tableland, made up of clusters of hills and peaks, and interspersed with moorland and valleys. Its width varies from 15 to 30 miles; and the scenery is much bolder in parts than in others. The average height is about 2,000 feet, but many of the peaks rise far above this, *e.g.*, Cross Fell, the highest point, and the meeting-place of four counties—Northumberland, Cumberland, Westmoreland, and Durham, is 2,900 feet; and other peaks, Whernside, Micklefell, Ingleborough, and Penyghent are nearly 2,500 feet in height. The Peak, 1,800 feet, in Derbyshire, is the culminating point of a remarkable cluster of grandly formed elevations, representing a great variety of lovely scenery by the strange rugged peaks, deep caves, perpendicular cliffs, and broken clefts, which form the valleys between. Some parts are well wooded, and clear sparkling streams add not a little to the romantic scenery which is always an attraction to tourists, especially as the Pennines are, as a rule, treeless and barren, with the exception of a scanty rough herbage barely sufficient to feed sheep.

The real value of this range is that it forms an important watershed for the northern, and north-midland, counties of England. Its mineral wealth is also of importance, for on either side of the chain there are rich coalfields, in addition to iron, lead, and building stones; so that we naturally find the districts surrounding the Pennine Range, *viz.*:—the counties of Northumberland, Durham, Yorkshire, Lancashire, Cheshire, Derbyshire, Nottingham, and Stafford, exceedingly rich in trade and manufactures of various kinds.

*The chief Rivers which have their source in the Pennine Range are:—*

    *A.* The Tyne (S. Tyne), Wear, Tees, Ouse, and Trent, flowing eastwards into the North Sea.

    *B.* The Eden, Lune, Wyre, Ribble, and Mersey, flowing westwards into the Irish Sea.

3. *The Cumbrian Group* includes the mountains of Cumberland, Westmoreland, and Lancashire, which form the Lake District, so renowned for its beautiful scenery. This is a grand group of more than a dozen peaks, all above 2,000 feet in height, and having the most picturesque valleys intervening, in which lie the silver surfaces of the lovely lakes, while tiny cascades and huge torrents pour down their streams from the heights above. Rich woodland, and rugged crag, vie with each other to perfect the scene, while villages, or mansions, peep out here and there,

making the whole one vast fairyland of beauty. No wonder the Lake District has attracted our poets, and artists, to dwell in this land of Nature's enchantment, for in few spots could her ever-varying changes be better studied than here. The principal peaks are Scafell, 3,230 feet, the highest mountain in England; Helvellyn, 3,055 feet; and Skiddaw, 3,022 feet high. Other peaks are Saddleback, Coniston Old Man, Fairfield, etc. *See also " Lakes" (Lake District) for a further description of this group.*

The only important rivers rising in the Cumbrian Group are the Derwent and the Kent, both of which flow westwards into the Irish Sea. A large part of the natural drainage of this district flows into the Lakes.

II. *The Cambrian, or Western System*, comprises the whole of the Welsh mountains. They principally consist of several short chains, branching out in different directions, which take their names after some peak occurring in them, *e.g.*, the Snowdon Range, the Plinlimmon Range, the Brecknock Beacons, etc.

Thus, they may be described as a cluster of mountain knots, linked together, either by varying ranges, or high tablelands, in which occur deeply-cut clefts and fissures, with steep valleys or glens, through which rush mountain tarns or rapid streamlets, with here and there a cascade to diversify the ever-changing beauties of this magnificent scenery.

The chief peaks include Snowdon, the highest mountain in England and Wales, 3,570 feet; Cader Idris, 2,929 feet Plinlimmon, 2,465 feet; and the Brecknock Beacons, a pair of twin heights about 2,900 feet high.

The view from the summit of Snowdon upon a clear day is both extensive and magnificent. The three Kingdoms of England, Scotland, and Ireland may be seen, together with a large portion of North Wales, also the Isle of

Man and Anglesea, including a grand stretch of the Irish Sea.

III. *The Third, and least important, of our Mountain Systems* is the Southern Range, known as "The Devonian," which includes the hills and highlands of Somersetshire, Devonshire, and Cornwall, so that Dartmoor, Exmoor, the Mendip Hills, and the Cornish Heights belong to this system.

This system of highlands are, strictly speaking, mountains, inasmuch as they are of igneous or volcanic formation, like the Northern and Cambrian Systems, and not of aqueous matter, like the oolitic, or chalk ranges, of other parts of England. Thus we find the same rough, rugged scenery as we meet with in Cumberland or Wales, though, generally speaking, more in miniature with regard to size and grandeur. Bold granite rocks, with rich slate beds, or layers, intervening, are found here, while the mineral yield is highly valuable, including tin, copper, lead, manganese, marble, and building stone of excellent quality.

*The chief Peaks in the Devonian Range are:—*
Yes Tor, 2,040 feet, and Cawsand Beacon, 1,800 feet, on Dartmoor; Dunkery Beacon on Exmoor, 1,700 feet; and Brown Willy, 1,368 feet, in Cornwall.

Exmoor, in North Devon and Somersetshire, is a chain of hills, in olden times covered with forests, but now chiefly clothed with rough pasturage and heather, with marshlands intervening.

Dartmoor, also originally a forest, is an elevated tableland, studded with rough tors or granite rocks, and intersected with streams, many of which are well known and frequented by anglers.

HILLS, etc.—We now pass on to the hills of England and Wales.

1. *The Central Heights* carry southwards the vertebral

column of England's structure in a less marked manner south of the Pennine Chain; but though the elevations are minor ones, yet the course may be distinctly traced until the Devonian Range is reached. These are all of aqueous formation, and therefore less bold in outline. This range of hills naturally divide England and Wales into two parts:— (1) To the North and West we find the chief manufacturing and mining districts; (2) To the South and East the agricultural and pastoral districts.

2. *The Cotswold Hills*, in Gloucestershire, stand first in importance here. They form a marked line of division between the two largest river-basins of England and Wales—the Thames and the Severn. They belong to the oolitic group of hills, which means that they are composed of minute egg-shaped particles of limestone, in contrast to the chalk ranges of Southern England.

Other oolitic ranges are: *The Edge Hills*, running from Oxfordshire through Warwickshire; *The Lincolnshire and Yorkshire Wolds*, running through those counties; and *The Yorkshire Moors*, running in a westerly direction from the coast near Whitby.

Then the several chalk ranges of Southern Britain include: *The Blackdown Hills and Dorset Heights; The Chiltern Hills* in Oxfordshire, a continuation of which range is known as the *East Anglican Heights*, as far eastward as the Wash; *The Gog and Magog Hills* in Cambridgeshire; and *The North and South Downs*, two somewhat parallel ranges, running East and West through Hampshire, Surrey, Sussex, and Kent. The Wrekin, in Shropshire, is an isolated peak; and Inkpen Beacon in Dorsetshire is in a similar position. Some smaller hills are the Clee Hills in Shropshire; the Clent Hills in Worcestershire; the Malvern Hills running through Worcestershire and Herefordshire, and the Quantock Hills in Somersetshire; the White Horse Hills, a continuation of the Chiltern Hills.

PLAINS.—Our next natural features, after the highlands of England, are the plains and lowlands. These we have referred to on page 110 under the head of "Surface." Two-thirds of England and Wales may be considered as plains and valleys.

1. The largest plain in England and Wales is *The Plain of York*, which extends through the central part of Yorkshire, on the eastern side of the Pennine Range. It is 160 miles long, and nearly 50 miles broad, with an area of about 1,000 square miles.

2. This plain is really the most northern portion of the *Eastern Lowlands*, which are continued southwards through the Fens of Lincolnshire (where the land sinks to the lowest level in the country) to the East Anglian Plain of Norfolk, Suffolk, and Essex.

3. *The Seaboard Plain*, or low pasture land, between the Wolds and the North Sea, is generally called *Holderness*.

4. *The Central Plain of England*, sometimes called *The Vale of Trent*, is somewhat higher in elevation than the Eastern plain. It comprises roughly the counties of Derby, Leicester, Warwick, and Stafford, which are situated south of the Pennine Range. In parts, this plain is 400 feet above the sea-level.

5. *A second portion of the Central Plain* yet continues as far south as the Thames; so that if we regard the two portions as one plain, we find it is bounded, roughly speaking, by four rivers—the Ouse, Trent, Thames, and Severn.

6. *The Cheshire Plain*, lying to the west of the Pennine Range, is also of importance. It includes parts of Lancashire and Cheshire.

7. *The Fens of Lincolnshire and Huntingdonshire* are a miniature representation of Holland. If we include *the*

*Bedford Level* in this area, it is extended over parts of several counties, bordering the Wash on the East Coast. The Fen country is damp and in parts unhealthy. Parts of it are still covered with reeds and coarse grass, where geese and sheep thrive, although, since the year 1629, much has been done to reclaim the land from the floods for agricultural purposes. The Fen District is about 60 miles long and 30 miles broad.

*The other smaller plains are :—*
1. The Cumbrian Plain, or Vale of Eden.
2. The Valleys of the Thames and Severn Rivers.
3. The Isle of Ely, or Eel Island, a raised plateau standing out from the Fen District, and in olden days always surrounded by water.
4. Salisbury Plain, which is more of a plateau than a low plain, resembling in a measure parts of Dartmoor in Devonshire in this particular.
5. The Vales of Worcester and Evesham in the West of England.
6. The Vale of the White Horse in Berkshire, with the more picturesque plains of Pewsey in Wiltshire and the Neath Valley in Glamorganshire.
7. The Weald of Kent is only a plain inasmuch as it lies between the two chalk ranges of hills known as the North and South Downs.

VALLEYS.—The Valleys of England and Wales deserve to be noticed here, owing to their singular beauty and natural fertility. In the North of England they are called "dales," but in the South they are known as "vales"—thus we speak of the dales of Yorkshire, and the vales of Somerset. As most of the principal valleys are well watered by navigable rivers, the chief of our large commercial and manufacturing towns have been placed therein.

RIVERS.—Nearly all the rivers of importance are navigable, which is a distinct advantage to the trade of the country, and there are a considerable number of excellent ports planted at their mouths, which give an uninterrupted communication with the interior. The rivers of England and Wales are both numerous and of considerable length for the size of the country. From the fact that no high mountains exist, and the hills have gentle slopes, they are generally slow-flowing. They drain the land both naturally, and artificially, for purposes of agriculture, and many of them provide water power for driving the machinery of mills, factories, etc.

The triangular shape of the coast-line of England and Wales, and the general position of the highlands, naturally arrange the river system into three divisions :—

    I. Rivers of the East Coast.
    II. Rivers of the South Coast.
    III. Rivers of the West Coast.

I. *The Rivers of the East Coast* flowing into the North Sea are first of importance if taken together for commercial and general purposes. They are the Coquet, Tyne, Wear, Tees, Humber, formed by the Yorkshire Ouse and the Trent, the Witham, Welland, Nen, Great Ouse, which enter the Wash after winding slowly through the central and eastern plains; the Yare, Orwell, Stour of Essex, Colne, Chelmer, and Blackwater flowing from the East Anglian Heights; the Thames, the Medway, and the Kentish Stour.

The six chief commercial rivers of this group are :—

A. *The Tyne*, which is made up of two streams, called the North Tyne rising in the Cheviots, and the South Tyne flowing from Crossfell in the Pennine Chain. These two streams join near Hexham in Northumberland. The river is 73 miles long, and its importance arises from its course running through the centre of the Northumberland colliery district, where both iron and coal abound. On this river stands Gateshead and Newcastle, with North Shields (Tynemouth) and South Shields at its mouth, where there are extensive shipbuilding yards.

*B. The Wear* is another important commercial river, with Sunderland at its mouth. Its length is 65 miles, and it flows from the Pennine Range, through a rich and increasing coal and iron district within the county of Durham. The city of Durham, with its magnificent cathedral, stands in a most picturesque position upon the banks of the Wear.

*C. The Tees* forms the southern boundary of the county of Durham, dividing it from the North Riding of Yorkshire. It rises in Crossfell like the Tyne, and its course is nearly 80 miles in length. This river is the principal outlet of the Cleveland iron district. On its banks stand Barnard Castle, Darlington, Middlesborough, and Stockton. The wide opening or estuary is known as Teesmouth.

*D. The Humber* is an important arm of the sea, or river estuary, from two to five miles wide, formed by the united waters of the Yorkshire Ouse and the Trent. It ranks high in importance as a commercial waterway, for on its northern shore stands Hull, or, as it is sometimes called, Kingston-upon-Hull, the third seaport in England, possessing an enormous trade with the Baltic in timber, corn, flax, hemp, wool, oil, tar, etc.; and forming an outlet for the manufactured goods of Yorkshire and the Midlands. Then there is Grimsby upon the southern bank, with its important docks and shipping, as well as its enormous fish trade with the interior.

1. *The Yorkshire Ouse, or Northern Branch of the Humber*, consists of the following tributaries—the Swale, Ure, Nidd,

Wharfe, Aire, Calder, Don, and the Derwent, in addition to the main stream, which begins at the junction of the Ure and the Swale. It waters the eastern plain of Yorkshire from the Pennine Range to the Humber. The valleys, or dales, are noted for their extreme beauty, the chief being Swaledale, Airedale, and Wharfedale, which are greatly visited by tourists.

On the banks of the Ouse and its tributaries are situated Richmond, Ripon, Ilkley, Leeds, Bradford, Halifax, Huddersfield, Sheffield, York, and Goole. The length of this river is 150 miles.

2. *The Trent, or Southern Branch of the Humber*, rises in the moorlands of Staffordshire, and flows onward for 180 miles to the Humber mouth through the counties of Stafford, Derby, Nottingham, and Lincoln. The chief tributaries are the Soar, and the Tame, on the right bank, and the Dove, and the Derwent, on the left bank.

The following towns stand upon the Trent and its tributaries—Burton-on-Trent, Nottingham, Newark, Derby, Leicester, and Stafford.

E. *The Great Ouse*, though it may not attain to such commercial importance as the above-named rivers, has a length of 145 miles. It rises in Northamptonshire, and drains the district of Buckinghamshire, Bedfordshire, Huntingdon, Cambridge, and Norfolk, until it finally enters the sea in the Wash. The chief tributaries are the Cam, Lark, Little Ouse.

The county towns upon its banks are Buckingham, Bedford, and Huntingdon, while Cambridge stands on a tributary, the Cam.

F. *The Thames* is the Queen of English rivers for importance and commerce. Its length is 215 miles, and it flows nearly across the southern part of the country from the Cotswold Hills in Gloucestershire, within ten miles of the

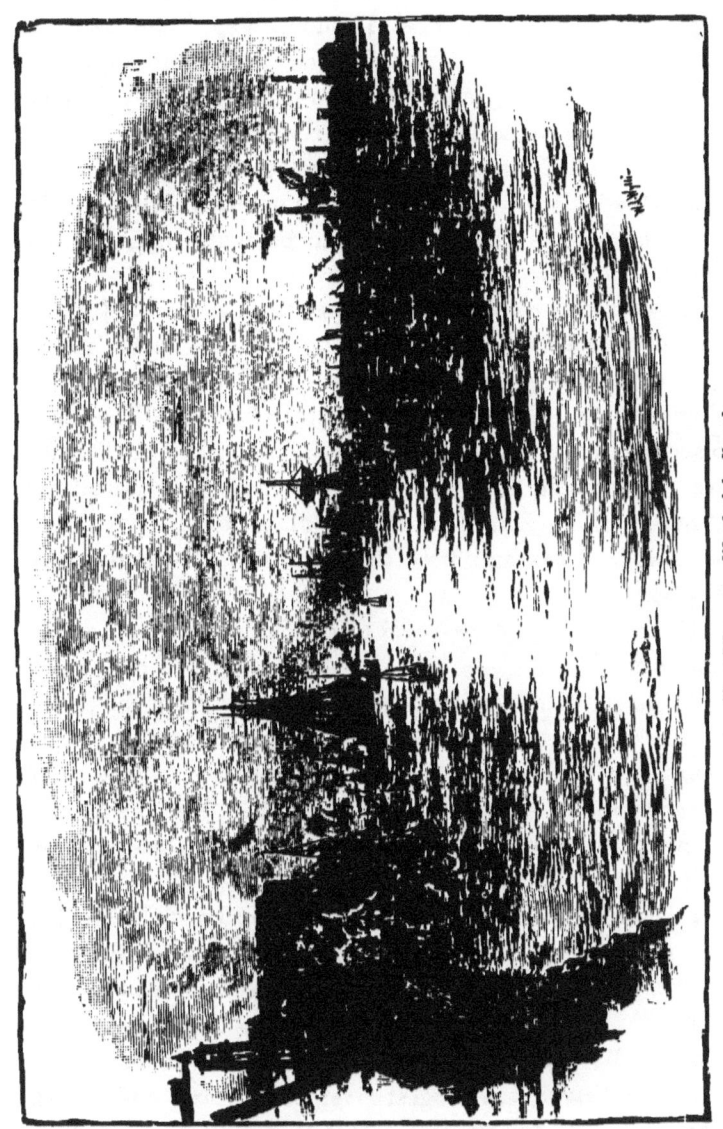

*The Thames—Woolwich Reach.*

Severn, to the North Sea. The chief tributaries on the right bank are the Kennet, Loddon, Wey, Mole, Darent, and Medway; and on the left bank the Windrush, Evenlode, Thame, Colne, Brent, Lea, and Roding. Below Oxford the Thames is called the Isis. No river in the world has the same amount of trade and commercial traffic as the Thames. Vessels laden with the produce and manufactures of nearly every country in the world are to be found in its grand docks, and numerous landing-stages.

This river is navigable for barges throughout the greater part of its course. The Thames and Severn Canal, which unites the two rivers, makes it possible to sail across England from London to the Bristol Channel. The chief places of importance standing on the banks of the Thames are Cirencester, Lechlade, Oxford, Abingdon, Reading, Windsor, Eton, Kingston, Richmond, LONDON, Greenwich, Woolwich, Gravesend, with Rochester and Chatham on the Medway.

II. *The Rivers of the South Coast flowing into the English Channel.*

These are of minor importance compared with the rivers of the East and West Coasts of England, owing to the nearness of the hills to the sea in this district. The chief are the Rother, Sussex Ouse, Arun, Itchen, Avon, Exe, and Tamar; and the smaller streams are the Dorset Ouse, Teign, Dart, and Fal.

III. *The Rivers of the West Coast* may be again divided into (*a*) those flowing into the Bristol Channel, as the Taw, Parrot, Avon, *Severn*, Wye, Usk, Taff, and Towy; (*b*), those flowing into the Irish Sea, as the Teifi, Wye, Dee, Weaver, Mersey, Ribble, Lune, Derwent, and Eden.

1. *The Severn*, the longest river in England and Wales, stands first in importance in this group. It rises in Plinlimmon, and by a circuitous course of 240 miles reaches the

Bristol Channel. A curious fact about this river is that the tide rises much higher here than in any other estuary in Europe. This sudden rising of the tide is called the *Bore*, or wall of water. It is caused by the meeting of the waters of the sea and the river at its mouth; so great is the

*In the Mersey.*

difference between high and low tide that it varies from 20 to 60 feet.

The principal tributaries of the Severn are the Wye, Usk, Upper and Lower Avon. Several towns of importance stand on its banks, as Welshpool, Shrewsbury,

Worcester, Bridgenorth, Tewkesbury, Gloucester, Ludlow on the Lune, Leamington, Warwick, and Stratford on the Avon.

2. *The Mersey*, only 68 miles in length, proudly owns Liverpool, the second seaport in Britain, near its mouth, with the shipbuilding yards and port of Birkenhead on the opposite bank. One great feature of its estuary is its depth, enabling ships of the largest size to pass up and down in safety. This opening is called the Liverpool Channel. It is an excellent harbour for the merchant vessels lying at anchor there.

The chief tributaries are the Irwell, upon which stands Manchester; and the Weaver, which flows through Nantwich and Northwich, the salt districts of Cheshire.

LAKES.—The two lake districts of England and Wales are situated in the northern counties of Cumberland, Westmoreland, and Lancashire; and in Merioneth, Carnarvon, and Brecknock in Wales.

There are also the Norfolk Broads, which are large shallow lakes connected with the rivers Bure, Yare, and Waveney. They are fringed with reeds and wild flowers, and they are noted as the favourite haunts of all kinds of waterfowl.

Thus we see that there are two kinds of freshwater lakes in this country; the first, planted in the mountain hollows, naturally formed by the drainage of the higher lands surrounding them; and the second, lakes, or meres, of the plain, formed by shallow depression in some river-basin area.

I. *The English Lake District Proper* is that of the Cumbrian Group of mountains. These delightful freshwater expanses add greatly to the grandeur and beauty of the wild mountainous districts in which they are situated. Thousands of tourists are to be met with here during the summer months.

There are seven well-known lakes surrounding Helvellyn, with numerous smaller ones.

1. *Windermere*, the largest in size, and sometimes considered the most beautiful, is about 14 miles long, and with an average breadth of 1 mile. It is situated between Lancashire and Westmoreland.

2. *Ullswater*, lying immediately at the foot of Helvellyn, which appears to rise immediately out of its waters, is the second in size.

3. *Derwentwater*, another beautiful lake, nestles under Skiddaw.

4. *Coniston Water* lies at the foot of the mountain called Coniston Old Man.

5. *Thirlmere*, which has been of late years utilised as the main water supply for the city of Manchester.

6. *Wastwater* is situated in a still wilder district, higher up the mountains than the other lakes of this group. It is considerably deeper than the above-named lakes.

7, 8. *Buttermere* and *Crummock Water* are other lakes in this district.

9, 10. Among the smaller lakes, *Grasmere* and *Rydal Water* take the highest place for their beautiful scenery. Here, too, are the associations of English poetry, rich and lasting, for this neighbourhood was the home of Wordsworth, Southey, the two Coleridges, and others.

II. The Welsh Lakes are smaller than those of the Cumbrian Group. The chief are :—

1. *Bala Lake* in Merionethshire, the largest and most important, is 4 miles long, and rather under a mile in width. It is beautifully surrounded by rockland and forest.

2. *The Lakes of Llanberis*, in Carnarvonshire, lying at the foot of Snowdon, are remarkably picturesque.

3. *Lake Vyrnwy* gives to Liverpool its water supply.

4. *Lyn Conway* is another beautiful lake in North Wales.

5. South Wales possesses but one lake of importance. It is called *Brecknock Mere*, as it lies near to the town of Brecknock.

III. *The Norfolk Broads, or Meres,* are lowland lakes of remarkable size and interest. Mr. G. C. Davies, in his "Rivers and Broads of Norfolk," says[1]: "From Yarmouth, looking inland, three main waterways radiate. The chief is the Yare, flowing from the westward; then comes the Bure, flowing from the north-westward, and having her large tributaries, the Ant and the Thurne, flowing from the northward. From the south-west come the clear waters of the Waveney. All these rivers are navigable for considerable distances, and on the Bure and its tributaries the greater number of the Broads are situated. These Broads are large shallow lakes, connected with the rivers, and are many of them navigable. Flat marshes follow the lines of the rivers, and while higher and well-wooded ground rises near the upper portions of the rivers, near the sea the country is perfectly flat, and vessels sailing on all three rivers are visible at the same time."

Other meres or lowland lakes of less importance are to be met with in Cheshire and the Fen District; but some of these are simply the effects of an imperfect system of drainage.

CLIMATE.—While the climate of England and Wales may be truly described as cool, temperate, and salubrious, yet it is distinctly variable. Though we may not be exposed to such extremes of climate as other countries situated in the same latitude on the mainland of Europe, owing to the influence of the Gulf Stream upon our coasts, yet great and sudden changes of temperature take place frequently, so

---

[1] "*Rivers and Broads of Norfolk.*"—*Jarrold.*

that often foreigners are disposed to describe it as "*unbearable*."

As a rule the inhabitants of our rural districts live to a far greater age than in other countries of Europe, so that it cannot be considered anything but healthy. Drought is seldom known, and too much rain seldom falls, so that it is equable in this respect, which aids vegetation greatly. The average rainfall varies from twenty inches on the East Coast to thirty inches on the West Coast. This is owing to the prevalence of the moist west winds of the Atlantic; and in consequence of the same influence, Ireland, or "Erin, the Green Isle," has a larger rainfall than England and Wales. That the climate is health-giving, to vegetation, as well as to man, may be seen in its abundant forests, which are unrivalled; its well-wooded plains; its richly-cultivated fields and pasturelands; its orchards and garden grounds; and its luxuriant hedgerows and wayside flowers.

The mean temperature of an English summer is 63', and of winter 37'·5", giving a mean annual temperature of 50'·55".

It has been wisely said that in no other country in the world do its inhabitants live out of doors so much as in England. It is undoubtedly this fact which enables our countrymen to dwell in other lands without great inconvenience to themselves, whether they be placed in the Torrid, Temperate, or Frigid Zones.

NATURAL PRODUCTIONS.—The natural productions of a country of necessity must rule its position in commerce and trade with other countries to a great extent. Though these are all important and extremely valuable, be they animal, vegetable, or mineral, in Britain, they have not alone contributed towards our National Greatness, inasmuch as the English people are "a Nation of Shopkeepers," which really means they are the Traders of the World.

In other words, the English, as a people, have so widened their interests and aims with regard to trade and commerce, that this country has become the manufacturing centre of the world's products, rather than of its own. The raw material imported is sent out again in the form of exported, manufactured goods, while her food supplies are far more gathered in from foreign nations than produced at home.

With these general remarks, we may introduce the natural productions of England and Wales under the three heads of Mineral, Vegetable, and Animal. This reversed order represents their value commercially.

I. *Mineral Productions :—*

The geological structure of England and Wales is both varied and valuable in its formation. The rocks are chiefly stratified, being rich in all kinds of mineral wealth, although granite, and other unstratified rocks, occur in Cornwall and Wales.

*The principal stratified rocks are :—*
1. Cambrian and Silurian, in Wales.
2. Devonian, in the South-Western Counties of Devon and Cornwall, and also in parts of Wales.
3. Carboniferous, in the North, Midland, and some Southern Counties.
4. Permian, in the Counties bordering the North-West Coast.
5. New Red Sandstone, chiefly in the Trent Valley, and the Vale of Cheshire.
6. Oolitic, a strong band extending through Central England in a south-westerly direction, from Yorkshire to Dorset, with traces also of this formation in the Weald of Kent.
7. Cretaceous, or Chalk Ranges. These are four in number:—*A.* Extending from Salisbury Plain to

Norfolk, and known as the White Horse Hills, the Chiltern Hills, and the East Anglian Heights. *B.* North Downs. *C.* South Downs. *D.* Dorset Heights.

A mixture of clay and sand is often found blended with the chalk. Alluvial beds occur in the valleys of the Trent, Severn, Thames, Great Ouse, etc.

MINERALS.—1. *The Coalfields* stand first in importance among English minerals. They spread over an area of 12,000 square miles. The annual yield is estimated at 150,000,000 tons, and the supply is considered well-nigh inexhaustible. The richest coalfield is that of Durham. Throughout the larger colliery districts iron abounds.

We may arrange the coalfields of England and Wales into three groups :—

    *A. The Northern Group*, comprising Northumberland, Durham, Cumberland, South Lancashire, and Cheshire, Yorkshire, Nottingham, and Derby Coalfields.

    *B. The Midland Group*, comprising the Coalfields of Leicester, Shropshire, Stafford, and Warwick.

    *C. The Western Group*, comprising the Welsh Colliery Districts, Shropshire and Gloucestershire, Somerset and Worcestershire.

Of late years several successful attempts have been made to open out coalfields in Kent, Sussex, and other places on the South Coast. Not one-fourth of the coal produced in England and Wales is exported to other countries. By far the greater portion is consumed at home, for smelting iron; for driving the machinery of our great manufacturing centres; for railways and steamships; for the making of gas; besides every kind of domestic and general use.

2. *Iron.*—The great advantage of iron being found in or near our colliery districts is that the cost of smelting is so much cheaper. Nearly all our great colliery districts abound in iron ore, so that an enormous yield of from 15 to 20 million tons is the annual result.

3. The other metals and mineral products found here are:—*Lead and Zinc* from Northumberland, Cumberland, Westmoreland, Durham, Yorkshire, Derbyshire, Shropshire, Devonshire, and in certain districts in Wales, where it is occasionally mixed with silver, etc.

4. *Copper and Tin* come principally from the south-western district of Devonshire and Cornwall. These mines have been worked from the earliest times, and they are still excessively rich in ore. Copper also is found in smaller quantities in Anglesea.

5. *Antimony and Manganese* are generally met with in the copper and tin mines.

6. *Plumbago* is chiefly obtained from the mines around Keswick, and Borrowdale, in Cumberland. Of late years the supply has been somewhat limited, so that artificial lead for pencils is now commonly manufactured both at home and abroad.

7. *Rock Salt* occurs in thick layers in Worcestershire and Durham, and *Common Salt* comes from the districts of Cheshire and Worcestershire; the chief centres being Northwich, Middlewich, Nantwich, and Droitwich, etc. Salt is also procured in Hampshire and Dorsetshire, where, by means of evaporation tanks, it is procured from the sea water, as is so common in other places on the Continent of Europe. The annual yield of salt from the western districts of Cheshire and Worcestershire exceeds 2,000,000

tons, which fully explains the cheapness of this most useful article for household purposes.

8. *Alum and Jet* are found at Whitby, in Yorkshire.

9. *Slate*, for roofing, and other building purposes, is obtained from the extensive quarries of Carnarvon and Merioneth in North Wales; also in Cumberland, Westmoreland, and other parts of the North of England; and in Cornwall. In the latter district, the slate slabs are enamelled to represent marble, and so used for decorative purposes, such as chimney-pieces, etc.

10. *The Granite* quarries of Cornwall, Devonshire, and Cumberland, are the first in importance. Next follow those of Wales and Leicestershire, where the Mount Sorrel Quarries are of importance, chiefly for road-making, etc.

11. *Building Stone* varies greatly in quality, and quantity, in different parts of England and Wales. The best-known building stones are:

 *A. Portland*, from the Isle of Portland, in Dorsetshire, where it forms labour for one of our chief convict settlements.

 *B. Bathstone*, so called from the Cotswold Quarries, in the neighbourhood of Bath, etc.

 *C. Purbeck Marble*, which is really a superior limestone, hard enough to take a finished polished surface when dressed. Other varieties are the Derbyshire and Devonshire marbles, some veins of which are exceedingly beautiful.

 *D. Alabaster* comes from near Tutbury in Derbyshire, in the Dove Valley, and other places.

 *E.* Other important quarries of building stone exist at Weldon in Northamptonshire; Ancaster in Lincolnshire; and Masham in Yorkshire; and in various local quarries throughout the country.

F. *China Clay*, which is generally soft and plastic, is found in Central England, Cornwall and Devonshire, etc.

G. *Fuller's Earth* comes from Redhill, in Surrey, etc.

H. Several mineral drugs used in medicine, such as arsenic, Epsom salts, soda, lime, and sulphur, etc., are also found in this country.

MINERAL SPRINGS.—*These are principally:—*

1. *Chalybeate, or Iron*, such as Cheltenham, Tunbridge Wells, Malvern, Clifton, Harrogate, and Scarborough.
2. *Saline*, that is springs impregnated with salts (lime, magnesia, soda, sulphur), such as Bath, Cheltenham, Buxton, Matlock, Harrogate, and Epsom, etc.
3. *Warm Springs*, which occur at Bath, Clifton, Buxton, Middleton, and Matlock. These are greatly frequented by invalids.

NATURAL CURIOSITIES.—Under the head of Mineralogy we may include those curious natural formations which form an attraction to travellers from other countries, as well as the native tourists of this country. Here may be mentioned as a few among numerous others:—

1. The Peak Cavern and Pool's Hole, in Derbyshire.
2. The Wynyats (Windgates) of Derbyshire.
3. Elden Hole, a wonderful chasm, near Buxton.
4. The Loggan (Balance Stones) of Cornwall.
5. The Warm Springs of Derbyshire.
6. Yorda's Cave, in Yorkshire.
7. Parliament House Cave, in Holyhead.

II. *The Vegetable Productions of England and Wales* are both rich and varied. They should be classed rather under the head of Cultivated Products than Natural Products, although the latter are of considerable importance, inasmuch as the whole country presents to a stranger the general appearance of a well-wooded and highly-cultivated land, divided into park, woodland, and farm, with here and there forests, moors, or commons of a wilder nature.

In olden days, Britain was undoubtedly the land of forest and marsh, when the wolf, stag, wild ox, wild cat, with innumerable wild birds and numerous smaller animals, roamed at will. These were a terror to the inhabitants, who lived nomadic lives, and attended but little to cultivation, but depended upon the chase and the natural or wild products for subsistence.

FORESTS.—Extensive forests still remain to us as traces of a past age, while new additional plantations have been made for centuries past for purposes of sport, trade, or scenery. Thus we have the New Forest, in Hampshire, once the favourite hunting-ground of the Norman kings and barons; Windsor Forest; Dean Forest, in Gloucestershire; Whittlebury Forest, in Northamptonshire; Wychwood, in Oxfordshire; Needwood Forest, in Staffordshire; Epping Forest, in Essex; Sherwood Forest, in Nottinghamshire, which brings us memories of bold Robin Hood and his followers. Dartmoor, once an extensive forest in South Devon, has been greatly broken up, as has also the Weald of Kent; but some forest districts still remain to tell the tale of other days.

*Our Forest Trees* include the oak, elm, birch, ash, beech, poplar, maple, alder, aspen, yew, Scotch and other firs, many of which are natural products, or indigenous to the soil of England and Wales. England has ever taken a high place for her oak forests, so valuable for shipbuilding, the roofing of churches, and other large buildings, etc. The varied beauties of her forest trees have been praised by poet and artist alike; and her valuable timber is a source of wealth to her landowners.

The botanist will also find throughout the forests

meadows, lanes, and hedgerows of England, many rare and beautiful specimens of flowers, ferns, grasses, and herbs, as well as the better-known commoner kinds; but as England is, above all things, a *land of cultivation*, these smaller examples of the vegetable kingdom naturally fall into insignificance when compared with her rich cereal or root crops, which provide ample food for both man and beast.

VEGETATION.—The vegetation of this country far exceeds in both the quantity and quality of its native productions that of other countries placed in the same belt of latitude. Although we have records of the vine having been cultivated in the open in England in times past, yet this is quite impossible now. Apples, pears, plums, cherries, nuts of various kinds, with the peach, fig, and apricot in sheltered situations, are among our orchard trees; while among the fruit bushes are the gooseberry, raspberry, currant, growing well in every part. The bilberry, cranberry, and blackberry are wild fruits.

An English garden is generally regarded as a scene of beauty. Among its flowers are roses, lilies, carnations, peonies, with a countless host of annual and perennial flowering plants. Many of the native fruits and flowers of warmer countries flourish here owing to the mildness and even temperature of the English climate. Its vegetables also comprise many valuable kinds, including potatoes, cabbage, cauliflower, asparagus, sea-kale, beans and peas, parsnips, carrots, and turnips, etc., so that even the poor in this country are amply provided with a large and varied stock of vegetables for their food supply.

CEREALS AND ROOTS.—Wheat stands first in importance among our corn plants, yet our harvests are rich and abundant with barley, oats, rye, pulse (beans and peas), mangel-wurzel, turnips, kohl rabi, and other valuable root plants. Hops are largely cultivated in Kent, Sussex,

Surrey, Worcestershire and Herefordshire; and rape on the Eastern Coast.

Not only does England stand in a high position among the nations of the world for her cultivated products, but she can further boast of a higher and larger area of cultivation than any other country in the world, *viz.*, only one-twelfth of the whole of this country is not under cultivation; two-fifths of the whole is pastureland; and the remainder of the cultivated districts is arable corn-growing land, etc.

The agriculture of England has risen to a very high state of perfection, owing to the vast improvements in machinery, and the application of steam power for agricultural purposes; as well as the remarkable advantages resulting from the extreme fertility of the soil, and the perseverance and industry of the people. Nearly every tract of land which will not admit of cultivation is covered with pasture for cattle and sheep. The chief pasturelands are situated in the South and West; and the chief mining and agricultural districts are situated in the centre, East, and North. In a few years our agricultural machinery, waggons and carts, may all be propelled with automotor power instead of steam or horses.

The present depression among farming interests is not in the least due to any neglect in cultivation, but rather to foreign competition lowering the standard prices of the English markets, by reason of imported vegetable and animal products not being taxed in accordance with those produced at home. (*See* note upon Roads and Taxation of Land, etc.) The fact that one-fifth only of the population of this country are entirely and solely interested in agriculture, renders it the more difficult for any Government to introduce measures to aid the landowner and farmer. The manufacturing and mining districts at once could send a vote of four-fifths of the population against such a measure, especially as the English people pride themselves upon what is known as Free Trade.

### III. ANIMAL PRODUCTIONS.

1. *The Wild Animals of England and Wales* are few and unimportant. They are generally small in size, and none are either dangerous, or savage. The fox, badger, otter, hare, rabbit, squirrel, stoat, weasel, polecat, hedgehog, mole, rat, and mouse, are the chief representatives. The stag, wild ox, bear, wolf, beaver, and wild cat, as wild animals are now unknown; although deer are still kept as ornaments in the noble parklands surrounding many country mansions; and at Chillingham Park in Northumberland there still exists a herd of wild cattle, yet as these are kept in an enclosure, they can scarcely come under the head of wild animals. The fox, badger, otter, hare, and rabbit, are still regarded as animals for either sport, or the chase; and in many districts they are carefully preserved for these objects.

2. *Of Wild Birds*, the heron, owl, hawk, wild goose, pheasant, partridge, grouse, waterhen, wild duck, magpie, carrion crow, crow and rook, jackdaw, jay, and wild pigeon are the largest. The numerous families of smaller wild birds are represented by the blackbird, thrush, starling, sparrow, linnet, lark, and finch tribes, robin and wren, with many others. England is a land of song-birds. Throughout the year the woods, meadows, lanes, and hedgerows are alive with the pleasant twittering of her feathered inhabitants, which are, for the most part, clothed in homely brown, or quiet grey plumage. The cuckoo, redwing, fieldfare, swallow, nightingale, and other birds, visit this country for a certain season, either during the spring, summer, autumn, or winter months; *e.g.*, the Broads, or Meres of Norfolk, are rich with visitants from Norway and Sweden and other parts of Northern Europe at certain seasons. The

eagle very occasionally visits our shores, although it is sometimes met with in the more isolated parts of Ireland and Scotland. Gulls and various other sea-birds frequent our coasts, and during stormy weather may be seen making incursions into the swamps, or marshy lands, of the interior.

The kingfisher still frequents certain streams, in spite of the cruel efforts of man to exterminate this richly-plumaged bird; and the bird of paradise has only been met with at rare intervals of late years for the same reason.

3. *Reptiles* are not numerous. The English viper is now very scarce indeed; the brown adder may occasionally be seen basking upon the close herbage of some out-of-the-way common. Of snakes, several kinds are still common in certain districts, but they are non-poisonous and most timid, always fleeing away at the approach of man. The tree-lizard, toad, frog, newt, snail, and earthworm are to be met with everywhere.

4. *Insects* are also small and inoffensive. The dragon-fly, hornet, wasp, bee, gnat, and house-fly are the best known. Many beautiful butterflies and moths abound.

DOMESTIC ANIMALS.—England is certainly rich in domestic animals. The horse, ox, cow, mule, ass, sheep, goat, pig, poultry of many kinds, with geese and ducks, are to be met with everywhere. The swan glides gracefully over the ornamental waters of the wealthy, and the peacock spreads out his rich plumes upon the garden terraces near by.

The great companion to an Englishman is his faithful dog. Rich and poor alike keep dogs for every conceivable use or fancy, insomuch that the dog almost vies with the domestic cat in claiming a share of the fireside in most English homes.

FISHERIES.—We have already described at some length

the great value and importance of the British fisheries under the head of "The British Isles." ("General Remarks," pp. 73-6.)

POPULATION.—The census of England and Wales in 1891 was upwards of 30,000,000. Of this number 28,000,000 were in England, and 2,000,000 in Wales.

The largest centres of population were London, Manchester, Liverpool and Birmingham, Leeds and Sheffield, each containing more than 300,000 inhabitants. (*See* page 162.)

PEOPLE.—The English people are a bold, enterprising, honest, hard-working race, possessing steady perseverance, with inquiring minds. No nation, either ancient or modern, has made such advancement in commerce, trade, manufacture, art, and science, as the English have, who proudly regard their country as the "workshop of the world."

In the chapter upon "Ethnology of the British People," we have named them a mixed race of the ancient Celtic and Teutonic families.

The original inhabitants were of the Celtic race. The Roman Invasion brought strangers into Britain from Gaul and Italy, who introduced new customs and manners, together with a new language, and from this period the work of civilisation steadily progressed. Following these came the Saxons and Danes, who settled in the country; they in turn became a part of the people of Britain, and so introduced their own language and ways of living. The Normans again made marked changes in the life, language, and manners of the English people, after the conquest of 1066, although they did not change them as a nation.

We find, therefore, that the English are a mixture of British, Saxon, Danish, and Norman. The Romans entirely withdrew from Britain to maintain their foreign wars. In

Wales, Cornwall, and the Isle of Man, the people have somewhat retained their ancient Celtic manners, with marked traces of the Erse, or Gaelic, language, more than in other parts of England and Wales.

IMPORTS AND EXPORTS FROM AND TO :—

UNITED STATES :—

*Imports.*—Corn and flour, tobacco, turpentine, timber, cheese, oils, skins, wool, fish, rice, etc.

*Exports.*—Cotton, woollen, and linen goods, silks, iron, steel, coal, hardware, machinery.

INDIA :—

*Imports.*—Rice, sugar, cotton, silk, wool, spices, fruits, coffee, tea, hemp, gums, dyes.

*Exports.*—Cotton, linen, and woollen goods, iron, machinery, beer, firearms, all kinds of manufactured goods.

FRANCE :—

*Imports.*—Silk, brandy, wines, sugar, fancy goods, eggs, fruits, gloves, toys, etc.

*Exports.*—Coal, iron, copper, woollen, linen, and cotton goods, horses, corn, flour, and machinery.

RUSSIA :—

*Imports.*—Flax, hempseed, cordage, tallow, hides, wool, timber, corn, etc.

*Exports.*—Woollen and cotton goods, porcelain, fancy goods, machinery.

AUSTRALASIA :—

*Imports.*—Wool, gold, corn, hides, skins, timber, metals, gums, spermaceti, meat, fruits, etc.

*Exports.*—Wearing apparel, cotton and woollen goods, tools, machinery, food supplies, manufactured goods.

GERMANY:—
    *Imports.*—Corn, timber, oil cake, rape and linseed oil, iron, flax, wool, fancy goods, toys, etc.
    *Exports.*—Machinery, cutlery, cotton and woollen goods, earthenware, herrings, and manufactured goods.

EGYPT:—
    *Imports.*—Raw silk, wool, tortoise shell, corn, cotton, gum arabic, coffee, rugs, rice, etc.
    *Exports.*—Cotton and linen goods, silks, books, fire-arms, machinery, tools, coal, iron, fancy goods.

NETHERLANDS:—
    *Imports.*—Butter, cheese, fish, poultry, corn, flax, wines, gin, tobacco.
    *Exports.*—Coal, machinery, barley, cotton and woollen goods, manufactured goods.

CHINA:—
    *Imports.*—Tea, silk, drugs, ivory, camphor, porcelain, gums, wool.
    *Exports.*—Iron and steel goods, firearms, beer and ale, clothing, machinery.

BRAZIL:—
    *Imports.*—Raw cotton, sugar, hides, timber, drugs, coffee, guano, wool.
    *Exports.*—Manufactured goods, colonial produce, fancy goods, machinery,

SPAIN:—
    *Imports.*—Wines, fruits, nuts, copper, metals, wool, cork, olive oil.
    *Exports.*—Iron and steel goods, coal, machinery, food supplies, glass and china.

BRITISH NORTH AMERICA :—
  *Imports.*—Skins, furs, train oil, blubber, timber, corn, fish.
  *Exports.*—Clothing, tools, manufactured goods, machinery, drugs, fancy goods.

WEST INDIES :—
  *Imports.*—Sugar, rum, cocoa, coffee, spices, arrowroot, fruits, sponge, timber.
  *Exports.*—Machinery, fancy goods, clothing, drugs, tools, and manufactured goods.

OTHER COUNTRIES :—
  *Imports.*—Natural produce both raw and manufactured, etc.
  *Exports.*—All kinds of manufactured goods, machinery, clothing, drugs, etc.

TRADE AND MANUFACTURES.—These form the backbone of English industry. In no country in the world may be seen such a variety of manufactured goods; and when we consider that this extensive system of natural industry has sprung up, more or less, during the past century, and that the national interests have been transferred from agriculture to manufacturing trade (as nearly four-fifths of the population are either engaged in trade, or in some way connected with it), we are the more amazed at the rapid progress made; the perfection of the goods produced; and the vast wealth invested in our manufacturing industries.

The following are a sample of the chief manufactures of England and Wales, with the centre of trade of each :—

  *Cotton Goods.*—Manchester, Blackburn, Bolton, Preston, Wigan, Oldham, Bury, Rochdale, and other Lancashire towns.
  *Woollen Cloth.*—Leeds, Bradford, and other towns in

the West Riding of Yorkshire, including Halifax, Huddersfield, Wakefield, Dewsbury, also the West of England centres.

*Flannel.*—Halifax in Yorkshire, Welshpool in Wales, etc.

*Blankets.*—Dewsbury and Huddersfield in Yorkshire, Witney in Oxfordshire.

*Worsted Goods.*—Bradford, Halifax, and other Yorkshire towns.

*Carpets.*—Kidderminster, Axminster, Huddersfield, etc.

*Mixed Goods.*—Norwich, Wales, with the towns of Yorkshire and Lancashire.

*Silk Goods.*—Macclesfield, Congleton, etc., in Cheshire, Derby, Coventry, and Spitalfields in London.

*Hosiery.*—Leicester, Derby, Loughborough, and Nottingham.

*Lace.*—Nottingham and Derby, etc.; also Honiton in Devonshire, with hand pillow lace throughout the Southern Midland Counties.

*Ironfounding.*—South Wales, Bilston, Wednesbury, and West Bromwich.

*Machinery.*—Birmingham, Manchester, Sheffield, Norwich, and nearly all large towns.

*Cutlery, Hardware.*—Sheffield, Birmingham, Dudley, Wolverhampton, etc.

*Nails, etc.*—Wednesbury, Dudley, Bilston, etc.

*Watches and Jewellery.*—London, Birmingham, Liverpool, Sheffield, Coventry, etc.

*Needles and Pins.*—Birmingham, Redditch, Bristol, etc.

*China and Pottery.*—Burslem, Stoke, and potteries in Staffordshire; Derby, Worcester, Torquay, and many other places.

*Glass.*—Birmingham, Stonebridge, Wolverhampton, Tutbury, etc.

*Paper.*— Maidstone, Rickmansworth, Sittingbourne, High Wycombe, and throughout England.

*Leather Tanning.*—Southwark, Newcastle, and other midland and northern towns.

*Shoes.*—Northampton, Kettering, Leicester, Wellingborough, and other midland towns.

*Gloves.*—Woodstock, Yeovil, Witney, London, Birmingham, etc.

*Bicycles.*—Birmingham, Coventry, etc., etc.

*Ale and Porter.*—Burton-on-Trent, London, Romford, and in most other large towns.

*Soap and Candles.*—London, Hull, Dudley, Lewes, etc.

*Straw Bonnets.*—Dunstable, Luton, St. Albans, and other parts of Hertfordshire and Bedfordshire.

*Pens, Fancy Goods, and Toys.*—London, Birmingham, Leeds, Manchester, Sheffield, and other towns.

SEAPORTS.—The principal seaports of England and Wales are :—

1. *East Coast.*—Newcastle, Gateshead, North and South Shields, Sunderland, Hartlepool, Hull, Grimsby, Yarmouth, Harwich, LONDON, Gravesend, Dover.
2. *South Coast.*—Folkestone, Newhaven, Portsmouth, Southampton, Weymouth, Plymouth, Falmouth.
3. *West Coast.*—Bristol, Swansea, Pembroke, Cardiff, Newport, Liverpool, *Manchester on the Ship Canal*, Whitehaven.

POLITICAL DIVISIONS :—

England and Wales are divided into fifty-two irregular portions called Counties or Shires. England has forty Counties, and Wales twelve.

*A.* The three largest Counties in England are Yorkshire, Lincolnshire, and Devonshire.

*B.* The three smallest Counties in England are Rutlandshire, Middlesex, and Huntingdon.

*A.* The most mountainous County is Cumberland.

*B.* The flattest County is Cambridgeshire.

*A.* The four Counties containing the greatest number of inhabitants are Middlesex, Lancashire, Yorkshire, and Surrey.

*B.* The four most thinly populated Counties are Rutland, Anglesea, Dorsetshire, and Westmoreland.

*A.* The Maritime Counties of England are twenty in number.

*B.* The Inland Counties of England are also twenty in number.

*A.* England is divided into five parts:—*Northern Counties*, six; *Eastern Counties*, four; *Southern Counties*, ten; *Western Counties bordering Wales*, four; *Midland Counties*, sixteen.

*B.* Wales is divided into two parts:—*North Wales*, six Counties; *South Wales*, six Counties. (*Nine of the Welsh Counties are Maritime, and only three are inland.*)

*A.* The most Northern County in England and Wales is Northumberland.

*B.* The most Southern County in England and Wales is Cornwall.

*C.* The most Eastern County in England and Wales is Norfolk.

*D.* The most Western County in England and Wales is Cornwall.

ENGLAND[1]:—

   *A*. The Shires of England are twenty-eight in number. They include two Northern; one Eastern; six Southern; four Western; and fifteen Midland Counties; and all the Inland Counties except Middlesex.

   *B*. The Counties are six in number; being lands or kingdoms.

   *C*. The Folk are two in number (East Anglia proper).

   *D*. The Sexes are three in number (South, East, and Middle people). The old kingdom of Wessex founded by Ordic, lying south of the Thames, no longer remains.

   *E*. The foreign portion is Cornwall, or West Wales.

WALES[1]:—

   The Welsh Counties, excepting Anglesea, "The Ea or Isle of the Angles," are called Shires. The ancient Celtic name for Anglesea = " Mona."

---

[1] These notes are important, inasmuch as the old English word "Sciran," to cut, shows how these divisions were apportioned in early times for purposes of Law, Government, etc.; whereas some older settlements were left untouched at this later division of the country, having been the ancient estates of Counts or Earls. (*See* "Derivation of English Counties," p. 147.)

## POLITICAL DIVISIONS: FORTY COUNTIES OF ENGLAND.

| No. | Counties. | Area, Square Miles. | Population. 1891. | Capital and other Towns. | On what River. |
|---|---|---|---|---|---|
| 1 | Northumberland | 1,871 | 506,030 | *Newcastle*—N. Shields, Alnwick | Tyne |
| 2 | Cumberland | 1,523 | 266,549 | *Carlisle*—Whitehaven, Keswick | Eden |
| 3 | Westmoreland | 762 | 66,098 | *Appleby*—Kendal | Eden |
| 4 | Durham | 1,097 | 1,016,559 | *Durham*—Sunderland | Wear |
| 5 | Yorkshire | 5,836 | 2,213,364 | *York*—Leeds, Sheffield [pool | Ouse |
| 6 | Lancashire | 1,766 | 3,906,721 | *Lancaster*—Manchester, Liver- | Lune |
| 7 | Lincolnshire | 2,611 | 473,912 | *Lincoln*—Boston, Gainsborough | Witham |
| 8 | Norfolk | 2,024 | 463,287 | *Norwich*—Yarmouth, King'sLynn | Wensum |
| 9 | Suffolk | 1,515 | 361,790 | *Ipswich*—Bury St. Edmunds | Orwell |
| 10 | Essex | 1,533 | 784,258 | *Chelmsford*—Colchester, Harwich | Chelmer |
| 11 | Kent | 1,557 | 808,736 | *Maidstone*—Canterbury, Roches-ter, Chatham [Hastings | Medway |
| 12 | Sussex | 1,466 | 548,979 | *Lewes*—Chichester, Brighton, | Ouse |
| 13 | Hampshire | 1,625 | 611,425 | *Winchester*—Southampton | Itchen |
| 14 | Dorsetshire | 1,006 | 194,517 | *Dorchester*—Weymouth | Frome |
| 15 | Devonshire | 2,585 | 631,808 | *Exeter*—Plymouth, Torquay | Exe |
| 16 | Cornwall | 1,330 | 322,571 | *Bodmin*—Launceston, Falmouth | Camel |
| 17 | Monmouthshire | 496 | 258,054 | *Monmouth*—Chepstow, Newport | Wye |
| 18 | Herefordshire | 863 | 115,949 | *Hereford*—Ross, Leominster | Wye |
| 19 | Shropshire | 1,343 | 236,329 | *Shrewsbury*—Ludlow, Bridge-north | Severn |
| 20 | Cheshire | 1,052 | 743,869 | *Chester*—Birkenhead, Maccles-field, Stockport | Dee |
| 21 | Derbyshire | 1,028 | 520,914 | *Derby*—Chesterfield, Belper | Derwent |
| 22 | Nottinghamshire | 837 | 445,753 | *Nottingham*—Newark, Mansfield | Trent |
| 23 | Staffordshire | 1,184 | 1,087,161 | *Stafford*—Wolverhampton | Sow |
| 24 | Leicestershire | 806 | 375,092 | *Leicester*—Loughborough | Soar |
| 25 | Rutlandshire | 149 | 20,659 | *Oakham*—Uppingham | Wreak |
| 26 | Northamptonshire | 1,016 | 290,508 | *Northampton*—Peterborough | Nen |
| 27 | Huntingdonshire | 372 | 54,069 | *Huntingdon*—St. Ives, St. Neots | Gt. Ouse |
| 28 | Cambridgeshire | 857 | 121,961 | *Cambridge*—Ely, Wisbeach | Cam |
| 29 | Warwickshire | 897 | 838,030 | *Warwick*—Birmingham, Coventry | Avon |
| 30 | Worcestershire | 723 | 385,309 | *Worcester*—Dudley, Kidderminster | Severn |
| 31 | Gloucestershire | 1,258 | 645,574 | *Gloucester*—Cheltenham, Bristol | Severn |
| 32 | Oxfordshire | 756 | 191,191 | *Oxford*—Banbury, Witney | Isis, or Thames |
| 33 | Buckinghamshire | 738 | 160,700 | *Buckingham*—Aylesbury | Gt. Ouse |
| 34 | Bedfordshire | 463 | 160,704 | *Bedford*—Dunstable, Luton | Gt. Ouse |
| 35 | Hertfordshire | 630 | 224,550 | *Hertford*—St. Albans, Hitchin | Lea |
| 36 | Middlesex, including LONDON | 282 | 4,792,130 | LONDON—Brentford, Uxbridge | Thames |
| 37 | Berkshire | 752 | 236,163 | *Reading*—Abingdon, Newbury | Kennet |
| 38 | Surrey | 759 | 521,551 | *Guildford*—Croydon, Kingston | Wey |
| 39 | Wiltshire | 1,307 | 264,997 | *Salisbury*—Devizes, Chippenham | Avon |
| 40 | Somersetshire | 1,629 | 438,710 | *Taunton*—Bath, Wells | Tone |

### TWELVE COUNTIES OF WALES.

| 1 | Flintshire | 244 | 77,277 | *Mold*—Flint, Holywell, St. Asaph | Alyn |
|---|---|---|---|---|---|
| 2 | Denbighshire | 633 | 118,843 | *Denbigh*—Wrexham | Clwyd |
| 3 | Caernarvonshire | 544 | 117,233 | *Caernarvon*—Bangor | |
| 4 | Anglesea | 271 | 50,098 | *Beaumaris*—Holyhead | |
| 5 | Merionethshire | 663 | 49,212 | *Dolgelly*—Bala, Harlech | Maw |
| 6 | Montgomeryshire | 839 | 58,003 | *Montgomery*—Welshpool | Severn |
| 7 | Cardiganshire | 675 | 63,467 | *Cardigan*—Aberystwith | Teifi |
| 8 | Radnorshire | 426 | 31,791 | *Presteigne*—New Radnor | Lugg |
| 9 | Brecknockshire | 754 | 51,393 | *Builth*—Brecon | Usk |
| 10 | Glamorganshire | 792 | 467,054 | *Cardiff*—Merthyr Tydfil, Swansea | Taff |
| 11 | Caermarthenshire | 974 | 130,566 | *Caermarthen*—Llanelly | Towy |
| 12 | Pembrokeshire | 610 | 88,296 | *Pembroke*—Milford, Haverford-west | |

### DERIVATION OF THE NAMES OF ENGLISH COUNTIES :—

**Six Northern Counties.**

1. *Northumberland.*—The land north of the Humber. This county once comprised the wider area of this district.
2. *Cumberland.*—*Cumbria,* the land of the *Cymb,* or *Cymri,* or *Celts;* or it may be *Coomb,* a valley. The place of valleys.
3. *Durham.*—*Dune-holm,* or the hill on the island ; or home of wild animals, *e.g., Deor-ham (A. Saxon).*
4. *Westmoreland.*—The West-moor-land of Northumbria.
5. *Lancashire.*—Roman *Castra,* or Camp on the Lune.
6. *Yorkshire.*—Roman *Eboracum,* derivation unknown ; or *A. Saxon, Eura-wick,* or place on the Ure (*Ouse*).

**Four Eastern Counties.**

7. *Lincolnshire.*—Roman *Lin,* a pool, and *colonia.* The Colony by, or on, the pool.
8. *Norfolk.*—North Folk. ⎫ Two families of Angles.
9. *Suffolk.*—South Folk. ⎬ Hence "East Anglia," old name.
10. *Essex.*—*East Seaxe,* or Saxons, as opposed to Middlesex and Wessex.

**Ten Southern Counties.**

11. *Kent.*—Corner county, from Celtic *Cann.*
12. *Surrey.*—South kingdom or people—*Suth-rice.*
13. *Sussex.*—*South Seaxe,* or South Saxons.
14. *Berkshire.*—Probably *Bare Oak Shire.* Originally public meetings were held under a bare, or polled, oak in Windsor Forest.
15. *Hampshire.* — South Hamp Shire, probably from Southampton, the *South-town-home.*
16. *Wiltshire.*—Probably a contraction of *Wiltonshire* from the town of that name on the Wily.
17. —*Somersetshire.*—Derivation unknown.
18. —*Dorsetshire.*—Probably a contraction of *Dorchestershire. (See Wiltshire.)*
19. *Devonshire.*—Derivation unknown.
20. *Cornwall.*—The land of the *Wealhas (Saxon name for strangers);* or *Welsh (West),* on the corner or jutting out land.

**Four Western Counties.**

21. *Cheshire.*—*Castra* or *Cester*, a camp (*Roman*) on the Dee.
22. *Shropshire.*—Probably *Scrubshire*, the land of brushwood, or scrub.
23. *Herefordshire.*—The ford of the Army, on the Severn.
24. *Monmouthshire.* — Literally *Munnow*, or *Minnow* Mouth; so called from the River Munnow, a tributary of the Wye.

**Sixteen Midland Counties.**

25. *Nottinghamshire.*—*A. Saxon*—*Snotenga*, Caves, and *ham*, home. The home or place of caves.
26. *Leicestershire.*—Legion Camp, a large central camp of the Romans.
27. *Derbyshire.*—Wild beast, or deer country (*Norse derivation*).
28. *Staffordshire.*—The ford of the *Staff* or *Stave*. The ford or river crossing was made here by means of leaping with a pole from stone to stone.
29. *Rutlandshire.*—*Ru*, *Rud*, or Red land county.
30. *Worcestershire.*—Probably *Wigra Castra*, a war camp; but uncertain.
31. *Warwickshire.*—*A. Saxon*, *Wering-wic*, a fort dwelling.
32. *Northamptonshire.*—*A. Saxon*—*Ham*, a home, and *ton* a town—the North town home; as Southampton—the South town home.
33. *Huntingdonshire.*— The hunter's place—*Dun-hill* (*A. Saxon*).
34. *Cambridgeshire.*—The bridge or ford over the River Cam.
35.—*Gloucestershire.*—Welsh *Gleau*, strong, and *cestra*, camp.
36.—*Oxfordshire.*—The ford of Oxen through the Thames or Isis.
37. *Buckinghamshire.* — *A. Saxon*—*Boc*, a beech-tree, and *ham*, a home.
38. *Bedfordshire.*—Probably *A. Saxon*—*Bedican*, a fortress, and *ford*. The fortress at the ford or river.
39. *Hertfordshire.*—*A. Saxon*—*Hart*, a stag, and *ford*. The crossing of stags.
40. *Middlesex.*—The land of the *Middle Seaxe* (Saxons).

*N.B.*—The word *county* literally means the rule or estate of a Count or Earl. *Shire*, from *A. Saxon* "*Sciran*," to cut. The Sheriff was the Shire-riff presiding over the Shire Court of each county.

The Twenty Maritime Counties are :—

1. *Northumberland*, the most northern of the English counties, is both a mining and a manufacturing district. Coal and iron abound; lead also is found, and occasionally building stone. The chief manufactures are iron smelting, glass, shipbuilding, and chemical works. The coast yields some good fishing, and the country underlying the Cheviot Hills and the Pennine Range offers pasturage for cattle and sheep. The chief towns are *Newcastle*, Tynemouth, North Shields, Berwick-on-Tweed, and Hexham.

2. *Durham*, like its more northern neighbour, is the centre of a rich coal-field, and possesses manufactures of importance, including shipbuilding and hardware goods. Durham is the county town, university, and cathedral city; but Sunderland is considerably larger in both size and population. Other busy towns are South Shields, Gateshead, Darlington, Stockton, Hartlepool, and Jarrow.

3. *Yorkshire.*—The prince of counties for size and importance is subdivided into three Ridings—North, East, and West. The latter contains the chief centres of trade and population. York is the capital and cathedral city. It was once the capital of Britain, and it still remains one of the oldest and most beautiful of our cities. The Yorkshire coast fisheries are large and valuable, and the moors and valleys are rich in pastures and agricultural produce. The coal and iron-fields of England are of the highest importance, and this county is the centre of the woollen trade.

The other towns in Yorkshire are :—
- *A. West Riding.*—Leeds, Bradford, Huddersfield, Wakefield, Halifax, Sheffield, and Ripon (a second cathedral city).
- *B. North Riding.* — Middlesborough, Scarborough, Whitby, and Northallerton.

*C. East Riding.*—Hull, Beverley, and Bridlington.

4. *Lincolnshire.*—This county, though in area it takes the second place, presents a remarkable contrast to busy Yorkshire. Its inhabitants are chiefly agricultural, and its population small. Lincoln is the capital and cathedral city; but Great Grimsby, on the coast, is the town of chief importance. Other towns are Grantham, Boston, Gainsborough, Stamford, and Louth.

5. *Norfolk*, again, must be classed as an agricultural county, although some manufactures are carried on. The coast fisheries are exceedingly rich, and both pastures and arable land stand in value above the average. Norwich is the capital, chief town, and cathedral city. The other towns of importance are King's Lynn on the Wash, Yarmouth, Cromer, and North Walsham.

6. *Suffolk*, which forms the sister county in East Anglia, is strictly an agricultural district, with important coast fisheries. The capital is Ipswich. Other towns are Lowestoft, Bury St. Edmunds, and Sudbury.

7. *Essex*, if considered without that portion of the great Metropolis known as "London over the Border," is also an agricultural district. The fisheries are unimportant. The capital is Chelmsford, but Colchester is a much larger town. Harwich, Saffron Walden, Braintree, Romford, Ilford, and Maldon are other towns.

8. *Kent*, ofttimes called "the Garden of England," is a district of garden, orchard, and farm lands. Here grows much of the fruit supply for the London markets, such as apples, pears, cherries, plums, strawberries, raspberries, gooseberries, and currants. There are also nut groves and hop gardens, interspersed with rich corn districts, and pleasant pastures. Canterbury is the capital, as it is the chief cathedral city of England. Other places of importance are Maidstone; the five towns of Chatham, Rochester, Strood,

Brompton, and Luton, which form one group; Woolwich, Gravesend, Greenwich, Dover, Folkestone, Sheerness, Margate, Ramsgate, Sandwich, Sevenoaks, Ashford, Tunbridge and Tunbridge Wells, Deal, and Hythe.

9. *Sussex*, the next coast-lying county, bids fair for the same title as Kent. The scenery throughout is varied and beautiful. It is strictly agricultural, and rich in fashionable watering-places or seaside resorts, such as Brighton, Hastings and St. Leonards, Eastbourne, Worthing, Bognor, and Littlehampton. Chichester is the cathedral city and capital, but Lewes is the county town. Other towns are Battle, Shoreham, Horsham, and East Grinstead.

10. *Hampshire*, another agricultural district, is more densely wooded than either Kent or Sussex. Although the soil is somewhat poor, yet agriculture is carried on to a large extent with cereals, roots, fruit, and pasturage. Winchester is the most ancient city. It was, for a short period, the capital of England, and its cathedral is a noble relic of England's power in the past. The largest towns are Portsmouth and Southampton. Aldershot, Basingstoke, Bournemouth, Christchurch, Lyndhurst and Lymington are places of some importance.

The beautiful *Isle of Wight* forms part of Hampshire for political and religious purposes. Its chief towns are Newport (the capital,) Ryde, Cowes, Ventnor, Shanklin, and Freshwater. Osborne House, near Cowes, is a favourite home of our great and good Queen Victoria.

11. *Dorsetshire* is sparsely populated throughout. Its interests are purely agricultural, and its inhabitants somewhat poor. Dorchester is the capital, but Weymouth is of the most importance; Wimborne, Poole, and Lyme Regis are other towns.

12. *Devonshire*, the third largest county in England, justly deserves the name of "lovely Devon" sometimes

accorded it. It contains the high land of Exmoor, with the forests and plateaux of Dartmoor. We now have entered into the district of mines, and some few manufactures again; yet, on the whole, Devonshire is an agricultural county. The soil here is much richer than the neighbouring districts of Dorset and Hampshire, so that a higher state of cultivation exists. A marked feature in the scenery of South Devon is the numerous orchards, which have been planted for the purposes of cider-making. The fisheries on the south coast are of considerable value; and this county is rich in seaports and health-giving wateringplaces. Exeter is the capital and cathedral city; but there are several other important towns, *viz.*, Plymouth, Devonport, Dartmouth, Exmouth, Sidmouth, Teignmouth, Ilfracombe, Barnstaple, Bideford on the coast, and Tiverton, Crediton, Tavistock, South Molton and Axminster in the interior.

13. *Cornwall* is certainly still the "land of the strangers." In no other part of England are the people so foreign-like in their habits and customs. This county also contrasts with any other in its geological formation and physical aspects. It is chiefly a mining district. Copper, tin, silver, manganese, etc., are still procured in large or small quantities; and the immense slate and granite quarries are a source of great wealth. The people on the coast are mostly engaged in the pilchard and mackerel fisheries. In olden days the rocky, dangerous nature of the Cornish coast formed a rich harvest-ground for smugglers. The largest town is Penzance. Bodmin is the old capital; but Truro, the new cathedral city, is generally now regarded as the chief town. Other towns of importance in Cornwall are Falmouth, St. Austell, Launceston.

*The Scilly Isles* (*see* separate notice, "Islands of England and Wales," p. 105) are generally included in Cornwall.

The capital is Hugh Town, on St. Mary's Island. Large quantities of vegetables, fruit, and flowers are sent to London every year from these islands.

14. *Somersetshire.*—This county is almost entirely agricultural. Its pastures are proverbially rich and productive. It is most pleasantly situated along the shores of the Bristol Channel, and there are but few towns of any size or importance as regards trade or commerce. The capital is Taunton; but Bath is of more importance by reason of its warm mineral springs, which attract large numbers of invalids and visitors every year for the waters. It is one of two cathedral cities, the other being Wells, from which the bishop takes his second title. Other towns are Bridgwater, Frome, Yeovil, Weston-super-Mare, and Glastonbury.

15. *Gloucestershire* is both an agricultural and a mining district. There are also woollen cloth manufactories in the neighbourhood of Stroud and Dursley. The coal-fields are called by the names of the Forest of Dean Colliery in the West, and the South Gloucester Colliery in the Avon Valley. Gloucester is the capital and cathedral city. The other towns are Bristol and Clifton, Cheltenham, Cirencester, Stroud, and Tewkesbury.

16. *Monmouthshire.*—This county, like Gloucestershire, is both mining and agricultural. Both iron and coal are found here, as it borders closely on the important South Wales colliery district. The scenery of the Wye here, as in Hertfordshire, is remarkable for its great beauty. The capital is Monmouth, but the largest town is Newport, which is a seaport of considerable importance. Other towns in Monmouthshire are Tredegar, Abergavenny, Pontypool, and Chepstow.

17. *Cheshire.*—Although this county is purely agricultural in nature, yet of late years the extensive cotton

manufacturing district has spread its area over the northern portion of it, and its small county towns have been changed into cotton centres, as Stockport and Stalybridge. Other manufacturing districts of Cheshire are silk-weaving at Macclesfield; salt works at Nantwich, Middlewich, and Northwich; shipbuilding at Birkenhead, which is considered to be a suburb of Liverpool. The capital is Chester, an ancient cathedral city, which takes us back to Roman times, with its castle and fortifications. Other towns are Runcorn, Altringham, and Crewe, where are situated some of the most important railway works in the kingdom, belonging to the London and North-Western Railway Company.

18. *Lancashire.*—This county is the main seat of the cotton manufacture. It is the most densely populated portion of the United Kingdom, next to the Metropolis of London, as Manchester and Liverpool rank next in size and population. As Manchester is the central pivot of the English cotton trade, so Liverpool is the cotton port. It ranks as the second port of the world's commerce. The Manchester Ship Canal (*see* p. 69) now brings this important city within the lists of our seaport towns, as vessels of a certain size and freight are able to convey their cargoes direct to its warehouses. The principal cotton towns are Preston, Blackburn, Bolton, Oldham, Rochdale, Warrington, Wigan, Ashton-under-Lyne, Chorley, Bury, and Salford. Barrow-in-Furness has large steel and iron works; St. Helens and Colne are busy places of trade and manufacture. Lancaster is the old capital, and the cathedral cities of Manchester and Liverpool have each a bishop to preside over the teeming population surrounding them. There are rich and extensive coal-fields throughout Lancashire, which add materially to the wealth of the county.

19. *Westmoreland.*—But a very small portion of this county touches the sea, yet it must be included among our maritime counties. It is the land of mountains, lakes, valleys, and pastures, so that it ranks as a pastoral, rather than an agricultural, or a manufacturing, district. Appleby is the old county town. It is of little importance beyond its beauty, as it is said to be the smallest county town in England. Kendal is somewhat larger, as there are several manufactories of minor importance. Ambleside is a popular tourist resort for the Lake District.

20. *Cumberland,* another mountainous district, lies to the west of the Pennine Range. The scenery is bold and beautiful. Excellent coal is obtained from the Whitehaven Colliery district lying along the coast. Carlisle is the capital and cathedral city. Other towns are, Whitehaven, Workington, Cockermouth, Maryport, Keswick, and Penrith.

The Twenty Inland Counties are :—

1. *Nottinghamshire* is well wooded and picturesque in many parts. It is both an agricultural and a manufacturing district. Coal is also plentiful. The chief trade is carried on in lace-making and stockings, although there are other various manufactures. Nottingham is the capital, but Southwell represents the cathedral city of the district. Other towns are Newark, Mansfield, Worksop, and Retford.

2. *Derbyshire* combines the mining, manufacturing, and agricultural interests. The northern part is mountainous, and noted for its scenery—called the Peak District. The South Yorkshire Coalfield is continued in the eastern portion, and the chief manufactures are iron ware, cotton goods, and hosiery. Some lace-making is carried on around Derby, which is the capital. Other towns are Chesterfield, Glossop, Ilkeston, Buxton, and Matlock; also Belper, Wirksworth, and Ashborne.

3. *Staffordshire* is a thickly populated district of mines

and manufactures. There are two coal-fields, and the series of towns called *The Potteries* are to be found here. Numerous ironworks and furnaces, with every kind of hardware manufactures, have given the Wolverhampton district the name of *The Black Country*. The capital is Stafford, but the cathedral city is Lichfield. Wolverhampton is the most populous and the busiest centre of trade; with its neighbouring towns of Walsall, Wednesbury, Bilston, and West Bromwich. There are six pottery towns, *viz.*, Stoke-upon-Trent, Hanley, Burslem, Etruria, Longton, and Newcastle-under-Lyne; and on the eastern side of the county stands Burton-on-Trent with its world-renowned breweries.

4. *Shropshire* is sometimes called "Salop." It is situated partly in the central plain, and partly in the higher lands bordering upon Wales. These districts are divided in a somewhat marked way by the River Severn. Shrewsbury is the capital; other towns are Wellington, Bridgnorth, and Coalbrookdale in the mining districts, where coal and iron are abundant. Oswestry has woollen manufactories, and the smaller towns are Ludlow, Wenlock, and Bishop's Castle.

5. *Leicestershire.*—The chief industries of this midland county are coal-mining, woollen hosiery, and boot-making, with extensive dairy and cheese farming. Besides these important manufactures, a large portion of Leicestershire is given up to agriculture. The Leicester breed of sheep are considered excellent, both for their large size and the quality of their mutton. The capital is Leicester. Other places of importance are Loughborough, Melton Mowbray, the centre of the famous hunting district, Ashby-de-la-Zouch, Hinckley, and Lutterworth.

6. *Warwickshire*, sometimes called the central county of England, is a fair spot, if taken as a whole, although the

colliery and manufacturing districts around Birmingham do scarcely come under this description. Warwickshire proudly owns the finest castle in England; the birthplace of England's greatest poet; and the largest hardware manufacturing city in the world. It is a county of contrasts. In a short space of time you may travel, from modern busy Birmingham, to old-world Warwick, or silent Stratford-on-Avon, and forget about its existence altogether. Coventry, of ancient silk ribbon renown, now makes cycles of all kinds, watches, and clocks, etc. The other towns are Leamington, Rugby, and Nuneaton.

7. *Herefordshire*, one of the western counties on the Welsh border, is 38 miles in length, and 32 in breadth. The surface is pleasantly diversified. Hills, dales, woodlands, meadows, hop gardens, and bright orchard plots follow each other in rapid succession, so that a tour through Herefordshire is always a treat to a stranger. It is a lovely agricultural district, as the soil is rich and productive. The capital and cathedral city is Hereford, picturesquely situated on the Wye. Other towns are Leominster, Ledbury, and Ross.

8. *Worcestershire* is a well-wooded midland county, partly mining, partly manufacturing, and partly agricultural in its interests. It is somewhat smaller in size than Herefordshire. It may justly be described as an important county, inasmuch as it possesses excellent coal and iron mines in its northern division, which forms part of the Black Country; and the manufactures of the towns include carpets, cloth, lace, gloves, nails, and hardware goods, pottery and glass, cider and perry, leather, needles, salt, and oil-cake. Like Herefordshire, its hop gardens and large orchards are a pleasant feature in the landscape. The capital and cathedral city is Worcester, standing on the River Severn. Other important towns are Kidderminster,

Dudley, Stonebridge, Droitwich, Malvern, Redditch, Bewdley, Bromsgrove, Stourbridge, and Evesham.

9. *Rutland*, the smallest county in England, is chiefly agricultural, and may be considered a corn-growing district. It is only 152 square miles in extent. The whole county consists of small, even ridges or uplands, with well-watered valleys lying between. Oakham is the capital, and it is the only town of importance. At Uppingham there is a large public school.

10. *Northamptonshire*, another agricultural county, possesses the chief centres of the boot-and-shoe trade, but few other manufactures of importance. It is a pleasant district, well diversified with hill, dale, and woodland. The farming interests are of value. The area is 1,016 square miles. The capital is Northampton, on the river Nen, and the cathedral city is Peterborough. Other towns are Kettering, Wellingborough, and Higham Ferrers.

11. *Huntingdonshire* is another small inland county, being only 30 miles in length by some 23 in breadth. Its interests are purely agricultural, and dairy farming is carried on extensively throughout. For excellent cheese (Stilton) and butter, Huntingdonshire stands almost without a rival. Its rich pastures are productive of fat stock, and sheep are reared on the flat fen-lands found in the northern district. The capital is Huntingdon, on the Great Ouse River, where Oliver Cromwell was born. Other towns are St. Ives, St. Neots, and Godmanchester.

12. *Cambridgeshire* is also a dairy-farming county. It closely resembles Huntingdonshire in the richness of its pastures and natural features. It is about 50 miles long and 30 miles broad. The northern portion is known by the name of the Isle of Ely, and the land here is low-lying and marshy. The capital is Cambridge, the second of England's wondrous seats of learning. Its colleges and

halls, some eighteen in number, date back from the thirteenth century, as Peterhouse was founded in 1257. The cathedral city is Ely, and other towns are Chesterton, Wisbeach, and Newmarket.

13. *Bedfordshire* is also a low-lying fen county. It is a small agricultural district, some 36 miles long by 22 miles broad. The only manufacturing interests of this county are straw-plait bonnet and hat making, and thread lace. The capital is Bedford, situated on the Great Ouse; and other towns are Luton, Dunstable, Leighton Buzzard, and Biggleswade.

14. *Hertfordshire* is an agricultural county, 38 miles in length and 20 miles in breadth. None of its towns are of large size, so that its manufactures are of less importance than those of other neighbouring counties. Yet, matting, straw-plaiting, hat and bonnet making, and ribbon weaving are carried on. Certain parts of Hertfordshire have extensive cherry and apple orchards. The capital is Hertford, on the River Lea. Other towns are St. Albans, Hitchin, Watford, Bishop Stortford, Barnet, and Ware.

15. *Buckinghamshire*, another agricultural and dairy county, has but few towns, and these are small and unimportant. The rich pastures of the Vale of Aylesbury produce excellent butter and milk, and much hay is grown for the London markets in this county. The only manufactures of Buckinghamshire are butter, condensed milk, turnery and wood ware, chairs, and some straw-plaiting. The capital is Buckingham, on the Great Ouse. Other towns are Aylesbury, Wycombe, Stony Stratford, and Great Marlow. The first of England's public schools is at Eton, which joins Windsor by a bridge.

16. *Berkshire* is an agricultural county, being 48 miles long, and so irregular in shape that its width varies from 7 to 28 miles. The scenery throughout is picturesque;

beautiful woods, including the Royal Park and Forest of Windsor, are situated in this county; and the Thames valley lends a special charm to the scenery. The corn-growing and dairy districts are excellent. Among the manufactures are biscuits, machinery, matting, chairs, etc. The capital is Reading, on the Kennet. Other towns are Maidenhead, Windsor, Abingdon, Wallingford, Newbury, and Wokingham.

17. *Oxfordshire* is an agricultural county, with some few manufactures. The natural features vary considerably. In the north-western district the monotony of stone walls, instead of green hedges, entirely spoils the otherwise picturesque scenery. The chief manufacturing interests are blankets, gloves, and lace. The capital and cathedral city is Oxford, England's oldest seat of learning, as it dates from the time of Alfred the Great. There are twenty-five colleges and halls, with many other public and educational buildings. Other towns are Woodstock, Banbury, Chipping Norton, Henley-on-Thames, and Witney.

18. *Wiltshire* is a large county, chiefly agricultural and pastoral. Its manufactures include the famous West of England cloth, which is woven at Bradford, Trowbridge, and Westbury in this county. Excellent butter, cheese, and dairy produce also come from Wiltshire. Carpets and kerseymere are also made. The capital and cathedral city is Salisbury, on the River Avon. Other towns are Devizes, Chippenham, Bradford, Trowbridge, Calne, Swindon, Marlborough, Westbury, Wilton, and Warminster.

19. *Surrey* is generally considered one of the most beautiful of the southern counties of England. It is perhaps fair to regard it as the garden of London, inasmuch as immense supplies of fruit, flowers, and vegetables are conveyed every day to the Metropolis from the fields of Surrey. One of its chief interests is market gardening. The whole of South London, or London south of the

Thames, is situated in this county. This, with the additional suburban towns of Croydon, Clapham, Putney, Barnes, Mortlake, Dulwich, Norwood, Richmond, Kingston, Kew, Surbiton, etc., make it one of the most populous districts in England. The capital is Guildford, on the River Wey. Other towns are Epsom, Dorking, Godalming, and Sutton, besides the above-named suburban districts.

20. *Middlesex* is but 233 square miles in area, yet it contains the highest population in the British Isles, as the chief portion of London, the Metropolis of the World, stands in this county, with its northern and western suburbs of Willesden, Kilburn, Tottenham, Highgate, Hampstead, and Hornsey. Other towns are Brentford, Uxbridge, Ealing, Harrow, with England's second great public school, Staines, and Enfield.

THE COUNTY COUNCIL is a modern innovation, which has been legalised for administrative purposes of local government. In addition to the government by the County Council of the 52 counties of England and Wales, London, the Metropolis, has been constituted a county, with an area of 120 square miles, and a population of nearly $5\frac{1}{2}$ million inhabitants.

The following 61 provincial boroughs have also for local government purposes been formed into administrative counties:—

Barrow, Bath, Birkenhead, Birmingham, Blackburn, Bolton, Bootle, Bradford (York), Brighton, Bristol, Burney, Bury, Canterbury, Cardiff, Chester, Coventry, Croydon, Derby, Devonport, Dudley, Exeter, Gateshead, Gloucester, Great Yarmouth, Halifax, Hanley, Hastings, Huddersfield, Ipswich, Kingston-upon-Hull, Leeds, Leicester, Lincoln, Liverpool, Manchester, Middlesborough, Newcastle-upon-Tyne, Northampton, Norwich, Nottingham Oldham, Plymouth, Portsmouth, Preston, Reading, Rochdale, St.

Helens, Salford, Sheffield, Southampton, South Shields, Stockport, Sunderland, Swansea, Walsall, West Bromwich, West Ham, Wigan, Wolverhampton, Worcester, and York.

TOWNS.—It is not generally known that more than half the people of England and Wales reside, and work, in the towns. This may be the better understood when we have considered the population of London, which equals a sixth of the whole of the inhabitants of England and Wales.

The last census returns for 1891 gave the following statistics (in round numbers), which are most interesting, inasmuch as they point out the great centres of population, trade, wealth, and labour :—

| | | |
|---|---|---|
| 1. London, | 5,500,000 | inhabitants. |
| 2. Liverpool, | 730,000 | ,, |
| 3. Manchester, including Salford, | 703,000 | ,, |
| 4. Birmingham, | 429,000 | ,, |
| 5. Leeds, | 368,000 | ,, |
| 6. Sheffield, | 324,000 | ,, |
| 7. Bristol, | 222,000 | ,, |
| 8. Bradford, | 216,000 | ,, |
| 9. Nottingham, | 212,000 | ,, |
| 10. Hull, | 200,000 | ,, |
| 11. Newcastle-on-Tyne, | 186,000 | ,, |
| 12. Portsmouth, | 159,000 | ,, |
| 13. Leicester, | 142,000 | ,, |
| 14. Oldham, } 15. Sunderland, } | 131,000 | ,, |
| 16. Cardiff, | 129,000 | ,, |
| 17. Blackburn, | 120,000 | ,, |
| 18. Bolton, | 115,000 | ,, |
| 19. Brighton, | 115,000 | ,, |
| 20. Preston, | 108,000 | ,, |
| 21. Norwich, | 101,000 | ,, |
| 22. Birkenhead, | 100,000 | ,, |

*N.B.*—In 22 of our largest towns in England and Wales the population was, in 1891, 10,440,000 inhabitants, out of a total for the whole country of 29,002,525.

LONDON, from Celtic *Llyn*, a pool, the town near the pool, is the Metropolis of the world, or in other words, it is the great social, political, moral, philanthropical, intellectual, literary, artistic, and commercial centre of civilised nations.

# ENGLAND AND WALES.

All alike feel its influence, wealth, and power. Not only the products of the world are gathered together here, but representatives of all nations visit this wonderful city every year. London is probably one of the most ancient of English cities. Situated on both banks of the River Thames, about 60 miles from the sea, its far-stretching area of hundreds of square miles, with its teeming population of millions of inhabitants, place it among the modern wonders of the world.

Strictly speaking, London is now a county for all legal and parliamentary matters. It contains two cities, London and Westminster, and seven parliamentary boroughs, *viz.*, Marylebone, Finsbury, Southwark, Lambeth, Chelsea, Hackney, and the Tower Hamlets. It is represented in the House of Commons by 59 Members.

The City of London proper is divided into 26 wards under a Lord Mayor, a Court of Aldermen, Sheriffs, and a large body of other important officers, and these have their jurisdiction and power within the old city wall boundaries, not including the metropolitan area.

There are two cathedrals, St. Paul's in the City, and St. Peter's, or the Abbey, at Westminster[1]; besides the Roman Catholic Cathedral of St. George at Southwark; The Brompton Oratory, etc. Then, again, nearly every conceivable religious body has its place of worship within its area. For educational purposes, its universities, colleges, museums, art galleries, science schools, hospitals, lecture halls, and technical instruction rooms are unrivalled. For amusement, its 67 theatres and music halls, its exhibitions and bazaars, include more than 100 holiday resorts open daily.

Its principal parks are nine in number: Hyde Park; Regent's; St. James'; Green; Kensington Gardens; Victoria; Kensington; Battersea, and Southwark Parks; besides other

---

[1] *N.B.—A third cathedral is S. Saviour's, Southwark.*

# ENGLAND AND WALES.

*Millwall Docks.*

open spaces allotted for public use and recreation in the metropolitan area. These are carefully kept, and planted with choice flowers, and shrubs, to suit the varying seasons.

Its squares, public buildings, clubs, monuments, shops, and stores of trade are exceedingly numerous, and display many styles of design and architecture. Its provision and food markets outnumber those of any other city in the world; while its docks, bonded warehouses, cellars, and immense storehouses are crowded with the produce of the world's markets, and workshops. Its manufactures and trades are so numerous, and varied, that it would be well-nigh impossible to enumerate them all. There are railways above and underground, and, in addition, thousands of omnibuses, tramcars, and cabs, cross and re-cross each other's tracks, to convey passengers to every part.

London, the largest city in the world, covers, within a circle of fifteen miles from Charing Cross, about 700 square miles of area, and its inhabitants exceed 5,500,000. More than 100,000 foreigners from every part of the world are to be found in London. Here we may find "more Jews than there are in Palestine; more Roman Catholics than in Rome; more Irish than in Dublin; more Scotch than in Edinburgh. Its port and dock registers record thousands of ships of every kind and craft. The growth of its population is estimated at more than 50,000 each year, *e.g.*, a birth and a death taking place within its area every few minutes. Many miles of new streets are added to its boundaries each year. It is, indeed, a city of contrasts. It contains more wealth and more poverty; more philanthropy and more crime; more industry and more idleness; more religion and more unbelief, than any other city in the world. Its immense water supplies; its perfect system of sanitation; its lighting of streets and buildings; its fire brigades; and police arrangements, are maintained at an immense cost

*The Port of Liverpool.*

to ensure health and security to the millions of people dwelling there."—*Leisure Hour.*

Probably the most astonishing fact concerning London is its continuous and never-failing food supply. The greater the increase of population the better they are provided for. It now stands in four counties—Middlesex, Surrey, Kent, and Essex—and one naturally marvels to think what will be the population, and its needs and requirements in the future, if the present rapid growth continues. In the twelfth and the thirteenth centuries famine and plague were of frequent occurrence; but now in the nineteenth, with the command of the world's markets, and the incomparable system of provision for the ever-increasing masses, these appear to be quite an impossibility.

*Liverpool*, from "*Lyrpool*" or "*Llerpwll*"—Celtic, "*the place on the pool*," with a population in 1891 of 730,000, ranks as the second city, and commercial port, in Great Britain. The docks and warehouses, which receive, in the main part, the produce and manufactures of the western world of America, etc., are among the finest in the world, as they comprise some 25 miles of quay and landing stages, with more than 250 acres of docks and storage sheds.

Liverpool is a well-paved city. Its streets are well drained and lighted, and its public buildings are magnificent. In 1690, or rather more than 200 years ago, the population of Liverpool was under 5,000, and its port of but little commercial value; now its annual tonnage amounts to 10,000,000. Its southern suburb of Birkenhead is connected by a submarine tunnel. The great American lines of steamships have their centre here for both goods and passengers, and thus it is regarded as the chief emigration port of the empire. Again, Liverpool receives nearly the whole of the raw cotton and wool sent to this country for manufacturing purposes, as it is situated on the verge of the cotton and woollen industries of Lancashire and Yorkshire. Its merchants are rich and prosperous, and probably in no other

*Lime Street, Liverpool.*

place upon the earth's surface could be found the same extensive trade interests, and private wealth, as upon the

Liverpool Exchange and Chamber of Commerce. Liverpool was made a Bishop's See in 1880.

*Manchester*, from "*Main*," a stone, and "*Castrum*," a camp or fort, is therefore "*the place upon the rock.*" Its population in 1891, including Salford, was 703,000, thus placing it in order as the third city in Great Britain. It is the court and home of King Cotton. It is now a port, having in 1894 been joined to the River Mersey by the famous Manchester Ship Canal, which allows of vessels of a certain size to enter the port of Manchester, instead of trans-shipping their cargoes as heretofore. This fine municipal and parliamentary city contains many costly and beautiful public buildings, among which may be mentioned the Royal Exchange, Town Hall, Chamber of Commerce, Banks, Post Office, Athenæum, Assize Courts, Free Trade Hall, Cathedral, and many magnificent Churches, Owen's College, Schools, Institutes, Hospitals, etc. Its manufacturing interests are world wide. Hundreds of thousands of operatives are employed in the cotton and other mills and factories, where every conceivable article of clothing, consisting of cotton, silk, or woollen material, is made; besides firearms, machinery, and various other things.

*Birmingham*, the fourth city in Great Britain, numbered 429,000 persons at the last census of 1891. Standing as it does in the centre of the great midland iron and coal districts, it practically commands the principal of England's hardware goods manufactures; and its trade is of worldwide importance for firearms, tools, and machinery, besides glass, toys, jewellery, and fancy goods. The derivation of its name is uncertain, probably it was originally "*Brum-wych-am*," or "the home of the Brum or Brummings in the wood." Birmingham is more like London, than either Liverpool or Manchester, in the arrangement of its streets, yet its atmosphere is even more dense and cloudy owing to the numerous

*Queen's Dock, Hull.*

furnaces and manufactories surrounding it. The public buildings are very fine. It is not yet made into a Bishop's See, but it is included in the Diocese of Worcester.

*Leeds*, from either "*Loidis*" or "*Ledes*," of unknown origin, is the principal seat of the woollen manufactures of Yorkshire. Its population in 1891 was 368,000. All kinds of cloth are manufactured here, in addition to carpets, blankets, shawls, and other woollen goods. Leeds is a fine town, which is rapidly growing in importance. The streets and buildings are excellent. Its commercial value is said to exceed £12,000,000 per annum. The other manufactories of Leeds are machinery and iron goods, locomotive and agricultural engines, leather, chemicals, caps, shoes, glass, and paper.

*Sheffield* is the sixth and last town of England and Wales whose population exceeds 300,000 souls. In 1891 the census gave the number as 324,000. The derivation of Sheffield is undoubtedly "*Sheaf-field*," as the town stands at the confluence of the two streams, Don and Sheaf. It is far from being pleasant in appearance. The choking fumes and dense clouds of smoke, from its many factories, render both people and buildings of a dreary, sallow aspect. Everything appears to be seen either through a fog, or a tainted atmosphere. This town is the grand centre of our cutlery and silver-plating manufactures. All kinds of iron and steel work are carried on here, so that Sheffield makes the best cutlery in the world.

The Welsh Counties are twelve in number. The natural divisions are :—

> *North Wales.*—Six counties: Anglesea, Caernarvonshire, Denbighshire, Flintshire, Merionethshire, and Montgomeryshire.
> 
> *South Wales.*—Six counties: Cardiganshire, Radnorshire, Brecknockshire, Caermarthenshire, Pembrokeshire, and Glamorganshire.

## ENGLAND AND WALES. 173

They may be further divided into nine maritime counties and three inland counties.

*Southampton Docks.*

Montgomeryshire is the largest in area; and Flintshire is the smallest county in Wales.

Glamorganshire is the most thickly populated district, and Radnorshire the least in population.

The area of Wales is 7,442 square miles, and the population only 1,501,103. Generally speaking, more than half of the inhabitants speak their native language of Welsh in addition to English, which is now taught in the schools throughout the country.

Wales is a mountainous district throughout, so that the agricultural interests are far below those of mining and manufactures. The hills, however, afford good pasturage for sheep and cattle, and the chief farming industry rests in rearing these animals.

The mining interests are valuable and extensive. Coal and iron are plentiful in Glamorganshire, Flintshire, and Denbighshire. Excellent building stone, granite, and slate are quarried in large quantities; and lead, copper, and tin, with some silver and gold, are produced. Besides the manufacture of metal goods, etc., the trade in slate dressing, flannel, carpets, etc., is flourishing and important.

The counties and chief towns arranged alphabetically are:—

1. *Anglesea*, 275 sq. miles.—Beaumaris and Holyhead.
2. *Brecknockshire*, 734 sq. miles.—Brecon, Brynmawr, and Builth.
3. *Cardiganshire*, 692 sq. miles.—Cardigan, Aberystwith, Lampeter.
4. *Caermarthenshire*, 919 sq. miles.—Caermarthen, Llandovery, Llanelly, and Kidwelly.
5. *Caernarvonshire*, 563 sq. miles.—Caernarvon, Bangor, Llandudno, Conway, Pwllheli.
6. *Denbighshire*, 664 sq. miles.—Denbigh, Wrexham, Ruthin.
7. *Flintshire*, 256 sq. miles.—Mold, Flint, Rhyl, Holywell.

8. *Glamorganshire*, 790 sq. miles.—Cardiff, Swansea, Merthyr Tydfil, Llandaff, Cowbridge, Aberavon, Neath.
9. *Merionethshire*, 668 sq. miles.—Dolgelly, Barmouth, Bala.
10. *Montgomeryshire*, 797 sq. miles.—Montgomery, Welshpool, Llanidloes, Llanfyllin.
11. *Pembrokeshire*, 613 sq. miles—Pembroke, Haverfordwest, Tenby, Milford.
12. *Radnorshire*, 471 sq. miles.—Radnor, Presteigne.

CHIEF BATTLE-FIELDS OF ENGLAND AND WALES :—

*Northumberland.*—Berwick, 1296 ; Otterburn or Chevy Chase, 1388 ; Homildon Hill, 1402 ; Hexham, 1464 ; Flodden Field, 1513.
*Durham.*—Neville's Cross, 1346.
*Yorkshire.*—Stamford Bridge, 1066 ; The Standard (Northallerton) 1137 ; Boroughbridge, 1322 ; Branham Moor (York) 1408 ; Wakefield, 1460 ; Towton, 1461 ; Marston Moor, 1644.
*Lancashire.*—Atherton Moor, 1643 ; Preston, 1648.
*Cheshire.*—Rowton Heath, 1645.
*Lincolnshire.*—Lincoln, 1141 and 1217 ; Stamford, 1470.
*Nottinghamshire.*—Stoke, 1487.
*Leicestershire.*—Bosworth Field, 1483.
*Staffordshire.*—Blore Heath, 1459.
*Northamptonshire.*—Northampton, 1460 ; Naseby, 1645.
*Shropshire.*—Shrewsbury, 1403.
*Worcestershire.*—Evesham, 1265 ; Worcester, 1651.
*Herefordshire.*—Mortimer's Cross (Leominster) 1461.
*Gloucestershire.*—Tewkesbury, 1471.
*Warwickshire.*—Edgehill, 1642.
*Oxfordshire.*—Chalgrove Field, 1643 ; Cropedy Bridge 1644.

*Hertfordshire.*—St. Albans, 1455-61; Barnet, 1471.
*Berkshire.*—Newbury, 1643-4; Reading, 1643.
*Kent.*—Sevenoaks, 1450; Blackheath, 1497.
*Sussex.*—Battle (Telham Hill) 1066, commonly called Hastings; Lewes, 1264.
*Somersetshire.*—Sedgemoor, 1685.
*Cornwall.*—Stratton, 1643.

IMPERIAL BRITAIN. MAP VII.

# PART IV.

## SCOTLAND.

NAME.—Scotland, it is evident, means "The Land of the Scots," a northern Irish tribe of warriors who took possession of the southern and western portions of the country at a very early period. The Romans described Scotland as Caledonia. It has also been called in early times North Britain, and occasionally Albyn, or Albion, or white rock land. It is strange to find this latter title still used by the older inhabitants of the Highland districts.

POSITION.—The northern portion of the Island of Great Britain is called Scotland. It is very irregular in shape, having its narrow parts towards the north and the south; being only about 35 miles wide from the Firth of Clyde to the Firth of Forth.

Scotland forms one of the few peninsulas of the old world pointing northwards. The sea entirely surrounds it, with the exception of the narrow neck of land about 60 miles in breadth which connects it with England on the south. This country is situated between the parallels of latitude 54° 88′ and 58° 41′ north of the Equator; longitude 1° 45′ and 6° 14′ west of Greenwich.

AREA AND EXTENT.—The area of Scotland is 30,000 square miles, or about half the size of England and Wales. The greatest length, measured from Cape Wrath in Sutherlandshire in the North, to the Mull of Galloway in Wigton in the South, is 280 miles; and the extreme breadth, from Peterhead in Aberdeenshire in the East, to Ardnamurchan Point in Argyllshire in the West, is 175 miles.

POPULATION.—In 1891, the last census taken gave the

population as 4,025,647, showing a slight increase of 8 per cent. during the past ten years. However, Scotland is a thinly populated country compared with England and Wales; being only one-ninth of that of the whole of Great Britain, and giving only an average of 134 persons to each square mile of territory. Again, it will be seen that the population of London alone exceeded the population of the whole of Scotland in 1891 by 1,474,353 persons.

The Highlands of the North are much less populated than the Lowland centres of trade, where most of the large towns are situated.

BOUNDARIES.—Scotland is bounded on the North by the Atlantic Ocean; South by England and the Irish Sea; East by the North Sea or German Ocean; and West by the Atlantic Ocean, and the North Channel.

COAST-LINE.—This is considerable for such a small country, being 2,500 miles in length, not including the 788 large and small islands which so thickly fringe and stud the Western and Northern Coasts. This enormous coast-line gives about 1 mile of coast to every 12 square miles of area, and so irregular is the boundary line that no part of Scotland is 50 miles from the sea.

The Eastern Coast is much less indented than the Western, owing to the prevalence of the Atlantic storms beating upon the latter shores, so that the coast-line of this side of Scotland is less picturesque, as it is less bold than on the western side. It possesses, however, special advantages for navigation, trade, and commerce, in consequence of which the principal seaports, with the exception of Glasgow, situated on the Clyde, are to be found on the Eastern Coast.

CAPES AND HEADLANDS.—The chief capes are:—
*On the East Coast travelling from South to North—*
St. Abbs Head in Berwick; Fifeness; Buchanness;

Peterhead; Kinnaird's Head in Aberdeen; Tarbetness in Cromarty; and Noss Head in Caithness.

*On the North Coast—*
Duncansby Head, and Dunnet Head in Caithness; Strathy Point and Cape Wrath in Sutherland.

*On the West Coast, travelling from North to South,* the capes and headlands are too numerous to mention, owing to the serrated nature of this coast. The chief are:—
Point of Stoir in Sutherland; Rhu Rea, and Red Point in Cromarty and Ross; Ardnamurchan Point, and the Mull of Cantire in Argyll; the Mull of Galloway and Burrow Head in Wigton.

BAYS AND INLETS.—*On the East Coast* there are the Firths of Forth; Tay; Murray; Cromarty; with Dornoch, and Sinclair Bays.

*On the North Coast.*—Pentland Firth is a strait lying between Caithness and Orkney, although it is frequently classed as an inlet. Dunnet Bay and the Kyle of Tongue are the chief inlets.

*On the Western Coast* there are a multitude of inlets, among which may be mentioned Lochs Broom; Torridon; Linnhe; Eil; Leven; Fyne; Long; with the Firth of Clyde, and Loch Ryan.

*On the South Coast,* Luce Bay, Wigton Bay, and the Solway Firth.

STRAITS.—The principal straits are:—
1. The Pentland Firth, in the North, between Caithness and the Orkney Islands.
2. The Minch, } between the Hebrides and the
3. The Little Minch, } Mainland.
4. The Sounds of Sleat; Mull; Jura; Islay; and Harris, between the Hebrides.
5. The North Channel, lying between Scotland and Ireland.

ISLANDS.—The total number of islands, large and small, surrounding the coasts of Scotland, are 788 in number, yet only about 200 are inhabited. These are arranged in four groups or clusters, called:—

1. The Shetland Isles, 80 in number.
2. The Orkney Isles, 67 in number.
3. The Inner Hebrides, } 300 in number.
4. The Outer Hebrides, }
5. There are, besides, the islands of the Clyde, forming Buteshire, 4 in number, *viz.*, Bute; Arran; Great and Little Cumbrae.
6. With the following less important isolated rocks or craigs, *viz.*:—
   *A.* Ailsa Craig, a solitary rock in the Firth of Clyde.
   *B.* Inchcolm and Inchkeith, two small islets in the Firth of Forth, noted for the remains of a religious monastery, as well as being the burial place of several Scottish kings.
   *C.* Bass Rock, also in the Firth of Forth, upon which is placed a lighthouse.
   *D.* Bell Rock, in the Firth of Tay, noted for the lighthouse which bears its name.

The islands of Scotland are of such importance that they deserve a chapter to themselves, but, for convenience sake, we will treat of the several groups in order here.

The most northern groups are the *Shetland* and the *Orkney Isles*. The area of the combined groups is 1,320 square miles, and the united population was 59,164 in 1891. The two groups together form one of the Scotch counties. Commencing with the most northern group, the Shetland, or Zetland Isles, are 80 in number, of which 32 are regularly inhabited, although the fishermen occasionally occupy others to carry on their trade at certain seasons of the year. This cluster of islands is situated in the

IMPERIAL BRITAIN.        MAP IX.

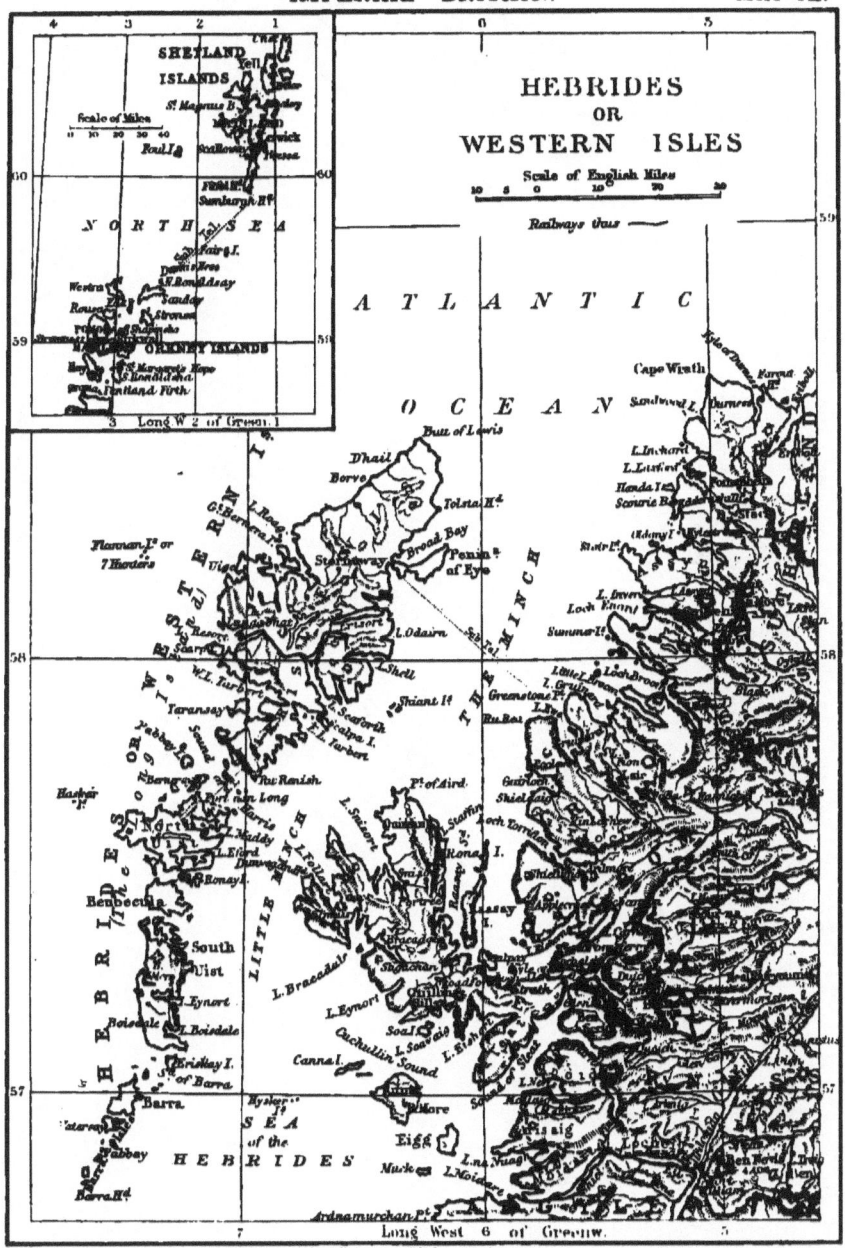

*Bass Rock.*

North Atlantic Ocean, about 100 miles to the north-east of the mainland of Scotland; and lying between the parallels of latitude 59° and 61° north of the Equator, and longitude 0° 44′ and 1° 44″ west of Greenwich. The physical features are marked. Most of the islands are irregular in shape, and the surface is rugged and somewhat barren, so that agriculture is in a neglected state. The climate is cold, and much wet weather prevails. The inhabitants are the original successors of the old Celtic race. They are strong, hardy, honest, thrifty people, of simple manners and habits, and with but little education. For the most part they are engaged in the coast fisheries, or in the rearing of black cattle, sheep, ponies, and goats. The Shetland ponies are exported to all parts.

Wild fowl, sea-birds, game, and fish are abundant. Occasionally the Arctic sperm whale and the seal visit these islands, when there is quite a stir among the inhabitants to secure these prizes for the market.

The chief islands are Pomona or Mainland; Yell; Unst; Thule; and the chief towns are Lerwick, and Scalloway.

The imports are chiefly food supplies, tools, clothing, and manufactured goods.

The exports are barley, whisky, cattle, ponies, fish, seal-skins, knitted goods, feathers.

The total area of the Shetlands equals 551 square miles, and the population in 1891 was 28,711; of which 5,930 were inhabitants of Lerwick, the capital.

The Shetlands, together with the Orkneys, were originally governed by native earls or sea-kings, under the Crowns of Norway and Denmark. James I., by his marriage in 1590 with Anne of Denmark, received these as his possession.

*The Orkneys*, or *Orcades Islands*, number 67 islands, of

which but 30 are inhabited. This second group is situated to the south-west of the Shetlands, at a distance of six miles only from the North Coast of Scotland, lying between the parallels of latitude 58° and 59° north of the Equator, and longitude 2° 22' and 3° 26' west of Greenwich. The surface of the Orkneys is generally rocky and barren. The same irregularity of shape as was noted in the Shetland group is seen here, but in addition many of the smaller islands are mere rocks, called "holms." The climate is less severe than the Shetlands, but the winters are long and trying, and much wet weather prevails. The soil and agriculture are in an advanced state compared with the Shetlands. Vegetables and barley are produced, and the moors afford pasturage for cattle and sheep. The Orkneys literally teem with animal life. On the moors are grouse, snipe, wild fowl, geese, and ducks. Several species of eagle visit these islands, and the coasts are alive with gulls and other sea birds. Seals, sea otters, and fish are abundant.

The people are the same as the Shetlanders.

The chief islands are Mainland; Hoy; Ronaldsha; Sanda; Englisha; Burray; Stronsa; and Westra; and the chief towns are Kirkwall, and Stromness.

Both imports and exports are similar to those of the Shetland group.

The total area of the Orkneys is 376 square miles, and the population in 1891 was 30,453, of which 3,926 were in Kirkwall, the capital.

For the history of these islands, see note on the Shetlands (p. 182).

*The Hebrides*, or *Western Islands*, number some 300 islands, of which only 80 are inhabited. The area of the entire group is 2,750 miles. This group occupies a most exposed position in the Atlantic Ocean, lying off the West Coast of Scotland, between the parallels of latitude 55° and

59° north of the Equator, and longitude 5° and 8° west of Greenwich.

These islands may be sub-divided into an outer and an inner group, which are divided by the channel of the Minch and the Little Minch. The formation of the outer group shows distinctly that the whole have been united, though now so broken up into rocky mountainous islets beyond the main island of Lewis in the north of the group.

The physical features of the whole group may be described as rugged and mountainous. All the islands are irregular in shape and covered with pasturage, but by reason of the absence of trees and woodlands they are somewhat barren in appearance. The water supply is excellent, and the lakes and rivers are well stocked with fish and wildfowl. The climate is generally mild and somewhat humid, severe weather, of any length, being a rare occurrence. The soil is decidedly poor, so that agriculture is not in a flourishing state; but large herds of kyloes, or black cattle, are reared for exportation. These, with the coast fisheries, are the chief sources of living for the inhabitants, who belong to the old Celtic race, and being hardy, thrifty people, of simple manners and modest wants, they manage to exist upon but little beyond the bare necessities of life.

The outer group consists of the islands of Lewis; North and South Uist; Benbecula; and Barra; besides other smaller ones. The inner group has Skye; Mull; Islay; Jura; Tiree; Coll; Eigg; Rum; Canna; Colonsay; Iona and Staffa, with Fingal's Cave; also numerous smaller ones.

The chief towns are Stornoway, in Lewis; Portree and Broadford, in Skye; Port Askaig, in Islay; and Tobermory, in Mull.

The imports are chiefly food supplies, clothing, and

manufactured articles; and the exports include cattle, fish, game, skins, hides, barley, and oats.

The Hebrides were once a Norwegian colony. They were probably first inhabited in the eighth century. In 1264 the Macdonals, a powerful Scottish clan, took possession of them, and assumed the title of "Lords of the Isles." In 1748 they were finally given up to the Crown of Great Britain as a part of the Dominion of Scotland.

The four islands of the Clyde forming Buteshire consist of:—

1. *Bute Island.*—Length, 18 miles; breadth, 5 miles. This island is separated from the mainland of Scotland by the narrow, winding, picturesque channel called the Kyles of Bute, so frequently visited by tourists because of its lovely scenery.

The chief town, Rothesay, is a neat little seaport overlooking the mouth of the Clyde.

2. *Arran Island* is the largest in the group, being 20 miles long and 11 miles broad. It lies to the south-west of Bute. The surface is most mountainous. Goat Fell, its highest peak, is the highest mountain in the South of Scotland. The people are agriculturists and fishermen. The chief town is Brodick.

3, 4. *Great and Little Cumbrae* are two smaller islands, situated in the Clyde, to the east of Bute, and included in that county. The chief town, Millport, is exceedingly pretty. The Earl of Glasgow founded a theological college here under the Bishop of Argyll and the Isles some years ago.

*N.B.*—The area of the whole of Buteshire equals 218 square miles, and the population in 1891 was 18,404.

PHYSICAL FEATURES.—Few countries of the same size and area as Scotland present such diversified surface features. High mountain masses rather than ranges, with spurs branching out in every direction; deep and rugged glens or narrow valleys intersecting each other at every conceivable angle; hemmed-in mountain lakes, into which pour numerous torrents, some as cascades, and others as mere riplets, falling from the rocks above; irregular and deeply-cut arms of the sea running far up into the land, with the order reversed of long, irregular tongues or points of the land stretching out to the sea. These, among others, are the special features of Scotland, and give to this northern portion of Britain a romantic beauty, wild and picturesque in the extreme. No wonder that Burns hath sung its glories in such stirring words of farewell:—

> "Farewell to the Highlands, farewell to the North;
> The birth-place of valour, the country of worth;
> Wherever I wander, wherever I rove,
> The hills of the Highlands for ever I love.
> Farewell to the mountains, high covered with snow;
> Farewell to the straths and green valleys below;
> Farewell to the forests and wild hanging woods;
> Farewell to the torrents and loud pouring floods.
> My heart's in the Highlands, my heart is not here,
> My heart's in the Highlands a-chasing the deer;
> A-chasing the wild deer, and following the roe,
> My heart's in the Highlands wherever I go."

The whole country of Scotland is more or less mountainous or hilly, yet no regularity exists as to the position of the high-lands, so that no definitely marked watersheds are to be found, and the rivers are necessarily shorter and more rapid in motion than those of England and Wales. Only two large plains are to be noted, although there are others of smaller dimensions. These are the broad valley of Strathmore ("Great Valley"), dividing the Highland district from the Lowlands; and the "Great Glen" of Glenmore, through which passes the Caledonian Canal.

Thus the Great Glen of Scotland divides the country into two parts. It extends from the shores of Caithness on the north-east, through the counties of Inverness and Argyll as far as the Atlantic shores. It also cuts the table-land of the Highlands into two distinct parts.

The general surface of Scotland is divided into three parts:—

 *A*. The Northern Highlands.
 *B*. The Central Lowlands.
 *C*. The Southern Uplands.

Yet a further division should be added: the Plain of Ayr, which stretches away from the Southern Uplands towards the South-Western Coast.

MOUNTAINS.—The mountain system of Scotland consists of three principal clusters or masses of mountain groups, rather than district ranges, *viz.*, *The Northern; The Central;* and *The Southern Systems;* or, as they are sometimes described, *The Northern Highlands; The Grampians;* and the *Southern Uplands,* which latter include the Cheviot and Lowther Hills, with the smaller ranges of the Moffat Hills, the Moorfoots, and the Lammermoors.

Besides the above-named mountains, there are the—

 *A*. Sidlaw Hills, running south of the Grampians in a north-easterly direction through Perth and Forfarshire.
 *B*. The Campsie Fells, running from the Forth to the Clyde through Stirlingshire.
 *C*. The Ochil Hills, running through Kinross and Fifeshire.
 *D*. The Pentland Hills, stretching from the south-west of Edinburgh through Midlothian.
 *E*. Arthur's Seat near Edinburgh.

The Scotch mountains are generally barren, bleak, and precipitous, and their rugged, cheerless appearance greatly contrasts with the lovely and varied scenery of the valleys and glens intersecting them, many of which contain forests, with picturesque lakes or rivers, fed by the numerous cascades and streamlets, which leap from the rocky regions above.

1. *The Northern Highlands* traverse the counties of Inverness, Ross, Cromarty, and Sutherland, from west to east across the country.

The chief peaks are Ben Nevis, 4,373 feet, the highest mountain in the British Isles; Ben Attow, 4,000 feet; Ben Wyvis and Ben Dearg, each about 3,600 feet.

2. *The Grampians*, which comprise the great central mountain system of Scotland, are sometimes subdivided into two ranges—the Grampians proper, and the South Grampians. They run from west to east through Argyll, Perth, Inverness, Forfar, and Kincardineshires.

The chief peaks are Ben Macdhui, 4,300 feet; Cairntoul and Cairngorm, each a little over 4,000 feet; with Ben More and Ben Lawers, 3,000 feet; Ben Avon, 4,000 feet; Ben Ledi and Ben Lomond, 3,200 feet. The two latter are situated near that lovely portion of Perthshire known as "The Trossachs." The Grampians form the principal watershed of Scotland. Other peaks are Ben Cruachan and Ben Voirlich.

3. *The Southern Uplands* lie in the district south of the River Forth. The two chief branches are the Cheviot and the Lowther Hills, which for some distance form the boundary line between England and Scotland, and then abruptly branch off at right angles in a north-westerly direction.

The chief peaks are Mount Cheviot, 2,670 feet; Broadlaw, 2,700 feet; Lowther Hill, 2,500; Hartfell, 2,260 feet. This system forms the second important watershed of Scotland.

*The Forth Bridge.*

PLAINS.—These are small in size and unimportant. The chief plains are :—

1. *The Great Valley, or Strathmore*, lying to the south of the Grampians, and extending from the Forth to the German Ocean. It is about 80 miles long, and varies in breadth from 2 to 20 miles. This valley marks most distinctly the southern limits of the district of Scotland called "The Highlands."

2. *The Plain of Forth and Clyde*, as its name implies, is situated between the two rivers, forming their united river basins. It is only about 30 miles in length.

3. The *Clyde Vale* is a level tract in Lanarkshire through which flows the lower course of the Clyde River.

4. *The Plain of Ayr* is a fertile district near the West Coast.

5. *The Dales of Solway* border the Firth of that name.

6. *Glenmore*, or "the Great Glen," extends from Loch Linnhe on the Western Coast to the Moray Firth on the Eastern Coast. By a series of long narrow lakes now united by the Caledonian Canal, of which Loch Ness is the largest, navigation has been opened from the Atlantic to the North Sea, and thus the northern portion of Scotland has become an island, although geographically it is not regarded as one. Other minor plains are the Plain of Tweed, Plain of Caithness, Plain of Cromarty, and the Carse of Gowrie.

RIVERS.—The river system of Scotland is naturally divided into two parts, *viz.* :—

    *A.* Rivers flowing eastward to the North Sea.

    *B.* Rivers flowing westward into the Atlantic Ocean and Irish Sea.

In this way a journey round the Coast of Scotland, from Berwick-upon-Tweed to the Solway Firth, would show the following important rivers among other smaller ones :—

*The Tay Bridge.*

1. *The Tweed*, which is 96 miles in length, forms the boundary line between England and Scotland for some distance. This river rises in the South of Peebles, and by a circuitous route enters the North Sea by the ancient and independent town of Berwick, which is of great historical interest in connection with both countries. The chief tributaries are the Ettrick; Yarrow; Teviot; Till; Leader; and the Black and White Adder. Other towns on the Tweed are Coldstream, Kelso, Melrose, Peebles, and Hawick.

2. *The Forth* is about 60 miles long. It rises near Ben Lomond in Stirlingshire, and flows in an easterly direction into the opening of the sea called the Firth of Forth, which in position somewhat resembles the mouth of the Thames, and like that river it runs through the chief town, Edinburgh, with its docks and port (Leith) lying below it. At Queensferry the Forth Bridge crosses the Forth at an immense height, so that large ships are able to pass under it. The tributaries are few and of minor importance, *viz.*, the Firth, Allan, and Devon. Other towns are Alloa and Stirling on the Forth.

3. *The Tay*, which is the longest river in Scotland, being 110 miles, carries the waste waters of Loch Tay, etc., to the sea. On its banks stand Perth and Scone, of historical importance as the ancient crowning place of the Scottish kings. The tributaries of the Tay are the Lyon, Tummel, Ardle, Isla, Earn, and Almond. This river is noted for its excellent salmon fishing. Dundee is an important trading seaport at its mouth.

4. *The North and South Esk* flow from the Grampians into the North Sea near Montrose.

5. *The Don and the Dee* flow into the sea at Aberdeen. *The Dee* is 90 miles long. It rises at some considerable height in Cairngorm in the Grampians. This stream is

noted for its lovely scenery, excellent salmon and other fishing. Balmoral, the Royal Highland residence of Queen Victoria, is situated near its banks. The town of Aberdeen, which really stands on a tongue of land between

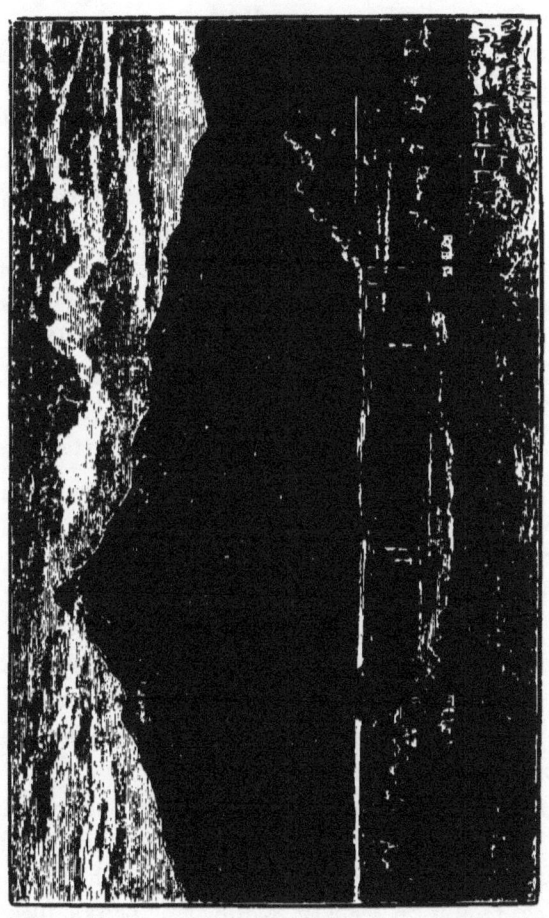

*Ben and Loch Lomond.*

the Don and the Dee, takes its name from the latter river, as "Aber-deen" means "Dee mouth."

6. *The Spey*, oftentimes called the "Thundering Spey,"

is more rapid than the other Scotch rivers. It is nearly 100 miles long, flowing from Loch Spey to the North Sea, near to the Moray Firth. It is useless for purposes of navigation, as it receives numerous mountain streams in its course, yet it affords the highest sport for the angler, and its salmon fisheries are excellent.

The smaller rivers on the East Coast are the Tyne, Eden, Deveron, Findhorn, and Ness.

The only river of importance flowing westwards is the *Clyde*. It is 98 miles in length, and it is always considered the chief commercial river of Scotland, as it flows through the principal mining and manufacturing districts. Glasgow, the largest manufacturing and commercial city of Scotland, stands near its mouth; and other towns on its banks are Lanark, Renfrew, Dumbarton, Greenock, and Port Glasgow. Near Lanark are the celebrated Falls of Clyde, where the river leaps by a double fall about 100 feet amid the surrounding rocks. This river rises in the Lowther Hills near to the Tweed, which flows in the opposite direction.

Other smaller rivers on the West Coast are the Ayr, to the west of the Clyde basin; the Southern Dee, Nith, Annan, and Esk, which drain the southern slopes of the Lowland Hills, and empty themselves into the Solway Firth.

LAKES.—One of the grandest features of Scotland is its lakes. These are both numerous and of considerable size. Their united area equals 700 square miles.

The lakes are principally to be found in the Highlands. Certain of the mountainous districts abound in lakes, which are extremely beautiful, nestling, as they do, amid the wildest mountain scenery, while their banks, like Loch Katrine and others, are well wooded in parts.

1. *Loch Lomond* is the largest lake in Great Britain. It is 24 miles long, from 5 to 7 miles wide, and possesses an

SCOTLAND.                                    195

area of 45 square miles. Its surface is broken by about thirty picturesque islands, and the mountain scenery around it is exceedingly grand, so that it may justly claim the proud title of the "Queen of the Scottish Lakes."

2. *Loch Katrine* lies a few miles to the north-east of

*Loch Katrine.*

Loch Lomond. This small, though beautiful, lake provides Glasgow with its water supply. The principal island here is "Ellen's Isle," of renown in Sir Walter Scott's "Lady of the Lake." It is 9 miles long, and has an average width of

1 mile. It is situated in the narrow valley of "The Trossachs."

3. *Loch Awe*, 23 miles long, and about 2 miles wide, is another beautiful lake surrounded by bold and lofty mountains.

4. *Loch Ness*, in Inverness-shire, is a long, narrow lake in Glenmore. In parts, it is 800 feet deep, and its extreme length is 22 miles. The celebrated Falls of Foyers are close by.

5. *Loch Shin* is another long, narrow lake situated in the Northern Highlands. It is nearly 20 miles in length.

6. *Loch Maree* is another large lake in the Northern Highlands. It has a number of small islands near its centre.

7. *Loch Leven*, in Kinross, contains four islands, upon one of which stands the ruins of Loch Leven Castle, where Mary Queen of Scots was imprisoned.

Other smaller lakes are Lochs Rannoch, Tay, Lydoch, and Earn, called the Perthshire cluster; Lochs Lochy and Spey are very much frequented by tourists because of their wild and romantic scenery.

CLIMATE.—Compared with England, the climate of Scotland is more trying, by reason of being much colder and more damp. This is explained by its more northern position in the first place, and secondly, by its being more exposed to the expanse of the Atlantic Ocean.

Scotland is an exceedingly healthy country. The Gulf Stream so far effects the climate as to render the winter season less severe than in other countries situated within the same degrees of latitude on the mainland of Europe. The annual rainfall varies from 20 to 23 inches on the East Coast, and from 30 to 45 inches on the West Coast.

It is a curious fact that the cold is oftentimes more severe in the Thames Valley than in the Hebrides or Shetland Isles. This is owing to the prevalence of warm and moist sea-breezes.

AGRICULTURE.—The soil of Scotland is generally described as poor, although there are many rich and fertile tracts. The Scotch people are a most industrious and persevering race, so that, wherever it is possible to cultivate the land, crops are produced. About one-fifth of the whole country is under cultivation; two-thirds may roughly be estimated as pasturage, and the remainder is waste land. Barren and sterile districts are to be met with throughout the Highlands.

The first impression a stranger has of Scotland is its somewhat barren appearance, by reason of the dearth of trees in the southern moorlands, and the bold, rugged nature of the mountainous districts of the North. One also misses, in the more remote parts, the home-like appearance of cottage gardens, with fruit trees, flowers, and vegetables. The soil is more adapted for the growth of oats and barley, than wheat or roots.

The most fertile districts are Strathmore, portions of Fifeshire, Teviotdale and the Vale of Ayr, and part of Berwickshire, although many smaller tracts of fertility are known. The hilly districts of the Lowlands produce excellent pasturage for sheep and cattle. The chief dairy districts are the south-western counties of Ayr, Wigton, Kirkcudbright, and Dumfries.

NATURAL PRODUCTIONS.—These, with but few exceptions, are similar to those of England, and in the same way the reversed order of mineral, animal, and vegetable products, represents their market value, or extent, as productions.

1. *Minerals.*—The geological structure of Scotland is less varied than that of England and Wales. Granite prevails throughout the country; that of Peterhead, in Aberdeenshire, on the East Coast, is the finest in quality. Both the

Silurian and the Devonian formations occur in the South, while gneiss, schist, etc., are found in the mountainous regions of the North. The Central Plain of Strathmore is composed of red sandstone, which is greatly mixed with local formations. Good building-stone is abundant in almost every part, and there are some good lime-stone quarries in Lanarkshire.

The Coalfields of Scotland are of considerable value. They are restricted to one great district lying around the Rivers Clyde and Forth. The chief coalfields are the Fife, situated to the north of the Forth River; the Lothian, to the south-east of Edinburgh; the Lanarkshire, around Glasgow; with several less important fields in Dumfries. The annual yield of coal has been estimated at more than 20 millions of tons.

In the Vale of the Clyde and Forth, one large coal-bed extends through a district of nearly 1,000 square miles in extent, thus affording an almost endless supply. Lanark is the chief centre of this mining district, and, in consequence, here we find the principal manufactories of Scotland, and this district is more thickly populated than other parts of the country.

Within the coal district of Lanark, iron ore is most plentiful, so that smelting furnaces are quite a feature in the landscape. Iron is also found in Fife, Stirling, and Perth. Marble is met with occasionally in Sutherland, Perth, Argyle, and West Lothian. Lead, in large or small quantities, exists in the Lowther Hills,—a part of which range is called the Leadhills,—Lanark, and Dumfries; also at Dollar in Clackmannan; Strontian in Argyle; Belville in Inverness; and Leadlaw in Peebles. Slate is found in the quarries of Argyleshire. Some local gems, known as Scotch agates, are to be found in several districts.

2. *Animals.*—The wild animals of Scotland are the same

## SCOTLAND.

as those of England, with but few exceptions. The species are smaller and more numerous, owing to the larger area of uncultivated districts, especially in the Highlands, and they consist principally of deer and game, which are largely preserved.

The nightingale is seldom heard in Scotland, while many birds from colder countries, which are unknown to us in England, visit this country, such as eagles, solan geese, and several kinds of sea and water fowl.

In domestic animals, Scotland can scarcely compete with England either in respect to their size, breed, or numbers; but several special breeds of cattle, sheep, and horses are reared there; *e.g.*, the horses of Galloway and Clydesdale are most valuable; and the small ponies from the Shetland Isles are much in demand for pleasure purposes, and children's use. Another breed of cattle comes from Ayrshire; and the Cheviot sheep are also excellent.

The fisheries of Scotland are extremely rich. The species of fish taken are nearly the same as are found on the shores of England, but the yield is often more abundant.

Off the North Coast, seals, herring, cod, and haddock are frequently taken; and from Peterhead, and other towns on the East Coast, besides the Islands of Orkney and Shetland, whale ships are each year despatched on their perilous adventures.

Most of the rivers and lakes of Scotland yield large quantities of salmon, trout, and other fresh-water fish.

3. *Vegetable Productions.*—These certainly take the lowest place among the natural productions of Scotland. The more northerly position of this country, compared with England, and the poor nature of the soil, quite explains this fact. The natural vegetation comprises some hardier species than we find in England, *e.g.*, the conifera

or pine family are more numerous, and more varied in kind than ours; while the heather family are far more luxuriant in growth upon the moors or mountains than anything of the kind we possess. Oaks, beeches, and elm trees, with many thorns, are met with in the valleys and lowland districts, but there are whole neighbourhoods quite void of our common forest trees.

NATURAL PRODUCTIONS.—Wheat, and many of our English flowers and fruits, do not attain to perfection here, yet it must not be thought that Scotland does not possess a Native Flora; on the other hand, the Native Flora is an exceedingly rich one, numbering more than 2,000 indigenous plants, although, as we have remarked above, many of these resemble those of colder regions—as the heather, mountain moss, firs, and pines, etc. In some parts of the Northern Highlands enormous pine and fir forests may be seen, not unlike those of Norway. Of late years much has been done to improve the barren appearance of many parts, by the landowners making very large plantations of forest trees, which, in addition to improving the natural scenery, form important covers for game.

MINERAL SPRINGS.—These are few and unimportant compared with those of England. The best known are the following:—

Dunblane, in Perth; Oban, in Argyle; Glenelg, in Inverness; and Ballater, in Aberdeen. But of course there are iron springs in many other districts.

NATURAL CURIOSITIES.—Scotland, being still "a land of rugged and wild Nature," presents many natural curiosities. The chief are:—

1. *Fingal's Cave.*—This wonderfully formed basaltic cavern, or chamber of gigantic size in the Isle of Staffa, is one of the greatest curiosities in the world. The sides or walls of this cave are composed of regular basaltic columns

placed closely together, which support a beautifully formed arched roof, in appearance like unto mosaic work. The sea forms the floor, so that it is somewhat difficult of approach, except in calm weather. It is sometimes called "The Musical Cave," as the sea flowing into it produces sounds resembling distant harmony. This cave is 227 feet long, 42 feet wide at its mouth, and 66 feet high.

2. *The Bullers*, or Boulder Rocks, on the Coast of Aberdeen, are remarkable for their regular curved appearance.

3. *The Skye Caverns* are most remarkable. In fact the whole of Skye consists of "serrated ridges, streets of lava, cup-shaped caldrons, silvery cataracts, mountain lakes, and spar caverns."[1]

4. *The Clyde Falls*, in Lanark, are most interesting. Here the River Clyde rushes over a cascade of rocks, 100 feet high, by a double fall.

5. *Foyers Fall*, in Loch Ness, is another remarkable cascade.

6. *Petrifying Springs* occur at Hamilton, and Slane Castle, and Mosset Well, in Annandale, which springs suddenly from a rock, and possesses great mineral properties.

These are only just a few examples of Scotland's natural curiosities. The tourist in the Highlands, or Western Isles, will gather more information upon this subject in a few weeks than would fill a volume, so rich is the whole country in Nature's wonders. This part of Scotland is now most accessible to travellers by reason of the Highland Railways, which traverse the chief districts of interest.

PEOPLE, RACE, AND LANGUAGE.—See "Great Britain" (p. 43), and "England and Wales" (p. 138).

---

[1] *See* Professor Meiklejohn's "Geography—Scotland," p. 79.

RELIGION.—See "Great Britain" (p. 77).

EDUCATION.—The Scotch as a nation are an educated people, although there may be numerous examples where this is wanting in the Western Islands, or the wild mountainous Highland districts of the North.

There are four Universities in Scotland, which date from medieval times. These still continue to do excellent work in the higher Arts and Sciences. They are—St. Andrews, founded in 1411; Glasgow, in 1450; Aberdeen, in 1494; and Edinburgh, in 1589. The Scotch public and other large schools for the upper and middle classes are annually tested by a Government Board of Examiners, who have power to issue leaving certificates to the students, which are not only a proof of their school attainments, but further frank the holders of them from passing the preliminary examinations at the Universities, including Oxford and Cambridge, the Medical and Law Faculties, etc. The National School System of Scotland is uniform with that of England, but it works under a special code of regulations, called "The Scotch Education Act."

GOVERNMENT.—The same as England.

Scotland returns 72 Members to Parliament, and 16 Scottish Peers have seats in the House of Lords.

NAVAL PORTS.—None of importance. Vessels of the British fleet are stationed at intervals along the coast, which is alike protected by coastguard stations, and studded with lighthouses and lightships,* or floating lights, for the safety of vessels passing by, or approaching, the shores.

SEAPORTS.—1. *On the East Coast* there are Berwick-upon-Tweed, Eyemouth, Dunbar, Leith for Edinburgh, Bo'ness, Grangemouth, Alloa, Burntisland, Kirkcaldy, Perth, Dundee, Arbroath, Montrose, Stonehaven, Aberdeen, Peterhead, Fraserburgh, Banff, Inverness, Cromarty, and Wick.

## SCOTLAND.

2. *On the North Coast* there are no seaports.

3. *On the West Coast* the principal are Oban, Inverary, Campbelltown, Rothesay, Glasgow (the fourth largest port in Great Britain, and the commercial capital of Scotland), Greenock, Port-Glasgow, Ardrossan, Saltcoats, Irvine, Ayr, and Stranraer.

4. *On the South Coast* there are Wigton, Kirkcudbright, and Dumfries.

5. *The Island Ports* are Lerwick in Shetland; Kirkwall and Stromness in Orkney; Stornoway in Hebrides; and Tobermory in Mull.

INTERNAL COMMUNICATION.—For Railways, Roads, Canals and Rivers, Telegraph, etc., see "The British Isles" (pp. 60 and 70).

The roads throughout Scotland are proverbially good, owing to the unlimited supply of excellent stone in nearly all parts. Some 4,000 miles of main roads are kept in this way in thorough repair, and so travelling is made comparatively easy, even in the wildest and most out-of-the-way districts. The railways have considerably increased of late years, and the canal system is sufficient for the requirements of the mining and trade industries.

COMMERCE.—This is considerable, and increasing in importance and value each year. Not only is a large and varied coast trade carried on, but its western port, Glasgow, has a large trade with America, in addition to being one of the chief centres of shipbuilding in the British Isles.

The eastern ports, of which Leith, Dundee, and Aberdeen are the principal, possess an important Baltic trade, besides sending vessels to the chief trading ports of the world.

IMPORTS.—Raw cotton, hemp, wool, flax, food supplies, and colonial produce, with metals, timber, corn, and wines, are among the chief imports of Scotland.

EXPORTS.—Manufactured goods, including cottons, linens, woollens, sailcloth, cordage, also cattle, sheep, fish, iron, coals, and machinery, are the principal exports.

POLITICAL DIVISIONS.—Scotland is divided into thirty-three counties. These may be arranged under the heads of eleven northern; eleven central; and eleven southern counties.

Nearly all the counties are maritime, or touch the sea coast; the only inland counties being Lanark, Peebles, Selkirk, Roxburgh, in the extreme South, with Kinross and Clackmannan.

The most northern county on the mainland (not including Orkney and Shetland) is Caithness; the most southern county is Wigtown; the most eastern county is Aberdeen; and the most western (not including the Hebrides) is Argyll.

The largest county in Scotland is Inverness; the smallest county in Scotland is Clackmannan.

A curious arrangement of the political divisions exists in the manner the islands are included with portions of the mainland to form counties, or taken by themselves for the same purpose; thus we have Orkney and Shetland forming one county, and Buteshire, consisting of the Islands of Arran and Bute, with Great and Little Cumbrae in the Clyde.

Again, Argyllshire includes Islay, Jura, Mull, with numerous smaller islands; Inverness includes Skye, Harris, North Uist, etc.; and Ross-shire includes the northern part of Lewis and Harris, etc.

## SCOTLAND.

### POLITICAL DIVISIONS TABLE.

| No. | Counties. | Area. Square Miles. | 1891 Population. | Chief Towns. | Where Situated. |
|---|---|---|---|---|---|
| Eleven Northern Counties. | Orkney and Shetland, | 375<br>551 | 30,438<br>28,711 | Kirkwall, Lerwick, - | Mainland Island. |
| | Caithness, - - | 685 | 37,161 | *Wick*, Thurso, - - | .. .. |
| | Sutherland, - | 2,027 | 21,940 | *Dornoch*, Golspie, - | Dornoch Firth. |
| | Ross and Cromarty, | 3,129 | 77,751 | *Dingwall*, Tain - - | Dornoch Firth. |
| | Inverness, - | 4,088 | 88.362 | *Inverness*, Grantown,- | River Ness. |
| | Cromarty, - - | *See* Ross | *See* Ross | *Cromarty*, Ullapool, - | .. .. |
| | Nairn, - - - | 178 | 10,019 | *Nairn*, Cawdor, - - | Nairn River. |
| | Elgin, - - - | 475 | 43,448 | *Elgin*, Forres, - - | Lossie River. |
| | Banff, - - - | 686 | 64,167 | *Banff*, Keith, Cullen, - | Deveron River. |
| | Aberdeen, - - | 1,070 | 281,331 | *Aberdeen*, Peterhead, - | Dee River. |
| | Kincardine, - | 383 | 35,047 | *Stonehaven*, Laurencekirk,- | .. .. |
| Eleven Central Counties. | Fife, - - - | 492 | 187,320 | *Cupar*, St. Andrews, Dunfermline, - - - | River Eden. |
| | Forfar or Angus, - | 876 | 277,788 | *Forfar*, Dundee, Montrose, | .. .. |
| | Perth, - - - | 2,527 | 126,128 | *Perth*, Blairgowrie, - - | River Tay. |
| | Clackmannan, - | 47 | 28,433 | *Clackmannan*, Alloa,- | River Forth. |
| | Kinross, - - | 72 | 6,289 | *Kinross*, - - - | Loch Leven. |
| | Linlithgow, or West Lothian, | 120 | 52,789 | *Linlithgow*, Bathgate, - | .. .. |
| | Stirling,- - - | 447 | 125,604 | *Stirling*, Falkirk, - - | River Forth. |
| | Renfrew, - - | 244 | 290,790 | *Renfrew*, Paisley, Greenock, Port-Glasgow, - | River Clyde. |
| | Dumbarton, - | 241 | 94,511 | *Dumbarton*, Alexandria, - | River Clyde. |
| | Argyllshire, - | 3,213 | 75,945 | *Inverary*, Campbelltown, - | Loch Fyne. |
| | Bute, - - | 271 | 18.408 | *Rothesay*, Brodick, - - | Isle of Bute. |
| Eleven Southern Counties. | Ayr, - - - | 1,128 | 224,222 | *Ayr*, Kilmarnock, Irvine, - | River Ayr. |
| | Lanark, - - | 881 | 1,045,787 | *Lanark*, GLASGOW, - | River Clyde. |
| | Edinburgh, or Mid-Lothian, | 362 | 444,055 | *EDINBURGH*, Leith, - | River Forth. |
| | Haddington, or East Lothian, | 270 | 37,491 | *Haddington*, Dunbar, - | River Tyne. |
| | Berwick, - - | 460 | 32,398 | *Dunse*, Greenlaw, Coldstream, Berwick, - | River Tweed. |
| | Peebles, - - | 354 | 14,760 | *Peebles*, Linton, - - | River Tweed. |
| | Selkirk, - - | 257 | 27,349 | *Selkirk*, Galashiels, - | River Ettrick. |
| | Roxburgh, - | 665 | 53,726 | *Jedburgh*, Kelso, Melrose, Hawick, - - | River Teviot. |
| | Dumfries, - | 1,062 | 74,308 | *Dumfries*, Annan, Moffat, - | River Nith. |
| | Kirkcudbright, - | 897 | 39,979 | *Kirkcudbright*, Galloway, - | River Dee. |
| | Wigtown, - | 485 | 36,048 | *Wigtown*, Stranraer, Glenluce, Port Patrick, - | Wigtown Bay. |
| | Totals, | 29,906 | 4,033,103 | or 134 persons per square mile. | |

COUNTIES :—

1. *The Orkney and Shetland Isles* form a single county. (*See* Islands, p. 180.)

2. *Caithness* is a maritime county. The coasts are steep and rocky, and the interior barren and lacking trees. The town of Wick is the chief centre of the Scottish herring fishery. Stone is quarried throughout this county. The

most northern dwelling bears the name of " John o' Groat's House."

3. *Sutherland* is a Highland maritime county situated somewhat parallel with Caithness in latitude upon its northern shores. The population is scanty, as the interior is wild and rocky. Here there are large deer forests, and some sheep rearing is carried on. The inhabitants of the coast are employed in the fisheries.

4 and 5. *Ross and Cromarty* are generally taken together, as the latter county is made up of fragments, or scattered portions, distributed throughout Ross-shire. These are Highland counties greatly resembling Sutherlandshire in appearance. The northern division of the Island of Lewis belongs to Ross. The fisheries of the coast are important, and some sheep-farming is carried on in the interior.

6. *Inverness* is the largest of the Scottish counties. The surface is wildly beautiful and rugged. Here, too, deer forests and sheep tracts are abundant. To gain some idea of the grandeur of the scenery of Inverness, the traveller must visit Ben Nevis, the highest mountain in Great Britain, and then pass through the romantic Valley of Glenmore by the Caledonian Canal. Several of the larger of the Hebrides Islands are included in this county. They are Harris, North and South Uist, Skye, etc. The coast fisheries are rich and valuable, and both the sportsman and the angler have excellent pastime in the lochs, rivers, moors, and mountain districts.

7. *Nairn* is an agricultural coast county lying to the south of the Moray Firth. The soil is more fertile than in many other parts of Northern Scotland, and the coast offers good fishing.

8. *Elgin*, a small neighbouring county, is also fertile near the coast, which is a coast plain; but in the interior the

Aberdeen.

surface is more of the nature of the Highlands. It also possesses good coast fisheries. The old name for this county was Morayshire.

9. *Banff* is similar in its physical features and industries to Elgin and Nairn, its next neighbours.

10. *Aberdeen* is a maritime county, consisting of two distinctly marked districts, *viz.*, lowland and fertile in the north and east; and highland, wild, and mountainous in the south and west. Here we meet for the first time among the northern counties with considerable trade industries in the stone (granite) quarries, the paper mills, and shipbuilding yards. Farming is flourishing in certain districts, and cattle are reared for the London markets. At Peterhead the whalers are fitted out, and a considerable herring fleet is sent out. Aberdeen, the capital, is called the Granite City. It has an University and a Cathedral, with important manufactures in granite polishing, paper, linen, woollen, and iron goods.

The Highland residence of Queen Victoria (Balmoral) is in this county.

11. *Kincardine*, another coast county, situated immediately to the south of Aberdeen, is a sportsman's county. It contains the most easterly portion of the Grampian mountains. There are but few industries beyond agriculture and the fisheries. Stonehaven is another important herring-fleet station.

12. *Forfar*, or Angus, possesses a varied surface of hill and valley. Strathmore, one of the most fertile tracts of Scotland, is in this county, so that agriculture is in an advanced state here. Near, and around, Dundee and Arbroath, there are extensive linen and jute manufactures. Shipbuilding, rope, and carpet weaving are also carried on at Dundee and Montrose.

13. *Fife*, a lowland county, situated between the Firths

of Tay and Forth, is a busy manufacturing district. The flat district near the coast is much more fertile than the interior; hence James VI. compared Fife to "a beggar's mantle edged with gold." Towards the south-western side there lies a flourishing colliery district; but by far the most important part of the county is the coast belt, with its seaport, manufactories, and shipbuilding. St. Andrews University is the oldest in Scotland. It takes its name from the Patron Saint of the country.

14. *Perthshire* is the queen of Scottish counties. All parts are beautiful, whether we pass through the highland wilds or the lowland tracts. Grand and picturesque scenery will be found in the Trossachs, or the mountain heights of the West and South-west. Lochs Katrine, Achray, Vennachar, and Tay adorn the valleys, with numerous smaller ones; and the rich Carse of Gowrie contains the most fertile land in Scotland. The neighbourhood around the capital (Perth) is exceedingly beautiful, with its woods and hilly pastures; and the wild district of Blair-Atholl, at the foot of the Grampian mountains, is a favourite haunt for tourists. Scone, the ancient crowning place of Scotland's kings, is in this county. The coronation stone was removed from here to the Royal Chair in Westminster Abbey. There are no manufactures in Perthshire beyond dye works, ropes, and the hosiery trade of the capital.

15. *Clackmannan* is the smallest county in Scotland. It is a mining county, lying between the Ochil range and the River Forth. The coal and iron obtained here are of excellent quality, and large quantities are exported from Alloa, the port on the Forth, which is the largest town in the county. Excellent ale, and woollen tartans, are made here.

16. *Kinross*, another small county, is chiefly agricultural

in its interests. It is completely surrounded by the counties of Perth and Fife. Here lies the famous Loch Leven, where Mary, Queen of Scots, escaped from an island in the lake.

17. *Linlithgow*, or *West Lothian*, is both an agricultural and a mining county. Coal is abundant throughout the western portion, and paraffin oil is distilled from the shale of the eastern district. At Linlithgow Mary, Queen of Scots, was born. Queensferry and Bo'ness, near the Forth Bridge, are the chief ports of this county.

18. *Stirling.*—This county consists of two marked divisions. The eastward portion is mining and manufacturing, with a dense population; but the western part is agricultural, and but thinly peopled. Stirling and Falkirk are the two centres of trade. The Castle of Stirling stands upon a bold eminence at one end of the town, and near by may be seen the site of Bannockburn Battle. The Bridge of Allan, immortalised by the pathetic ballad of " The Miller's Daughter," is now a fashionable health resort.

19. *Renfrew.*—This small county is one of the most important in Scotland. Its industries comprise mining, manufactures, and shipping. Iron founding, and shipbuilding are the chief trades, although sugar refining, woollen, silk, and cotton goods, with soap, and large engineering works are to be met with at Renfrew, Paisley, Port-Glasgow, Greenock, and Johnstone.

20. *Dumbarton.*—This is a mountainous, rugged county, containing mining and manufacturing districts. Coal, iron, slate, and limestone are procured as natural products, and its manufactures include cotton, calico weaving, and printing, with shipbuilding on the Clyde, which really is the source of most of the trade of this part of Scotland. The chief centres are Dumbarton, Alexandria, and Helensburgh. The beautiful Loch Lomond is in this county,

with its ever varying scenery from Balloch to Ardlui in the Highland district of Rob Roy's country.

21. *Argyle* is a delightful district of mountains, lochs, peninsulas, islands, inlets, and capes. Its coast-line, by reason of the broken nature of the Western shores, is of considerable length, being about 600 miles from end to end, inclusive of the islands. Tourists, probably, visit this county more than any other of the Scotch counties, as Oban on the coast is the chief port for the Hebrides, and the Western Tours through the Highlands, and other districts. Granite is quarried in great quantities, and the coast abounds in excellent fisheries. Inverary, Oban, Campbelltown (noted for its whiskey distilleries), and Dunoon are the chief towns.

22. *Bute.*—The county of Bute consists of the islands of Bute, Arran, Great and Little Cumbrae in the Firth of Clyde. (*See* "Islands," p. 180.)

23. *Ayrshire.*—The dairy-farming district of Southern Scotland also possesses extensive coal mining districts in the North, and near the sea, so that its coast towns are of importance; the chief being Ayr, Ardrossan, Saltcoats, Troon, Girvan, and Ballantrae. Kilmarnock is a manufacturing centre for woollen and ironware goods. The poet Burns was a native of Ayr.

24. *Lanark.*—The most populous centre of manufactures and commerce along the banks of the Clyde is not altogether a pleasant county, although there is a pastoral district in the southern, or upper part, where there are extensive sheep farms. The Clydesdale horses and orchards are also well-known throughout the country. The lower portion includes the principal commercial and manufacturing districts of Scotland; the cotton and iron trade, in addition to the chief foreign trade and shipbuilding, centres around the Clyde in the towns and neighbourhood of

Glasgow, Hamilton, Coatbridge, Rutherglen, Motherwell, Lanark, Airdrie, etc.

25. *Edinburgh, or Mid-Lothian*, is an agricultural county, with some collieries and stone quarries. The chief town of importance is Edinburgh, the capital city of Scotland, which is often styled the "*Modern Athens*," by reason of its noble position, and its magnificent buildings. Its ports are Leith and Granton, Newhaven, Portobello, and Musselburgh on the Forth; and the first corn market of Scotland is at Dalkeith, situated at the junction of the North and South Esk in this county. There are important paper mills in the neighbourhood of Edinburgh.

26. *Haddington, or East Lothian*, is one of the best agricultural districts of Scotland. The surface is generally level, and the soil fertile, especially the lands bordering the Firth of Forth. There are a few coal mines in the western side of the county. Beyond this there are few industries, except in the towns of Haddington, the capital; Dunbar, a seaport; and North Berwick, which stands at the entrance to the Firth of Forth.

27. *Berwick, or Merse.*—This county is situated at the foot of the Lammermoor Hills, and stretches to the River Tweed, which forms its opposite boundary. The main part of this district is a fertile plain. There are many interesting ruins in Berwickshire, *viz.*, Coldingham Priory, Fast Castle, and Dryburgh Abbey, which last contains the burial-place of Sir Walter Scott. Greenlaw is the county town; but Berwick, or Aberberwick, is of more importance, situated as it is at the mouth of the River Tweed, although this, after many years of independence, is now regarded as an English town.

28. *Peebleshire*, or Tweeddale, is a pastoral county of regular undulating surface; green hills with fertile valleys succeed each other. The northern side of this county joins

## SCOTLAND. 213

the Midlothian coal district, but there are no industries here beyond agriculture and sheep farming. The chief town is Peebles, on the Tweed.

29. *Selkirkshire* is another pastoral district, but rather more hilly than Peebleshire. The noted vales of Yarrow and Ettrick, with the forest and river of the same name,

*Edinburgh, from Castle Hill.*

are in this county. Selkirk, the county town, has important woollen manufactures; and tweeds, tartans, and shawls are also made at Galashiels, which is now the chief centre for Scottish clan goods of this kind.

30. *Roxburghshire, or Teviotdale,* is a beautiful pastoral

and agricultural county, formed by the Vale of Teviot, and the basin of the Tweed River, and extending to the Cheviot range of hills. This is particularly the country of Sir Walter Scott, inasmuch as it contains Melrose Abbey, and Abbotsford his home. Besides the breeding of cattle and sheep, there are extensive manufactories of woollen goods and tweeds at Jedburgh, the county town; Hawick, and Kelso.

31. *Dumfriesshire* is divided into a hilly pastoral district in the north, and fertile lowlands in the south. Cattle, sheep, and pigs are reared in large numbers. The chief valleys are named after the rivers flowing through them, as Nithsdale, Annandale, and Eskdale, with Solway Strath, and Lochar Moss, in the extreme south. Dumfries is the capital. It is a fairly large town, and contains the chief market for the farmers of the south-western district of Scotland. Moffat possesses a mineral spring, and during the summer, tourists frequent this place for the waters.

32. *Kirkcudbrightshire* is another pastoral and agricultural county. The most fertile district is the lower portion bordering the Solway Firth. The inhabitants are chiefly engaged in rearing cattle and sheep. Pigs are also bred in large numbers. One part is very hilly and wild; Mount Merrick, the highest point, is 2,760 feet high. Near Creetown are large granite quarries. The capital is Kirkcudbright, which is a pretty seaport upon the estuary of the River Dee, where it enters the Solway Firth.

33. *Wigtownshire* is also a pastoral and agricultural county. The cattle here, and in Kirkcudbrightshire, are highly valued, and exported with agricultural produce from the capital and seaport Wigtown; also from Stranraer, and Port Patrick, where the Irish steamboats ply across the North Channel to Belfast. It is only 21 miles across

*The University, Edinburgh.*

the Channel here to Donaghadee on the Irish coast; that is about the same distance as from Dover to Calais across the Straits of Dover.

Towns.—The chief towns in Scotland are :—

Edinburgh, the capital, including the port of Leith; Glasgow, the largest commercial and manufacturing city; Dundee, Aberdeen, and Inverness, the capital of the Highlands, etc.

1. *Edinburgh.*—This city, which is both a royal and a parliamentary borough, as well as the metropolis of Scotland, is situated upon the southern side of the Firth of Forth. The town is divided into two parts, Old and New Edinburgh. In the old town, the streets are exceedingly narrow, and the houses are built very high, sometimes jutting out in queer angles and irregular shapes, so that the tops nearly touch each other; but in the new town the streets are among the finest in Europe; Princes Street being unrivalled for its beauty of scenery and imposing buildings. Edinburgh is the terminus for several railway systems, and the most perfect system of tramways connects every part with Princes Street. The Castle stands upon an imposing eminence overlooking the public gardens, museums, and galleries which form one side of Princes Street. No wonder that travellers have named Edinburgh "the Modern Athens," or the city of palaces.

The Palace of Holyrood was for a time the seat of royalty for Scotland's rulers, and its associations are rich in the history of the unfortunate Mary, Queen of Scots; while it was from here that James VI. of Scotland departed to claim the English throne as James I. of England. Edinburgh possesses two Cathedrals—St. Mary's Episcopal, and St. Giles, which is the chief centre of the Scottish Presbyterian Church. There is also a University.

Edinburgh has long been noted for its culture and

*The Trongate, Glasgow.*

literature. Its publishing trade still takes a high place, although of late years several of the leading firms have transferred their principal houses of business to London. Silk weaving, brewing, glass, chairs, fancy goods, jewellery, ropes, nails, shoes and boots, besides woollen and tweed goods, are among its manufactures. The population in 1891, including Leith, was 338,268.

Leith, the port of Edinburgh, was originally a separate town, but for some years past streets have been added until the two now form one city. The commercial trade of Leith is of the highest importance. Besides the coast trade with England, and other parts of Scotland, vessels now ply regularly with the Baltic; the Mediterranean; and other parts of the world; bringing in colonial and foreign produce in exchange for coal, iron, and home manufactures.

2. *Glasgow.*—This city is really the largest in Scotland. Its importance, so far as trade and commerce are concerned, place it far in advance of Edinburgh. It ranks as the sixth port in the United Kingdom, if we include the foreign trade of Greenock on the Clyde. From its unrivalled position, being situated on the greatest commercial river, and in the centre of the iron and coal districts, it is but little wonder that Glasgow claims to be the commercial capital of Scotland. Its manufactures comprise linen, woollen, silk, and cotton goods, muslins, machinery, steamships and railway engines, ironware and goods of all kinds, glass and pottery, calico printing, dyeing, brewing and distilling. In short, Glasgow has become the Birmingham, and the Liverpool, of Scotland combined in one city. Its busy streets are full of fine buildings, erected for the promotion of culture, education, art, science, and amusement. It possesses a fine University and Cathedral; a Free Church College; noble Municipal and County Buildings; Hospitals and Railway Stations; Markets and Theatres. Its Public Parks are ex-

*The University, Glasgow.*

tensive, and laid out with taste and skill. Its water supply is abundant, coming from Loch Katrine, some 30 miles distant. Its shipbuilding-yards are the wonder of nations; and its population in 1891 was 755,000.

3. *Dundee*, a flourishing seaport, situated in Forfarshire on the north shore of the Firth of Tay, on the East Coast of Scotland, is the third largest town in Scotland. For several years this town has been the chief centre of the linen and jute manufactures of the country, but of late there has been some decline. It also carries on a considerable trade in preserved provisions. The foreign trade is about £5,000,000 per annum. Here, too, is the chief seat of the whale and seal fishery trade. Ships are fitted out each year for this remunerative, though dangerous employment. The town has also an important coast trade, and fish-curing and drying give employment to many persons. The population in 1891 was 153,587.

4. *Aberdeen*, one of the chief cities of the North of Scotland, stands between the mouths of the Don and the Dee. It consists of the two towns of Old and New Aberdeen. Aberdeen is both a Cathedral City and a University. The chief manufactures are cotton and woollen fabrics, ropes, sailcloth, soap, and paper. Some shipbuilding is also carried on. Near to Aberdeen there are extensive granite works and quarries at Peterhead. The population in 1891 was 124,943.

5. *Inverness*, the capital of the Northern Highlands, stands on the River Ness, on a plain at the meeting of the basins of the Murray and Beauly Firths. It is hemmed in by mountain screens upon the land side, which add both beauty and grandeur to the scenery. It is a general meeting place for tourists for the many places of interest that are in the neighbourhood. The manufactures are small and unimportant, and as a port Inverness stands in a minor

position. This city contains a Cathedral, municipal buildings, and excellent hotels, which during the summer and autumn seasons are crowded with travellers from all parts of the United Kingdom. The population in 1891 was 20,855.

TRADE AND MANUFACTURES:—

| Trade. | Chief Towns and Centres of Manufacture. |
|---|---|
| Woollen Cloth ... | Galashiels, Selkirk, Stirling, Glasgow, Hawick, etc. |
| ,, Blankets | Hawick is chief centre for Scotch Blankets and Flannels. |
| ,, Tartans } ,, Tweeds } | Stirling, Galashiels, Bannockburn, etc. Dumfries. |
| ,, Shawls | Paisley, Kilmarnock, Galashiels, Glasgow, etc. |
| ,, Carpets | Kilmarnock, Glasgow. |
| Cotton Goods | Glasgow, Paisley, Galashiels and neighbourhood. |
| Linen Goods and Jute ... ... | Dundee, Dunfermline, Forfar, Arbroath, Montrose, etc. |
| Silk Goods ... ... | Paisley, Glasgow, Edinburgh, Calder, Shotts, etc. |
| Iron-founding ... | Falkirk (Carron) and neighbourhood, Devin, Muirkirk, Clyde, Shotts. |
| Shipbuilding ... | Glasgow, Greenock, Port-Glasgow, Ardrossan, Dundee, Aberdeen, Leith. |
| Ale and Beer ... | Glasgow and Edinburgh, etc. |
| Whisky ... ... | Campbelltown, Glenlivet, Balloch, Edinburgh, etc. |
| Cutlery ... ... | Kilmarnock, Glasgow, Falkirk (Carron), etc. |
| Fancy Goods ... | Paisley, Dundee, Glasgow, Edinburgh, Galashiels, etc. |
| Soap and Candles | Glasgow, Leith, Prestonpans, Aberdeen, Paisley, Dundee. |
| Glass and Pottery | Glasgow. |
| Paper ... ... ... | Penicuik in Midlothian, Edinburgh, etc., etc. |
| Haddock and Fish-Curing, etc., | Stonehaven, Findon, Bervie, etc. |

BATTLEFIELDS :—

*Inverness.*—Inverlochy, 1645; Culloden Moor, 1746.

*Nairnshire.*—Auldearn, 1645.

*Perthshire.*—Methven, 1309; Tippermuir, 1644; Killiecrankie, 1689; Sheriffmuir, 1715.

*Argyllshire.*—Glencoe, 1692.

*Stirlingshire.*—Stirling, 1297; Falkirk (1) 1298; Bannockburn, 1314; Kilsyth, 1645; Falkirk (2) 1746.
*Lanarkshire.*—Langside, 1568; Bothwell Bridge, 1679.
*Selkirkshire.*—Philiphaugh, 1645.
*Roxburghshire.*—Roxburgh, 1460; Ancrum Moor, 1545.
*Haddingtonshire.*—Dunbar (1) 1296; Haddington, 1548; Dunbar (2) 1650; Prestonpans, 1745.
*Midlothianshire.*—Pinkie, 1547.
*Elginshire.*—Forres Sweyno Stone, 1014.
*Ross and Cromarty.*—Glen Shiel, 1719.
*Ayrshire.*—Loudon Hill, 1307; Drumclog, 1679.
*Fifeshire.*—Inverkeithing, 1651.
*Dumfriesshire.*—Solway Moss, 1542.
*Aberdeenshire.*—Aberdeen, 1644.

HISTORY.—The original name for Scotland was Caledonia. The earliest known inhabitants were two Celtic tribes of a warlike nature, called Picts and Scots. Several of the Roman Governors of Britain, finding that they could not overcome these savage people, built large walls from coast to coast to prevent their frequent incursions. It was to destroy the power of these northern tribes that the British, after the withdrawal of the Roman armies, invited the Saxons to come to their aid. For several centuries a fierce warfare was carried on without much gain to the English. It was not till the reign of the warlike king, Edward I., that the brave and independent spirit of the Scotch nation was crushed, and then it proved to be a work of great difficulty to make headway against such noble leaders as Wallace and Bruce. During the weak Government of Edward II. everything was regained by the Scotch armies; and once more Scotland was proclaimed an independent dynasty, with its own ruler and Government. Matters remained in this state until the two Crowns were united in 1603, by the Scottish king, James VI., becoming James I. of England.

# PART V.

## IRELAND.

NAME.—The native title for Ireland is "*Ernia*" or "*Erin*—the Green Island," by reason of its supreme fertility and verdure. The Romans called the island "*Hibernia*, or The Wintry Land," because they considered it to be a damp, cold, and dreary place.

SHAPE AND AREA.—Ireland is an irregularly-shaped, oval island, containing about 32,520 square miles of territory, or about half the area of England and Wales.

EXTENT.—The greatest length is measured from Fair Head in the North-east to Mizen Head in the South-west, a distance of 300 miles; and the greatest breadth is from Down Head in the East to Slyne Head in the West, about 200 miles.

POSITION.—Ireland, the third largest island in Europe, being somewhat smaller than Iceland, is situated in the Atlantic Ocean, about 60 miles to the west of the island of Great Britain, this distance being reduced, however, in the narrowest part, the North Channel, to 21 miles. It lies between the parallels of—latitude, 51° 26′ and 55° 23′ north of the Equator; longitude, 5° 20′ and 10° 26′ west of Greenwich. The Atlantic Ocean surrounds the North-west and South shores; but in the East the sea has the different names of the North Channel, the Irish Sea, and the Bristol Channel.

COAST-LINE.—The exposed position of the North, West, and South Coasts of Ireland to the storms of the Atlantic is the cause of the broken coast-line. The rocks are precipitous, and in many parts well-nigh inaccessible from the sea on the North, West, and South Coasts; but the East Coast is more flat; although hidden rocks and sandbanks abound. The length of this irregular and much-broken coast-line is 2,200 miles, which gives an average of one mile of coast to each 14 square miles of area. The magnificent coast scenery of the North and West far surpasses that of any other part of the British Isles, and more resembles that of Norway than the scenery of our shores. There are two wonderful inlets on the North Coast, Loch Swilly and Loch Foyle; and here, too, we find the greatest natural curiosity of Ireland in the remarkable columns of basaltic rock, called Giant's Causeway, which extends along the coast for more than 2,000 feet. The same kind of formation is found in Fingal's Cave. (*See* "Scotland—Isle of Staffa.")

CAPES AND HEADLANDS.—From the preceding description given of the Northern and Western Coasts of Ireland, it will naturally be assumed that the rocky, bold, and rugged scenery is remarkable in these parts. The near proximity of the chief mountain groups to the coast, which in several points appear to project quite into the sea, produces a grandeur of scenery not to be surpassed in the British Isles. The high rocks, and the irregular nature of the whole coast-line of the North and West, give a peculiar wildness to the country as viewed from the Atlantic.

The principal Capes or Headlands are:—

*On the North Coast:*—Fair Head, Bengore Head, Inishowen Head, Malin Head, Horn Head, and the Bloody Foreland.

*On the West Coast:*—Dawros Head, Rossan Head, Malinbeg Head, St. John's Point, Knocklane Head, Rathlee Head, Downpatrick Head, Benwee Head, Erris Head, Saddle Head and Achill Head on Achill Island, Emlagh Point, Aghros Head, Slyne Head, Black Head, Hag's Head, Loop

Point, Dunmore Head, Bray Head, Bolus Head, Crow Head, Mizen and Brow Heads.

The Southern and Eastern Coasts are lower and less marked than the Northern and Western, although a number of important headlands exist there, which adds greatly to the beauty of the coast-line.

*On the South Coast*, if we continue our journey, we find:—Cape Clear, Galley Head, Old Kinsale Head, Power Head Blackball Head, Mine Head, Helvick Head, Hook Head, and Carnsore Point.

*On the East Coast* there are :—Greenore Point, Cahore Point, Mizen Head, Wicklow Head, Howth Head, Clogher Head, Down Head, and Garron Point.

BAYS AND HARBOURS.—These are numerous and important, the chief being on :—

*The North Coast:*—Ballycastle Bay, Lough Foyle (*see* Lakes), Lough Swilly, Sheep Haven, and Innishbofin Bay.

*The West Coast:*—Trawenagh Bay, Loughros More Bay, Donegal Bay, Sligo Bay, Killala Bay, Broad Haven, Blacksod Bay, Clew Bay, Galway Bay, Mal Bay, Mouth of the Shannon, Tralee Bay, Dingle Bay, Kenmare River, Bantry Bay, with many other smaller ones.

*The South Coast.*—Ross Bay, Courtmacsherry Bay, Kinsale Harbour, Cork Harbour, Youghal Harbour, Dungarvan Harbour, Waterford Harbour, and Barrow Bay.

*The East Coast.*—Wexford Harbour, Dublin Bay, Drogheda Bay, Dundalk Bay, Carlingford Bay, Dundrum Bay, Strangford Lough, Belfast Lough, Lough Larne.

*N.B.—The old Celtic word " Lough " is used in Ireland to represent either an inland lake, or a large opening on the coast.*

STRAITS.—The North Channel, separating Ireland from Scotland at its north-eastern point, is about 21 miles in breadth.

ISLANDS.—Numerous small islands stud the Northern and Western shores of Ireland. These are really detached portions of the mainland which have been separated from it by the violence of the Atlantic waves which beat upon these shores. The total area of these islands is 270 square miles, or about equal in size to Anglesea in North Wales.

The chief islands on the North Coast are Rathlin, Innishtrahull, and Tory; on the West Coast there are North Arran, Achill, Clare, Innishturk, Innishbofin, Innishshark, Arran Group, Bear, and Valentia, which forms the last telegraph station on land on the submarine cable route to America. On the South Coast the only three islands of note are Cape Clear Island, Spike, and Saltee; and on the East Coast there are Lambay Island, Ireland's Eye, and Dalkey. Several of these islands are uninhabited, but they form lighthouse and fishing stations, and are invaluable both to the coast inhabitants and to navigators.

The following detailed description of the six principal islands and groups will suffice to show their nature and use to the Empire, as well as to the inhabitants, who pick up but a scanty subsistence from fishing, or from collecting the wrack, or sea-weed, for medicinal purposes, and the making of kelp, or calcined ashes, used in the manufacture of glass.

*Rathlin Island*, situated off the North Coast of Antrim, is a small island some four miles from the shore. The surface is rocky, affording a rough herbage for sheep, which are the only animals on the island. The inhabitants are a poor, uneducated race, chiefly employed in fishing. It is a coast-guard station, and contains a lighthouse. Church Bay is the only village of importance on it. It is mentioned in history as being the hiding-place of King Robert Bruce of Scotland during his exile.

*Achill, or Eagle Island*, is situated on the Western Coast

of Mayo County. It is separated from the mainland by a narrow passage of about a mile in breadth. This is the largest of the islands of Ireland, being about 16 miles broad, and 7 miles long, with a circumference of 80 miles. Its surface is unequally divided into mountain and bog land. The inhabitants are either fishermen or shepherds; they are rude in their manners, and extremely simple in their ways of living. At Keel, the coastguard station, there is a church surrounded by small dwelling-houses. A small island called Achillbeg is included with Achill. These islands are named from a small species of eagle found there.

*Arran Islands.*—Area, 11,300 acres. Three small islands lying at the entrance of Galway Bay. Arranmore is the largest of this group. The people are engaged in the coast fisheries, or work in the marble quarries, of which there are several on the islands. Flocks of puffins, a curious kind of sea-bird, inhabit the rocks on the coasts. A lighthouse, 500 feet high, was built on Arranmore in 1817. In olden times these islands were a favourite resort for hermits and others who wished to lead a retired life.

*Valentia Island*, situated to the south of Dingle Bay in Kerry, is an exceedingly fertile and well-cultivated tract, and it is the most thickly-populated island in the country. Length, 6 miles; breadth, 2 miles. The town of Valentia is the most western port of the British Isles. It is the last British station of the Atlantic Submarine Telegraph Company, and from it the cable is laid between England and America. A great number of its inhabitants work in the stone quarries. They are a much more intelligent and cultivated race than the inhabitants of the other islands. Corn, flax, and vegetables are produced here.

*Clear Island, or Cape Clear*, is the most southern point of Ireland. The surface is rocky and barren, only a small part being under cultivation. The inhabitants, called Capers, are employed in fishing and working in the stone quarries; they were originally great smugglers. Vast flocks of sea-birds make their homes here.

PHYSICAL FEATURES.—The whole country resembles a slightly depressed plain in the centre, surrounded on all sides by coast mountains and highlands. This plain is most fertile, being well watered by numerous rivers and lakes which have given rise to the title of Emerald Isle, and justly so, because the natural verdure of the surface is seldom so universally met with in any other country.

Like Scotland, there are elevated highlands, vast lakes, and lovely streams in Ireland; but unlike Scotland, its mountains are clothed with verdure, and its lakes and rivers are generally surrounded by extremely fertile districts instead of wild moorlands. The bogs, which comprise about one-tenth of the whole area, are the most remarkable natural feature of the country. Many tourists visit Ireland each year.

MOUNTAINS AND HILLS.—The mountain system of Ireland is most irregular, for there are but few continuous chains. Roughly speaking, there are four groups or mountain districts, known by the suggestive titles of Northern, Eastern, Southern, and Western Highlands.

*The Northern Highlands* consist of the Donegal range with Mount Errigal, 2,460 feet, and the Mountains of Antrim, which are about 2,400 feet high; also a smaller range in Londonderry, the Carntogher Mountains.

*The Eastern Highlands* include the Mourne Mountains in the North-East, with Lugnaquilla, 2,039 feet high; the Wicklow Hills with Slieve-Donard, 2,796 feet.

*The Southern Highlands* are made up of several detached ranges, of which the principal are Knockmeledown Mountains, 2,609 feet; the Galtee Mountains, 3,015 feet; the

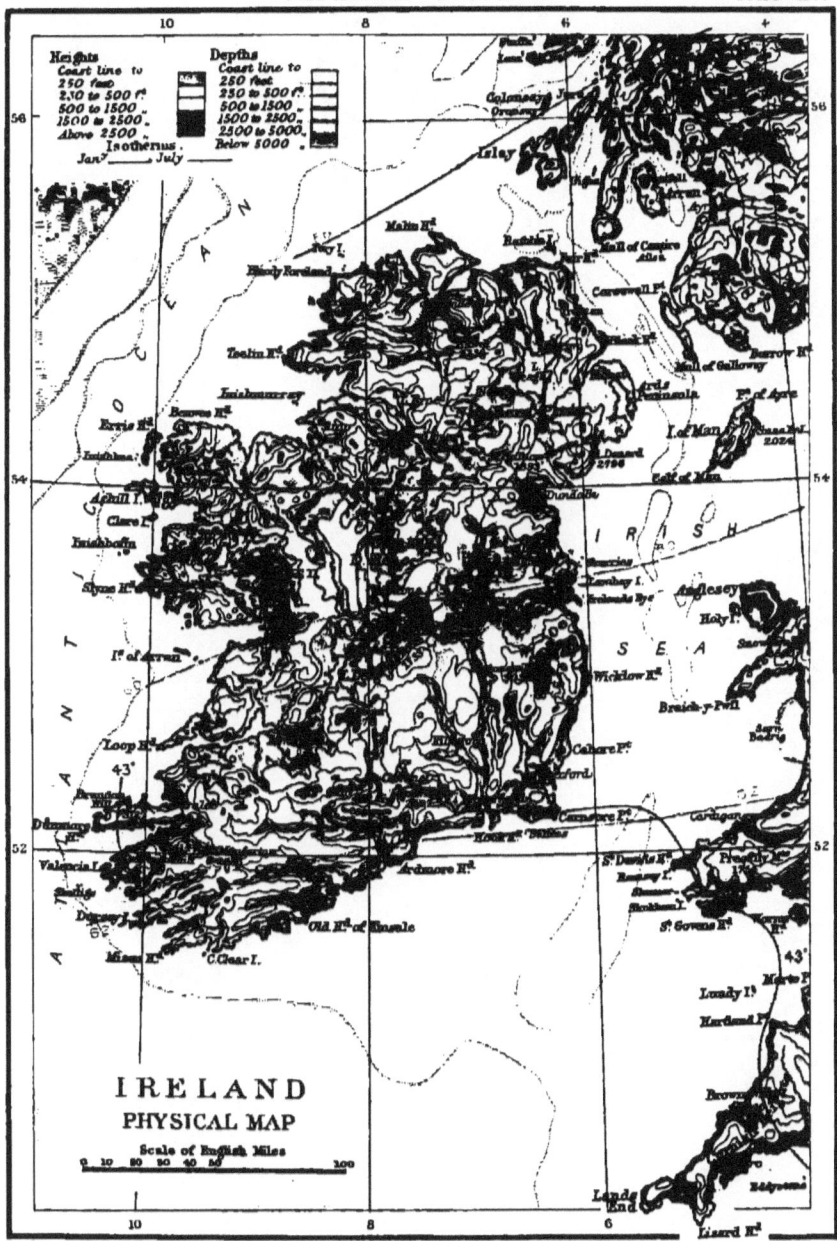

Silvermines, 2,273 feet; and Slieve Bloom, 1,733 feet.

*The Western Highlands* are more numerous and lofty than those of other parts. Here are situated the Kerry Ranges, including the Macgillicuddy Reeks, with Carrantual, 3,414 feet, the highest point in Ireland. The Mountains of Connaught, with Nephin Beg, 2,060 feet, and Croagh Patrick, 2,510 feet, in the County of Mayo; the Connemara Ranges, which also comprise the Twelve Pins Group and the Galway Mountains.

PLAINS.—There is, generally speaking, but one large central plain in Ireland. The natural arrangement of the mountains around the coasts gives to the country a saucer-like appearance, so that this plain extends from Galway Bay in the West to Dublin and Dundalk Bays in the East; and from Lough Neagh in the North as far as the Slieve Bloom Range in the South. Several of the river-basins or plains are of a fair size.

RIVERS.—Ireland possesses an excellent river system, but they are generally slow in motion, and small in size, as the central parts of the country are so flat. The principal rivers are :—

*A. The Shannon* is the largest river in the British Isles, although it is 14 miles shorter than the Severn, and it occupies a similar position to the Severn in England and Wales. It rises in the Fermanagh Hills to the north of Lough Allen, and flows in a curved south-westerly direction for a course of 224 miles, until it enters the Atlantic by means of a grand estuary. Its fall is not more than one foot to the mile, so that its waters are extremely sluggish. During its course its banks widen out to form several loughs or lakes, the chief being Loughs Allen, Ree, and Derg. Its tributaries on the right bank are the Suck, and Fergus; and on the left bank the Inny, Brosna,

Magne, and Deel. The towns of importance standing on its banks are Leitrim, Carrick, Athlone, Killaloe, and Limerick, which is situated at the head of the estuary, where it immediately widens out before entering the sea. This river is navigable for more than 200 miles of its course.

*B. The Barrow* is the second largest river of Ireland. It rises in the Slieve Bloom Mountains, and flows in a southerly direction for 114 miles, finally entering the sea in Waterford Harbour. It possesses only two tributaries of importance—the Suir and the Nore on the right bank. This river is navigable as far as Athy, some 60 miles from the sea. The other towns on its banks are Carlow and New Ross.

*C. The Suir*, which, though properly named a tributary of the Barrow, is sometimes considered as a separate river. It is 100 miles long, and flows in a south-easterly direction from the Slieve Bloom Mountains into the River Barrow, just before the latter enters Waterford Harbour. The towns on its banks are Thurles, Holycross, Calni, Clonmel, Carrick, and Waterford.

*D. The Blackwater* rises near the Lakes of Killarney in Cork County, and flows first eastwards and then southwards, a distance of 105 miles, until it falls into Youghal Bay. Its chief tributary is the Bride on the right bank. The towns situated on its course are Mallow, Fermoy, Lismore, and Youghal.

*E. The Liffey* is but 75 miles in length. It rises in the Wicklow Hills, near the East Coast, and by a circuitous course flows into the Irish Sea, through Dublin Bay. At its mouth stands Dublin, the metropolis of Ireland, which alone gives it importance, as no other large towns stand upon its banks.

*F. The Bann*, on the North Coast, drains Lough Neagh,

and after a course of 100 miles enters the sea through Lough Foyle.

Other smaller rivers are the Foyle on the North Coast; the Lagan, 40 miles, flowing into Belfast Lough; the Boyne, 80 miles; and the Slaney, 70 miles, on the East Coast, flowing into Wexford Harbour. The Boyne was noted for the famous battle of 1690, when William III. defeated James II. near Drogheda. On the South Coast, the Lee, 60 miles, the mouth of which river forms the famous Cork Harbour; and the Bandon, 40 miles, flowing into Kinsale Harbour. On the West Coast, the rivers, with the exception of the Shannon, are small and unimportant. Only two need be mentioned here—the Moy, which enters Killala Bay; and the Erne, which partakes of the double nature of both lake and river, which flows into Donegal Bay.

LAKES.—Ireland has been sometimes called the "Land of Lakes." The number and size of these large tracts of water may be accounted for by—

1. The heavy rainfall of the country.
2. The flatness of the interior.
3. The natural formation of the higher lands, mountains, and high rocks, which surround the coast-line.

In this way a large portion of the water of Ireland is prevented from immediately making its way to the sea, so that it naturally collects in the depressed districts, and forms inland lakes. The united area of the Irish lakes is estimated at 712 square miles.

1. *Lough Neagh* is the largest lake in the British Isles. Its area is 154 square miles in extent, being about 20 miles long, and nearly 10 miles broad, and its waters possess strange petrifying properties. Compared with the Lakes of Scotland and England, it is three times as large as Loch Lomond, and nearly fifteen times as large as Windermere.

The banks of this lake are low, and although a number of small streams flow into it, yet there is only one outlet, the Bann; so that after the rainy months, a very large additional area is flooded, and the lake appears to be nearly twice its natural size.

2. *Lough Erne* is 150 square miles in area. It is really two lakes—the Upper and the Lower Erne—connected by the River Erne. A pleasant feature of these lakes are the numerous islands. The fishing is of the highest importance.

3. *The Highland Lake Group* consists of Loughs Conn, Corrib, and Mask in Connaught. Lough Corrib is mysteriously connected with Lough Mask, the waters running through an underground channel. The irregular shape and picturesque wild scenery to be found in the neighbourhood of these lakes make them popular with tourists.

4. *The Shannon Lakes* are Loughs Allen, Ree, and Derg. They are merely extensions of the river banks over depressed areas.

5. *The Lakes of Killarney* are the Queen of Irish Lakes. This lovely group is situated in Kerry County. The three principal are called by the names of Upper, Middle, and Lower Lakes. Their united area equals 10 square miles. Here may be seen the finest scenery in Ireland, and, perhaps, by reason of its varied nature and freshness, the most beautiful in the British Islands.

The Lakes of Killarney have been thus described by the Rev. C. S. Ward, M.A., joint-editor of *The Thorough Guide Series*, " Ireland," Part II., pp. 111, 112 :—

" Nowhere else in these islands are woodland, lake, and mountain scenery, all of the utmost beauty, so exquisitely combined. It is, moreover, natural scenery almost untouched, certainly quite unimpaired, by man's handiwork; and the few ruins that there are around the lakes are picturesque adjuncts rather than noteworthy historical monuments. The one thing wanting in Killarney is verdant valley scenery, such as, by contrast, gives to the English Lake District its unique charm. What will probably most impress the visitor with a sense of beauty is the marvellous colouring, due, we imagine, to the sunshine passing through an atmosphere which, in ordinary seasons, is constantly being purified by passing showers."

Other smaller lakes are Loughs Arrow and Gill, in Sligo; Derravaragh, Owel, and Ennel, in West Meath; Oughter and Sheelin, in Cavan.

CLIMATE.—The Evergreen Island has received its title by reason of the salubrity and freshness of its climate, which is certainly both mild and temperate in the extreme. The summers are cooler and the winters warmer and more equable in temperature than in England, but the average rainfall is three days out of four, and this perpetual moisture produces the beautiful verdure of the fields and plants. The bogs are most extensive, occupying an area of no less than five millions of acres, or about one-tenth of the whole country. These, in no small degree, add to the humidity and mildness of the climate.

SOIL AND AGRICULTURE.—Generally speaking, the land is fertile and productive. Of course there are barren and poor districts, but potatoes, corn, flax, and nearly all root crops flourish beyond the average, where care and labour are expended upon their production. Unfortunately, political troubles have for many years past hindered the full progress of agriculture; yet statistics show a marked improvement in many parts, and as a large proportion of the inhabitants are dependent upon the land crops, or the rearing of sheep and cattle, this is an all-important matter, and the general prosperity of the country is influenced largely by it.

For many years the proper cultivation of the land was neglected, and in consequence the people suffered greatly from poverty. Much has been done to improve matters by the introduction of machinery and the opening up of fresh tracts of waste land for agricultural purposes, as well as by the encouragement of markets and centres for the sale of cultivated products. In certain districts the old customs of "Conacre" and "Tenant-right" still exist, and aid to maintain the high standard of agriculture. Yet, on the whole, the smaller holdings are among the drawbacks to Ireland's prosperity as a nation.

NATURAL PRODUCTIONS.—These naturally range themselves under the three heads of—I., Animal; II., Vegetable; III., Mineral.

I.—ANIMAL PRODUCTIONS.

*A. Wild Animals.*—In ancient times Ireland was much more thickly wooded than it is now. Dense forests stretched away far and wide over its surface, and these were inhabited by many obsolete wild animals, of which only the fossil remains, in the bogs or river-beds, are left to tell of their past existence. The bones of an enormous species of elk, together with the mammoth elephant, the sea-falcon, and several kinds of carnivorous animals now extinct, are occasionally to be met with. The native fauna now consists of the fox, badger, otter, hare, rabbit, squirrel, weasel, rat, and mouse, as in England. The birds are similar to those in Britain, with a few additional sea-birds, such as eagles and puffins, which are found on the Western Coast. Neither moles, nor venomous reptiles, are to be found in Ireland. An old legend ascribes their banishment from the island to the work of St. Patrick.

*B. Domestic Animals.*—These are the same as in England. The Irish cows, of various breeds, yield large quantities of excellent, rich milk, which is made into butter for home use and exportation to England. The pig probably ranks as the chief domestic animal. It is not an uncommon sight to meet with this animal in the country districts sharing the fireside of the cotter and his family. Geese, poultry, ducks, are to be met with everywhere. Enormous quantities of Irish eggs are for sale in the English markets.

*C. The Fisheries.*—The coast fisheries are not so ably worked as they might be. There is a marked want of enterprise and spirit in carrying out this important work, which is far from being so remunerative as it ought to be. The coasts literally teem with fish of the most valuable kinds. Most of the inland lakes also contain large quantities of excellent fish, and the numerous rivers produce excellent sport for the angler.

II. VEGETABLE PRODUCTIONS.—The native flora of Ireland comprises many rare and interesting species of plants beyond the well-known trees, shrubs, and flowers commonly met with in Great Britain. Some of the most striking and curious kinds are the Irish rose, the arbutus, which was introduced by the monks of Spain in the Middle Ages, and is now grown in full luxuriance in the neighbourhood of Killarney. This remarkable plant bears blossoms with green and ripe fruit at one and the same time, in a similar way to the orange plant. Other uncommon plants are the Irish furze, the yew, strawberry tree, numerous heaths, and sea-weed of all kinds on the coasts.

The forests of Ireland are now of minor importance, but the country is generally well wooded. The chief forest trees include the beech, oak, elm, chestnut, firs of all kinds, and maple. Trunks of enormous trees have been dug out of the bogs at a depth varying from 10 to 30 feet.

Among cultivated products, corn, especially barley, stands first for perfection of growth, while flax, hemp, rye, etc., thrive almost as well as in Russia. Root crops are rich and abundant. Tobacco, beetroot, and wheat are grown for exportation; but fruit does not ripen either so well, or so readily, as in England.

III. MINERAL PRODUCTIONS.

1. *Geology.*—The geological strata of Ireland may be divided into:—

    *A.* Rocks of primary formation found in the mountainous districts and highlands. These are greatly broken by igneous rocks of a volcanic nature.

    *B.* Other mixed formations are found in the interior, the most common being limestone, chalk, and old red sandstone. The bogs appear to have a foundation of clay and gravel intermixed with limestone.

The bogs are composed of peat, or soft turf, partly decomposed. No unhealthiness is produced by these damp vegetable formations, as they contain a great deal of tannic acid, which is the life principle of all vegetable astringents and is naturally conducive to health.

2. *Minerals.*—*A.* Coal is found in many parts, but it is of an inferior quality to that obtained in Britain. The largest coal centres are in the North-eastern, the Midland, and the South-western districts, but the produce is small in amount, so that coal is imported to the larger centres of trade and population from England. The chief coalfields are in Leinster at Wicklow, Kilkenny, Carlow, and Queen's County; other coalfields are Tyrone and Antrim in the north of Ulster; Cork, Kerry, Limerick, and Clare in Munster. Peat is the universal fuel of the country districts; and as this is plentiful, the scarcity of coal is not so much felt as otherwise it would be.

*B.* The iron mines are rich and productive in Cork, Down, Wicklow, and Carlow, where both copper and lead, with a little silver, are found. Marble, granite, building and other stone, limestone, fuller's earth, and manganese are widely diffused throughout the country.

3. *Mineral Springs.*—There are chalybeate springs at Golden Bridge near Dublin, Castle Connel near Limerick, Mallow in Cork, and Ballynahinch in Down.

4. *Natural Curiosities.*—*A.* By far the greatest natural curiosity in Ireland is the Giant's Causeway, situated on the North Coast. It consists of a regular succession of columns, pentagonal, hexagonal, and octagonal in shape, and fitting closely and compactly together. This formation is so complete and regular in structure, that it presents the appearance of having been constructed by hand. This line of columns stretches out for 3,000 feet into the sea; and a singular feature about it is that the same formation is met with on the opposite coast of Scotland. Probably the old legend that the Irish giants of ancient times constructed this pathway through the sea, for the purpose of travelling over it to subdue the natives of Scotland, originally gave to it the name of " The Giant's Causeway." One part of it, near Bengore Head, is called " The Organ," from its peculiar resemblance to that instrument.

*B.* The petrifying nature of the waters of Lough Neagh is so great as to change wood and other soft substances into stone.

*C.* The marble rocks of Lough Lene. These beautiful rocks are islands standing out of the lake, and to add to the charm of the natural scenery, the surface of these islands is clothed with luxuriant vegetation.

*D.* The Cascades of Bantry in Cork County, and Powerscourt in Wicklow, are remarkably fine ones.

*E.* "The Devil's Punchbowl is a deeply-set mountain tarn, about 600 yards long, and the scarped sides rise more or less abruptly from the water's edge, though not to such an extent as to make a rough scramble along the margin impossible." (Ward's "Ireland," *Thorough Guide Series*, p. 120.)

RACE AND LANGUAGE.—The old inhabitants appear to have belonged to the Celtic race. In the Northern Province of Ulster, they are the same race as the English and the Scotch. The people of Connaught are also of Celtic origin, and they still speak the Erse, or Gaelic, language. In Leinster and Munster they are of Celtic and Saxon descent, and generally speak the English language.

The Irish people are warm-hearted and kind by nature, but they possess a hasty, excitable temper, and as they are easily led by fanaticism into open rebellion, they have been considered fickle in purpose. Undoubtedly England has been much to blame in the past in not helping forward the trade and manufactures of the country. Ireland possesses but little national wealth, and English landowners and manufacturers have too often been content to draw wealth from the country, without encouraging the welfare and prosperity of the people in proportion.

POPULATION.—The population of Ireland in 1891 was 4,704,750. These figures show a decrease in the last ten years since 1881 of 9·1 per cent., probably owing to the large number of persons who have left their native country for America, Australia, South Africa, and other of our foreign possessions.

POLITICAL FACTS—COUNTIES.—Ireland is divided into

four large provinces, which are again sub-divided into 32 counties, as follows:—

    *A.* Maritime, 17.

    *B.* Inland, 15.

I. *Ulster*, in the North, contains 9 counties—*A.* 4 Maritime; *B.* 5 Inland.

    *A.* Antrim, Down, Londonderry, and Donegal.

    *B.* Armagh, Tyrone, Fermanagh, Monaghan, and Cavan.

II. *Leinster*, in the East, contains 12 counties—*A.* 5 Maritime; *B.* 7 Inland.

    *A.* Dublin, Wicklow, Wexford, Meath, and Louth.

    *B.* Kilkenny, Carlow, Kildare, Queen's County, King's County, West Meath, and Longford.

III. *Munster*, in the South, contains 6 counties—*A.* 4 Maritime; *B.* 2 Inland.

    *A.* Waterford, Cork, Kerry, and Clare.

    *B.* Limerick and Tipperary.

IV. *Connaught*, in the West, contains 5 counties—*A.* 4 Maritime; *B.* 1 Inland.

    *A.* Leitrim, Sligo, Mayo, and Galway.

    *B.* Roscommon.

The largest county is Cork; the smallest is Louth.

The most densely-populated county is Antrim; the least populated is Carlow.

## TABLE—POLITICAL FACTS, IRELAND.

| County. | Area. Square Miles. | Population, 1891. | Capital and other Towns. |
|---|---|---|---|
| **ULSTER—Nine Counties.** | | | |
| Antrim, | 1,190 | 427,698 | *Belfast*, Antrim, Carrickfergus, Larne, Lisburn, and Ballymena. |
| Down, | 957 | 266,893 | *Downpatrick*, Newry, Newtownards, Warren Point, and Donaghadee. |
| Londonderry, | 816 | 151,666 | *Londonderry*, Coleraine. |
| Donegal, | 1,870 | 185,211 | *Donegal*, Lifford, Ballyshannon, Moville. |
| Armagh, | 513 | 143,056 | *Armagh*, Lurgan, Portadown, Newry. |
| Tyrone, | 1,260 | 171,278 | *Omagh*, Strabane, Dungannon, Clogher. |
| Fermanagh, | 714 | 74,037 | *Enniskillen*, Newtown Butler. |
| Monaghan, | 500 | 86,089 | *Monaghan*, Clones, Carrickmacross. |
| Cavan, | 746 | 111,097 | *Cavan*, Cootehill, Belturbet. |
| **LEINSTER—Twelve Counties.** | | | |
| Dublin, | 354 | 419,111 | *Dublin*, Kingstown, Balbriggan. |
| Wicklow, | 781 | 61,934 | *Wicklow*, Bray, Arklow. |
| Wexford, | 901 | 111,534 | *Wexford*, New Ross, Enniscorthy. |
| Meath, | 906 | 76,616 | *Trim*, Kells, Navan, Dunboyne. |
| Louth, | 315 | 70,852 | *Dundalk*, Drogheda, Carlingford. |
| Kilkenny, | 796 | 87,154 | *Kilkenny*, Callan, Thomastown. |
| Carlow, | 346 | 40,899 | *Carlow*, Tullow, Bagenalstown. |
| Kildare, | 654 | 69,988 | *Athy*, Kildare, Maynooth, Naas. |
| Queen's County, | 664 | 64,630 | *Maryborough*, Mountmellick, Portarlington. |
| King's County, | 772 | 65,408 | *Tullamore*, Philipstown, Parsonstown. |
| West Meath, | 708 | 65,028 | *Mullingar*, Athlone. |
| Longford, | 421 | 52,553 | *Longford*, Ballymahon. |
| **MUNSTER—Six Counties.** | | | |
| Waterford, | 721 | 93,130 | *Waterford*, Lismore, Dungarvan. |
| Cork, | 2,890 | 436,041 | *Cork*, Queenstown, Youghal, Kinsale, Bantry, Bandon. |
| Kerry, | 1,850 | 178,019 | *Tralee*, Listowel, Dingle, Kenmare, Killarney. |
| Clare, | 1,294 | 123,859 | *Ennis*, Kilrush, Killaloe. |
| Limerick, | 1,064 | 158,563 | *Limerick*, Newmarket, Rathkeale. |
| Tipperary, | 1,659 | 172,882 | *Clonmel*, Carrick-on-Suir, Cashel, Thurles. |
| **CONNAUGHT—Five Counties.** | | | |
| Leitrim, | 613 | 78,379 | *Carrick-on-Shannon*, Leitrim. |
| Sligo, | 721 | 93,338 | *Sligo*, Collooney, Dromore. |
| Mayo, | 2,126 | 218,406 | *Castlebar*, Ballina, Killala, Westport. |
| Galway, | 2,452 | 214,256 | *Galway*, Ballinasloe, Tuam, Loughrea. |
| Roscommon, | 949 | 114,194 | *Roscommon*, Castlereagh, Elphin. |

## Trade and Manufactures:—

| Trade. | Chief Towns and Centres of Manufactures. |
|---|---|
| Linen Goods ... | Belfast, Drogheda, Lisburn, Lurgan, Newry, Ballymena, Coleraine. |
| Cotton Goods ... | Belfast, Dublin, Tullamore, and neighbourhood. |
| Coarse Woollen Goods ... ... | Dublin, Wicklow, Belfast, Kilkenny district. |
| Broad Cloth ... | Dublin and neighbourhood. |
| Ironfounding ... | Carrickfergus, Cork, Belfast district. |
| Shipbuilding ... | Cork, Waterford, Dublin, Belfast, Londonderry. |
| Ale and Porter... | Dublin, Belfast, Castlebellingham. |
| Spirits (Whiskey) | Cork, Dublin, Belfast, Clonmel, Roscommon, Limerick, Bushmills. |
| General Wares... | Dublin, Cork, Bandon, Londonderry, Belfast, Drogheda, Newry. |
| Mixed Goods ... | Waterford, Limerick. |
| Gloves and Lace | Limerick, Dublin, Cork, Belfast. |

Industries.—In addition to the above, the chief industry of the Irish people in the country districts is the rearing of cattle, pigs, sheep, horses, and poultry. The farm produce includes potatoes, oats, rye, and root crops. The ordinary English cereals do not abundantly flourish, as agriculture is at a low ebb. The bog land is also a drawback to farming in many districts.

Seaports:—

*North Coast:*—Londonderry.

*West Coast:*—Dingle, Tralee, Limerick, Galway, Westport, Sligo, Ballyshannon.

*South Coast:*—Castletown, Skibbereen, Kinsale, Cork, Queenstown, Youghal, Dungarvan, Waterford, New Ross.

*East Coast:*—Wexford, Kingstown, Dublin, Drogheda, Dundalk, Strangford, Belfast, Carrickfergus.

Naval Ports.—Queenstown, in Cork Harbour, is an important naval station. Vessels belonging to the British squadron are stationed at intervals along the coasts for protection and defence.

**MILITARY STATIONS.**—These are located at Belfast, Cork, Curragh, Dublin, etc.

*Kingstown Harbour, Ireland.*

TOWNS:—

1. *Dublin.*—The Metropolis of Ireland stands on both

banks of the River Liffey. It contains two Universities; two
Cathedrals (Christ Church and St. Patrick's); the Govern-

*Christchurch Cathedral, Dublin.*

ment Buildings and Vice-Regal Lodge, or residence of the
Lord-Lieutenant, as the Queen's representative is called;

the National Bank and post-office; many fine churches, and other public buildings, including barracks, clubs, law-courts, theatres, etc. The bridges, quays, and docks are

St. Patrick's Cathedral, Dublin.

of the finest architecture, and the streets—of which Sackville Street is the principal—are well paved and lighted.

*Sackville Street, Dublin.*

Its public walks and drives are indeed beautiful. One drive which completely encircles the town is nine miles in length. Phœnix Park is about 1,300 acres; and other public places are St. Stephen's Green; the Botanical Gardens; and Glasnevin Cemetery. The port of Dublin is Kingstown on Dublin Bay. An extensive passenger traffic and general trade is conducted from Kingstown, as it is the principal station and port for the mail steamers to and from Holyhead and Liverpool. Its manufactures and trade comprise stout and porter breweries, cabinetmaking, whiskey, poplin, cotton and linen goods, and fancy wares. The city, compared with other towns in the British Isles, takes an eighth place, being next in size to Sheffield, being less in population than Liverpool, Manchester, Glasgow, Birmingham, Leeds, and Sheffield.

The population of Dublin and the suburbs in 1891 was 311,209; and the port of Kingstown contains an additional 17,322 persons.

2. *Belfast.*—This important seaport is the second town in Ireland, and the chief commercial and manufacturing centre of the country. The town is situated on Belfast Lough, at the mouth of the River Lagan. It contains excellent streets, squares, and costly buildings. The foreign trade is considerable, and the landing quays are crowded with the produce from all parts of the world. The chief trade and manufactures consist of shipbuilding, linen and cotton goods, glass, chemicals, calico printing, distilling and brewing, ropes and sail-cloth, hats and tobacco, etc.

The population in 1891 was 255,950.

3. *Cork* is the third town of importance in the whole country, and the chief seaport in the South of Ireland. It stands on a commodious harbour called the "Cove of Cork." The streets and buildings are among the finest in the country. Its trade is extensive—comprising shipbuilding,

the export of grain, provisions, cattle, linen and cotton goods; and its manufactures include cutlery, mixed goods, gloves, whiskey, etc.

The population in 1891 was 75,345.

The Castle, Dublin.

4. *Limerick* stands upon the opening of the Shannon estuary. The inland trade is of considerable importance. The town, which is well arranged, paved, and lighted, is divided into three parts by the river, *viz.*, English Town; Irish Town; and New Town; which are connected by several fine bridges. The chief objects of interest are the cathedral, the court-house or gaol, the custom-house, the commercial buildings, several banks, breweries, and various manufactories. Its trade is shipbuilding, tanning, distilling, iron-founding, and the manufacture of lace, gloves, fancy goods, paper, etc.

The population in 1891 was 37,155.

5. *Londonderry*, or Derry, as it was originally called, is situated on the North Coast of Ulster, upon an arm of Lough Foyle. The city stood a remarkable siege in 1689. The hill upon which it stands is called Derry Island, and it is surrounded by massive walls, nearly 24 feet high. Several fine buildings ornament the streets. There are extensive flax mills, distilleries, breweries, flour and paper mills, which provide employment for a great number of people.

The population in 1891 was 33,200.

6. *Waterford* stands upon the Suir, about 12 miles from the sea. The town was founded by the Danes in 850, and soon grew into importance. The Quay, and the Mall, are the principal streets. The public buildings include the two cathedrals, several churches, the town-hall, court-houses, hospitals, etc. This seaport is the chief town of the export trade with Bristol.

The population in 1891 was 20,802.

GOVERNMENT.—The Government is semi-independent under the Crown of Great Britain, which appoints a Governor, called the Lord-Lieutenant, who holds office only during each successive Ministry, yet his power and his

IRELAND. 249

Court are almost Regal during his term of government. Ireland returns 103 members to the English House of Com-

*Londonderry.*

mons, and 32 out of 188 Irish Peers have seats in the House of Lords.

RELIGION.—Seventy-five per cent. of the people are Roman Catholics; the remainder are Protestants. Besides the Church of Ireland, nearly every religious sect is tolerated, but Dissenters are not nearly so numerous as in Great Britain. (*See* "British Isles," p. 77.)

    *A*. The Roman Catholic Church in Ireland is presided over by 4 Archbishops, 24 Bishops, and 3,429 Clergy.

    *B*. The State Church, or Church of Ireland, was disestablished in January, 1871, by Act of Parliament. It is governed by 2 Archbishops, 10 Bishops, and about 1,500 Clergy.

EDUCATION.—There are three Universities in Ireland, two belonging to the Church of Ireland and one to the Roman Catholic Church. Queen's Colleges have been established at Belfast, Cork, and Galway; and at Maynooth, in Kildare County, there is a large Roman Catholic Theological College.

The national system of education was in a backward state before 1860, when every possible means was employed to raise the standard. Commissioners, elected by the Government, took over the management and control of the schools and teachers, so that the national school system is now both extensive and complete in its machinery and arrangements to provide a good education for the children of the poorer classes.

REVENUE.—Ireland contributes about £6,895,807 to the National Exchequer of Great Britain.

INTERNAL COMMUNICATION.—Railways and Canals, etc. (*See* "British Isles," p. 60.)

COMMERCE.—Below that of either England or Scotland, yet considerable. The foreign trade of Belfast, Cork, Waterford, and Limerick is annually increasing. It is carried on with North America, the Mediterranean, the

West Indies, etc., in addition to the extensive home trade with Great Britain.

IMPORTS.—These are similar to Great Britain, consisting chiefly of raw produce, wool, cotton, silk, and flax, colonial goods and food supplies, coal, machinery, timber, salt, clothing, and manufactured goods, wine and brandy, also bark for tanning.

EXPORTS.—Food supplies, chiefly dairy and poultry produce, cattle, pigs, sheep, horses, poultry, oats, whiskey, stout, flax, ropes and cordage, leather, etc.

HISTORY.—The early history of Ireland is clouded in obscurity by the prevalence of ancient traditions having been transmitted from generation to generation, each of which probably contributed some additional superstition relating to both religion and national customs. The great Celtic Saint, Patricius, or St. Patrick, was Britain's first great missionary, and his sphere of work was Ireland, although it is often stated that he was preceded by Palladius, another missionary sent from Rome. St. Patrick was born in Britain towards the end of the fourth century. At an early age he was taken prisoner by some Irish pirates to their own land, and sold as a slave to Miliuc, an Irish chief, who treated him well. After seven years, he escaped to Britain, but some twenty years later, he returned as the apostle, or missionary, to the Emerald Isle, where he met with marked success, and converted hosts of all classes to Christianity; hence he was selected as the Patron Saint of that country.

To return to history, the conquest of Ireland commenced in 1170, and Henry II. of England claimed the subjugation of the Irish chiefs five years later. Yet this conquest was not completed until the fall of Limerick in 1691, when William, Prince of Orange, defeated the Irish, who had taken up the cause of James II. after his abdication of the

English throne. Order was finally restored for some years, after the Battle of the Boyne. Another rebellion was suppressed in 1798, and in 1801 the Kingdom and Crown of Ireland was incorporated with the Crown of Great Britain, and an Act was then passed uniting the two kingdoms under one Government.

BATTLEFIELDS. — Drogheda, in Louth, 1649 ; Londonderry Siege, 1688 ; Newtown Butler, in Fermanagh, 1689 ; Aughrim, in Galway, 1690 ; Battle of the Boyne, 1690 ; Limerick, 1691 ; Vinegar Hill, in Wexford, 1798.

# PART VI.

## BRITISH POSSESSIONS IN EUROPE.

1. ISLE OF MAN, IN THE IRISH SEA.
2. CHANNEL ISLANDS, OFF THE COAST OF FRANCE.
3. GIBRALTAR, AT THE ENTRANCE TO THE MEDITERRANEAN SEA.
4. MALTA, WITH GOZO AND COMINO ISLANDS, IN THE MEDITERRANEAN SEA.
5. CYPRUS ISLAND, IN THE MEDITERRANEAN SEA.

IMPERIAL BRITAIN. MAP XII.

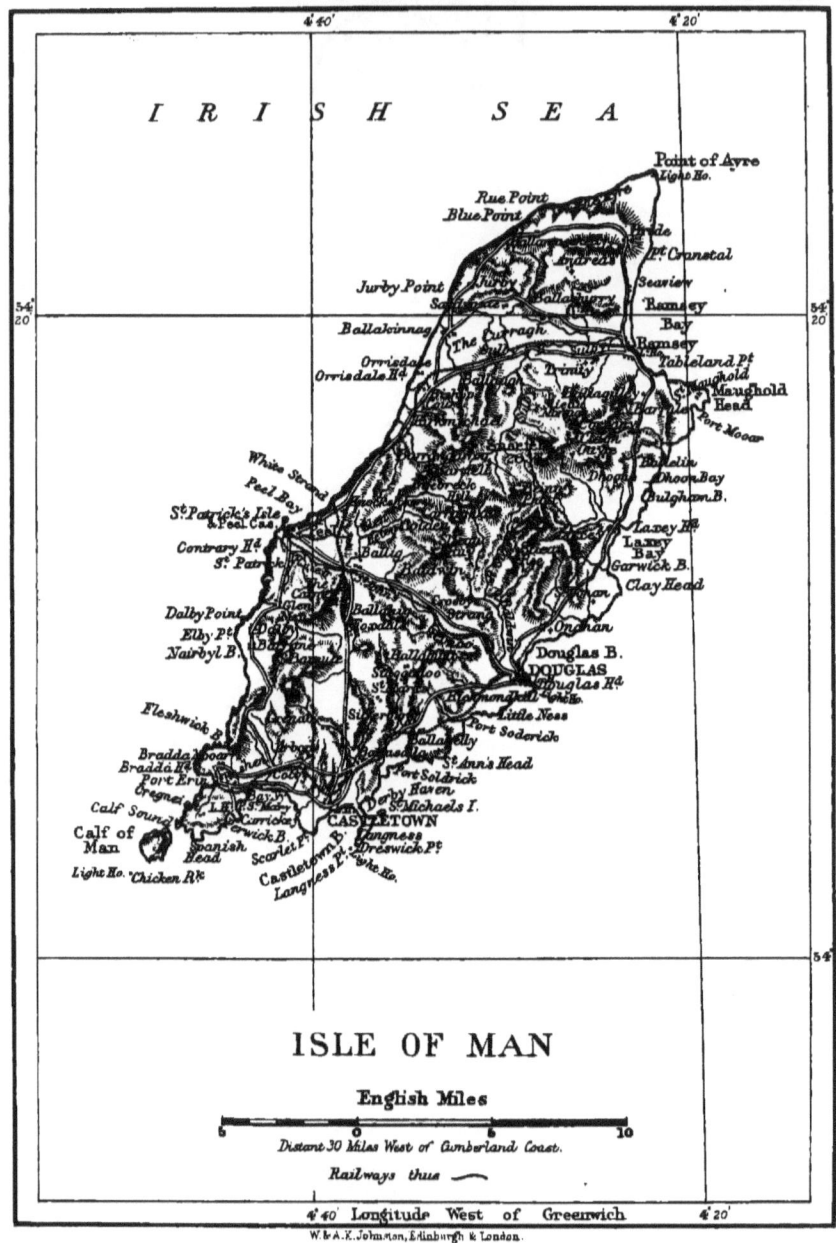

ISLE OF MAN

English Miles

Distant 30 Miles West of Cumberland Coast.

Railways thus

# PART VI.

# BRITISH POSSESSIONS IN EUROPE.

## ISLE OF MAN, OR MONA.

POSITION.—The Isle of Man occupies a central position in the Irish Sea, being nearly equi-distant from England, Scotland, and Ireland. It is situated between the parallels of latitude 54° 3′, and 54° 25′ north of the Equator; longitude 4° 18″, and 4° 47″ west of Greenwich.

AREA AND SHAPE.—This lovely island, which has been compared by Mr. Hall Caine to a "Manxman's Carrane" (pointed-toed shoe), is 34 miles long—north-east to south-west—from the Point of Ayre to Chicken Rock Lighthouse, and from 10 to 12 miles broad. In other words, it is an irregularly-shaped parallelogram. The total area is 230 square miles.

PHYSICAL FEATURES.—Those who have not visited Manxland have certainly missed one of the brightest spots in the British Isles. Mr. Hall Caine in his pamphlet, "The Little Man Island," says: "All islands are beautiful, when looked upon from the sea; but I know of nothing so lovely as the Isle of Man when you approach it from the English side towards the fall of night. The sun is then going down behind it, and from point to point the land lies grey on the blue line of the horizon, breaking it like the dim ghost of a snowstorm on a summer's evening. Coming nearer, the grey strengthens, the blue deepens, and the island sits on the water like a sea-gull in the late sunshine. As you get closer, and the sun dips behind the land, the mountains become purple, and a haze lies at your feet over a multitude of little peaks which you know to be the spires and towers of a town. Closer still, the spires and towers are thrown up into the luminous air, and the vast glass domes of Douglas catch the dying glory of the sky."

So it is that this island comprehends all the physical beauties of the British Isles with the exception of lakes. "It has a high, rockbound coast, rivalling in height and in grandeur of form the highest and wildest parts of the Western Coasts of Scotland or Ireland, against which the restless, changeful sea frets and foams ; with rugged cliffs and huge promontories, whose weather-blackened crags are hollowed by the waves into far-reaching caves, and narrow winding passages, and upon whose shelving ledges are perched myriads of sea-birds of various form and plumage. Above this Cyclopean sea-wall, the land slopes upwards into the mountainous interior ; the lower parts rich with cultivation, and thickly dotted with villa, farm, and cottage ; the higher parts green with perennial pasture ; the uplands a blaze of yellow gorse, or dark with purple heath, and weather-stained rock ; and above all, the long series of mountain peaks soaring high into the bright sunny air." [1]

This rugged coast-line is broken at intervals with sylvan glens of rare beauty through which sparkling streams find their way to the ocean. Far away in the mountains there are other fairylike glens and valleys ; such as Glen Rushen in the West ; Ravensdale, or Sulby Glen, or Glen Auldyn in the North ; or Balline, or Cornah, or Laxey Glen in the

---

[1] From "Manxland as a Holiday Resort," published by the Official Board of Advertising, Isle of Man.

## ISLE OF MAN, OR MONA.

East; or the Baldwin Glens, or Glen Moar, and the Rhenass Valley, or Glen Helen in the centre. The sides of these glens are mountain slopes, varying in height from 1,000 to 2,000 feet, and covered with heath, gorse, or trees,

*Bradda Head, Isle of Man.*

with here and there waterfalls and streamlets, flowing from above to perfect the ever-varying scenery.

MOUNTAINS AND HILLS.—From this description, it will be seen that the surface of the Isle of Man presents rich and varying features of mountain, hill, valley, and wooded glen. The chief heights are Snaefell, 2,034 feet; and other peaks are Injebreck, Mount Murray, Pen-y-phot, Cronk-ny-Indy Thaa, North and South Barrules, and the Greeba Hills. The famous Tynwald Hill, between Peel and Douglas, is the scene of the ancient open-air Parliament held each year on old Midsummer Day, July 5th, when nearly the whole of the inhabitants assemble to hear the Governor, the Bishop, and the Senior Deemster proclaim the laws in English, and in Manx, after a short religious service has been held in St. John's Church near by. The day is concluded as a general midsummer fair or holiday, in which officials, visitors, and people, all enter into the amusements provided for this annual gathering.

RIVERS.—These are small in size, but exceedingly picturesque, and they afford excellent fishing; trout and other small fish being most plentiful. Unfortunately, the Glenfaba, or Santon Burn, one of the most beautiful streamlets, has of late been poisoned by the washings from the Foxdale lead mines; but the Silver Burn which flows from South Barrule Hills; the Neb passing through Glen Helen; the Sulby River, which enters the Irish Sea at Ramsey; the Laxey from Snaefell; and the Glass, which forms Douglas Harbour, still remain in their primitive beauty and freshness.

CLIMATE.—In spite of the old legend that, in olden days, Mannanin, the famous magician, lived alone on the island by concealing it under a cloud of mist, the climate is in these days simply perfect. The air is dry, clear, and bracing, and there is almost perpetual sunshine. Its winter temperature is higher than that of Ventnor, in the Isle of Wight, and the island is remarkably free from sudden storms, or changes of a severe nature.

SOIL AND AGRICULTURE.—The soil is not only productive in the valleys and lowlands, but the inhabitants are most industrious, so that they make the most of their advantages. Corn, flax, pulse, potatoes, and vegetables are the chief productions.

The influence of the climate on vegetation here has been ably set forth by the President of the Natural History and Antiquarian Society, Dr. Tellet, F.E.G.S., who states:— "Exotic trees and plants . . . which have to be kept under glass—at anyrate during the winter months—grow and

*South Stack Light, Holyhead.*

flourish in the open air in the Isle of Man. I might instance the veronica, escallonia, macrantha, and the fuchsia, which thrives in almost any situation. The cordyline, Australis, Ti, or cabbage tree, introduced from New Zealand, grows to the height of twenty feet. The chanthus and geranium may be seen growing against walls, while the palm will grow in sheltered situations; the camellia, too, is quite hardy, and quite recently was in full bloom in February."

ANIMALS.—All the domestic animals of England are found here. Black cattle, sheep, horses, and goats are numerous. The elk and wild goat were once the undisputed rangers of the many hills, but civilisation has long since caused them to become extinct.

POLITICAL DIVISIONS.—The island is divided into six "sheadings" or counties, each of which is placed under the superintendence of a coroner, or civil officer. The three Northern sheadings are Ayre, Garff, and Kirk Michael; the three Southern sheadings are Middle, Rushen, and Glenfaba.

TOWNS.—The four towns are:—*Douglas*, the capital and largest town, now the seat of Government, on the East Coast; *Ramsey*, a quaint and pretty port on the North-East Coast; *Peel*, on St. Patrick's Isle, with its grand old ruins of the Castle and ancient Cathedral of St. Germain, on the West Coast; and *Castletown*, the ancient capital, also on the Coast, to the extreme South of the island. Of late years these interesting towns have been connected with a railway. Other rising places are Laxey, Port Erin, and Port S. Mary.

PEOPLE.—The Manx are a Celtic people, hardy, honest, and industrious. They are as much at home in their herring-boats as tilling their soil, so that they combine the sturdy hardihood of the mariner with the contented nature of the landsman; and, above all things, they love their island home and its primitive life and customs.

LANGUAGE.—This is a dialect of Erse, or Gaelic, mixed with Norwegian. It is called Manx. (*See* p. 87.)

GOVERNMENT.—The island is governed by a Lieutenant-Governor, who holds office under the Crown of Great Britain. He is ably assisted by a court of officials, forming one House of Parliament; and besides there is a House of

Keys, or Parliament of the People. These together form the Tynwald or Open-air Parliament, which is one of the most ancient legislative customs of the civilised world. All bills, after passing both Houses, receive the Royal assent, but do not become law until delivered in both the English and Manx languages on the Tynwald Hill.

REVENUE.—The public revenue, according to Whitaker, in 1896-7, was £77,287; and the public expenditure was £69,778; while the public debt amounted to £284,352.

RELIGION.—The island forms a diocese of the English Church under the title of Sodor and Man.

COMMERCE.—The trade of the island chiefly consists in exporting the productions, *viz.*, excellent lead, zinc, and slate, building stone, cattle, wool, hides, and herrings. The imports are the same as Great Britain.

HISTORY.—Few countries can boast of a more romantic past than this island, which has come down to us with its ancient constitution, legislature, and language, which was once the national tongue of Great Britain; its quaint folk lore; its antiquities; its Celtic Ogham inscriptions and Scandinavian runes, carrying us back to the earlier ages of Christian worship, and even to the heathen habits of a wild and uncivilised earlier period. By strange links the early history is connected with that of the Hebrides, and the kingdoms of Scotland, and Scandinavia. The old Norwegian pirates formed a settlement in the Western Isles of Scotland, and the Isle of Man, whose kings reigned supreme at Rushen Castle, and became most prosperous, until in 1263 the Scotch king, Alexander III., defeated their great chief, Haco, at Largs. Henry IV. of England seized the Isle of Man, and gave it to his favourite, Stanley, the ancestor of the present Earl of Derby. From them it passed to the Atholl family, until, in 1765, the English Parliament purchased the island for £70,000.

# THE CHANNEL ISLANDS.

NAMES.—The Channel Islands are the only remaining portion of the ancient Duchy of Normandy still retained by the Crown of Great Britain. These beautiful islands are not colonies. They belong to the Queen of England as the representative of the ancient Dukes of Normandy. Hence they are governed by their own laws, and the British Parliament rarely interferes with the internal affairs of Government. They are directly under the control of the Lieutenant Governor, who represents the Crown of Britain; and all business matters are transacted directly through the Home Office, and not through the Secretary of State for the Colonies. Professor Freeman describes this state of things thus :—" Practically, the islands have, during all changes, remained attached to the English Crown; but they have never been incorporated with the kingdom." ("Historical Geography of Europe," chap. xiii.)

The chief islands are Jersey, Guernsey, Alderney, Sark, Herm, Jethou, Little Sark, the Caskets, with smaller ones.

AREA.—The area of the whole group is 73 square miles.

POPULATION.—In 1891, 92,272, which gives the remarkably high average per square mile of 1,264 persons.

POSITION.—Alderney, the nearest island of the group, is situated 60 miles south of Portland Bill, and 7 miles west from Cape La Hague on the French Coast.

CLIMATE.—Very mild, and remarkably free from extremes of heat and cold. Snow seldom falls; there is an abundant rain supply, and strong sea-breezes make them

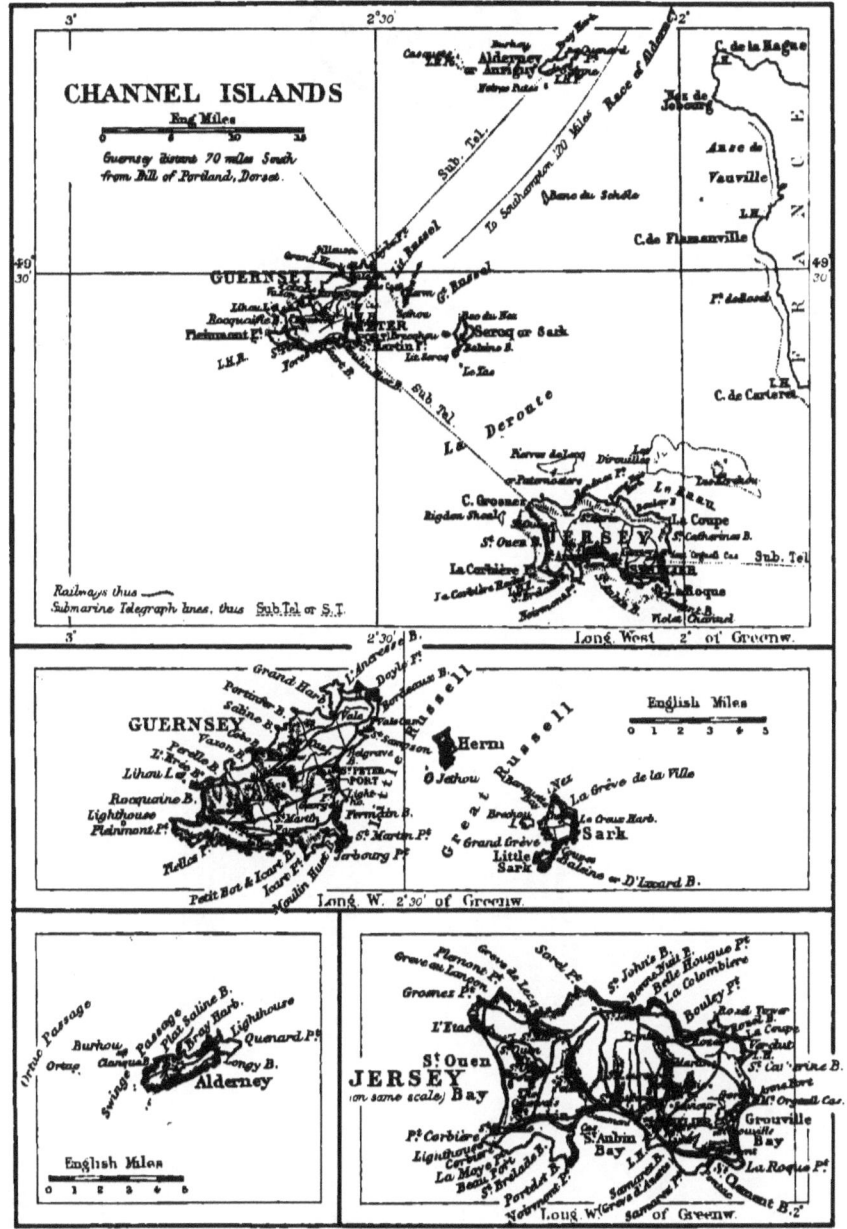

healthy. Hence they are attractive to visitors, and invalids resort here when other places are unsuitable.

PEOPLE AND LANGUAGE.—The inhabitants certainly resemble the French, more than the English, in language and manners. A large number of English people have settled in the islands, but these have unconsciously become a part of the older inhabitants, so far as habits and customs go. The native language is a broken Norman *patois*. The principal, or official, tongue is French; but English is understood in all parts.

RELIGION.—The State Religion is the Church of England. These islands are included in the Diocese of Winchester.

TRADE AND COMMERCE.—These are so important that the local taxation has been reduced considerably, and the islands are in a high state of prosperity by reason of the zeal and industry of the inhabitants. The passenger and goods traffic from England alone requires two daily steamboat services from Southampton (L. & S.W.R.) and Weymouth (G.W.R.); besides occasionally others during the summer months from London, Plymouth, etc.

GOVERNMENT.—In civil matters the Governor is assisted by the local legislature called "The States," the Crown Officer of which is called "The Bailiff," who presides over the fifty members, clerical and lay, constituting the Government. The Royal Court consists of twelve jurats elected by the inhabitants, and these form the judicial court.

HISTORY.—These islands were added to Normandy by the old sea-pirates, or Northmen, as early as the ninth century. By the Norman Conquest of England they became the home possessions of the Conqueror Dukes. Since 1066, they have remained a possession of the English Crown; although the French have repeatedly tried to regain them. In 1120, *The White Ship*, with Prince William and his sister, the children of Henry I., and more than a hundred young nobles, perished on the treacherous Casket Rocks; and upon the same spot in 1744, the *Victory*, with 110 guns and 1,100 men, went down. Jersey proved a refuge for the Earl of Richmond, afterwards Henry VII., in his flight after the Battle of Tewkesbury in 1471; and at a later date Charles II. visited this island during his exile. In 1781, St. Heliers, the capital of Jersey, was taken by the French, who held it for a short period, when it was retaken by the English. William IV. landed in Guernsey in 1831; and in August, 1846, Queen Victoria and Prince Albert visited the island, when the Victoria Tower was erected to commemorate the event.

## JERSEY.

This is the largest and chief island of the group, being about 45 square miles in area. It is situated about 15 miles from the French Coast. In shape it is quadrangular. The greatest length, from East to West, being 12 miles, and the breadth from North to South is about 7 miles.

Coast-line.—The coast-line is much indented, and there are several good harbours. Its length is 47 miles. The rocks on the coast are broken and generally precipitous; on the north side they rise to some 200 feet above the sea level. The approach to the island is extremely dangerous owing to the great number of small islands and hidden rocks which surround the coasts.

The Surface.—The interior is undulating and well diversified by woodland and streamlets, which, added to the rugged coast scenery, makes the island both picturesque and beautiful.

Agriculture and Productions.—A rich and productive soil well cultivated gives the whole island the appearance of one vast garden plot, in which fruit, flowers, vegetables

*Corbière Light, Jersey.*

and corn flourish. An active trade is maintained with England in vegetables, fruits, and flowers of nearly every kind. The domestic animals are excellent, including the famous Alderney and Jersey cows, small horses, pigs, sheep, and goats, and other English and French pets. The fisheries of Jersey are of great value. Lobster, cod, and oysters are abundant.

POLITICAL DIVISIONS.—The island is divided into parishes; the chief being St. Heliers, St. Owen, St. Lawrence, St. Clement, St. John, St. Brelade, St. Mary, St. Martin, St. Saviour, St. Peter, Trinity and Grouville, so named respectively after the churches standing in them.

TOWNS.—The chief towns are St. Heliers—the capital, which is a busy seaport, as well as a fashionable watering-place—St. Aubyn ranking next in importance, and there are numerous smaller places.

COMMERCE.—This is extensive, and increasing each year. Cattle, potatoes, oysters, cider, fruit, fish, and dairy produce are exported; while the inhabitants import woollen and cotton goods, machinery, glass and china, English manufactures, and hardware; wine and spirits from France, also colonial produce.

The population in 1891 was 54,518.

## GUERNSEY.

THE ancient Roman *Sarmia* is the "Green Isle" or Queen of the Group for both climate and coast scenery. It is about 9 miles long, 4 miles broad, with a circumference of about 27 miles, and an area of 24 square miles. The shape is an irregular triangle, with its longest side pointing from N.E. to S.W., and it possesses a similar coast-line to Jersey, only that the steep and dangerous rocks lie upon the southern side.

AGRICULTURE.—This is similar to Jersey. The chief feature which strikes a stranger is the division of the land into small holdings or farms, which elsewhere might hinder the prosperity of the inhabitants, but here by their energy and industry it is made both productive and profitable.

POLITICAL DIVISIONS.—Here the same arrangement of parishes, or districts, as in Jersey is met with, the principal being St. Peter Port, St. Saviour, St. Sampson, St. Peter in the Wood, St. Martin, St. Andrew, The Vale, The Forest, Câtel, and Torteval.

TOWNS.—St. Pierre, or St. Peter Port is the capital. It stands upon an excellent harbour, in a sheltered position upon the Eastern, or French Coast, side of the island. Other places are Torteval, Câtel, etc. The people, language, commerce, and trade are similar to Jersey.

The population in 1891, with Herm and Jethou Islands, was 35,339.

## ALDERNEY

ranks the third island in size of the Channel group. The French call it *Aurigny;* but its ancient Roman name was *Arinia*. It is only 4 square miles in area, being but 4 miles long, and 1½ miles broad, with a coast-line of nearly 12 miles.

The Channel, separating Alderney from the French Coast, is about 7 miles wide. It is called the Race of Alderney. The surface of this island is much elevated. The rocks on the coast are high and dangerous, and the whole island is surrounded with sunken rocks and small islands, of which the well-known group called *The Casquets* are the most formidable. The chief towns are St. Anne's and Brayé.

The population in 1891 was 1,857.

## SARK.

*Sark, from the West Coast.*

THE beautiful island of Sark, also called *Serk* or *Serq*, is another of the Channel Islands lying 6½ miles eastward of Guernsey. It consists of Great and Little Sark, which are united by a narrow neck or rock nearly 200 feet in height, and called "*The Coupée.*" The scenery here is simply magnificent. On either side the sea stretches out far and wide, while the numerous rocks which skirt the coast and make it dangerous to vessels, cause the waves to lash with fury upon the narrow belt of land as though they were threatening its immediate destruction.

This island is strangely weird and beautiful in its aspect, whether we view it from the land or from the sea. It consists only of one parish, and the inhabitants are fishermen, although they are largely employed in the cultivation of corn, vegetables, and fruit at such times as they are not engaged upon the water. The population in 1891 was 570.

IMPERIAL BRITAIN.     MAP XIV.

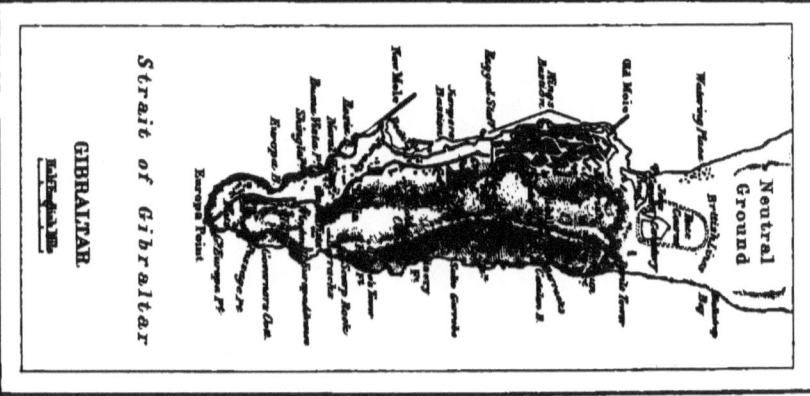

# GIBRALTAR.

NAME.—The ancient name for the strong, rocky peninsula which forms the western gate to the Mediterranean Sea was *Jebel Tarik*, or the "Rock of Tarik." From the map it will be seen that this impregnable fortress stands in a remarkable position. It is of the highest commercial value and maritime importance to Great Britain, inasmuch as it forms the principal key to the East by water through the Mediterranean Sea and the Suez Canal, while it secures our authority and upholds our power among the other maritime nations of Europe.

POSITION AND EXTENT.—The rock of Gibraltar is about two square miles in area. It forms a narrow, rocky promontory at the southern extremity of Spain, about three miles long and nearly three-quarters of a mile wide. It is connected with the mainland on the northern side by a narrow, sandy isthmus, which is known as "The Neutral Ground." Its southern end is called Europa Point, and its western shore forms one side of the Bay of Gibraltar, where

*Gibraltar.*

stands, or rather nestles, the busy seaport town so strongly protected by the overhanging garrison, lodged like a devouring bird of prey in the forbidding rocks above. The Strait, or narrow channel, of Gibraltar, which separates Europe from Northern Africa, is only about 15 miles wide.

GENERAL FEATURES.—The rocks of Gibraltar are a hard, grey, limestone marble. They are full of holes and caves, and the surface is both broken and precipitous. If we view the promontory from the sea, the rocks look bare, but they are fairly covered with vegetation, which serves to shelter large numbers of hawks, sea-birds, etc., while a strange family of tailless monkeys, or fawn-coloured Barbary apes, inhabit the numerous caves in company with rabbits, snakes, etc. In places the rocks rise abruptly from the sea to the height of 1,500 feet, and they are only accessible upon the western side. Fortified galleries have been made in the rocks at varying heights connecting the caves for a distance of more than two miles, and these gallery roads, protected by rock-bound walls on either side, are sufficiently wide to allow a wagon to pass along loaded with ammunition, or stores, to the batteries and fortifications above. At intervals of a few yards along the galleries port-holes have been cut through the outer rocks, and large guns mounted to guard the bay, and the neutral ground on the Spanish side. The crest of the rock also is an immense fortress, where about 1,000 cannon guard the entrance to the Mediterranean. A garrison is kept here of 5,300 men, yet so well planned are the arrangements that scarcely a gun can be detected, with the exception of a few placed upon the lower shore batteries. At night the scene is somewhat more enlivened by the many lines of dotted lights, which show the position of the barracks, forts, etc.; but as a visitor in the *Standard* has lately written: "It is only when he lands that the voyager discovers he has become a resident in a fortress, from whence, unless he behaves remarkably well, he may be turned out at very short notice. The custom-house does not trouble him, for Gibraltar is practically a free port. But is he a British subject? If not, he must get a pass from the town major, and if he wishes to remain a consul, or householder, must be surety for his conduct. If he wishes to visit the upper galleries, where nestle long rows of guns, he will have to get a pass from the Assistant Military Secretary; to see the lower ones only the Governor can grant leave. He cannot carry arms nor sketch, neither must he meddle with the monkeys, animals which are more frequently talked of than seen. . . . . . . . Everywhere there is order and prudent caution. Weapons of war are in every nook, or in carefully-labelled sheds. Cannon stand sedately behind clumps of aloes, or appear grimly where the pedestrian imagines he is only peeping into a dusty little garden. The narrow Waterport Street is full of soldiers; the best buildings are for their shelter, amusement, or instruction. At sundown the gates of Gibraltar are closed, and in or out no man can go until they are opened next morning. The gun-fire which wakes the sleeper is the signal for the toils of another day to begin. The gates are opened, and more than 2,000 people pour in from Spain to work; the band plays, and the tinkle-tinkle of the belled flocks of goats, driven from door to door to be milked, proclaim that Gibraltar has once more permitted civil life to exist for another twelve hours."

CLIMATE.—The climate is naturally hot and dry in summer, although the sea-breezes make it refreshing to Englishmen. In the winter it is pleasantly mild. The water supply is limited. Numbers of the houses have flat roofs to catch the rain as it falls, with tanks sunk below the surface to preserve and store the water for future use.

*Street in Gibraltar.*

THE TOWN is a free port, depot, and coaling station for vessels, some 7,000 of which call each year. It is built on the western side of the rock, nearly at its base. There are three principal streets running parallel to each other in which the buildings are marked by both English and Spanish architecture. The chief buildings are the Government Office, the Garrison, the Soldier's Institute and Home. A pleasant garden, called the Alameda, is situated in the centre of the town, in which may be found prickly pears and palms, white poplars, and pines, with figs and pomegranates among many smaller plants. Many of the officials have made small gardens near their houses by collecting soil upon the rock.

INHABITANTS.—The population in 1891 was 26,050, inclusive of a garrison of 5,300. The people are of a mixed character, consisting of English, Spanish, Moors, and Genoese. Both English and Spanish are spoken by the inhabitants.

GOVERNMENT.—Gibraltar is under the military rule of the Governor, who is an officer appointed by the Crown of Great Britain. The Government expenses are met in part by port duties, and the rents of property built by the Government. The town was made a Bishop's See in 1842. The diocese includes the English populations in Southern Europe, principally those surrounding the Mediterranean Sea.

HISTORY.—The town and promontory originally belonged to the Spanish, or more correctly speaking, the Moors in Spain. It was taken by the English in 1704, during the war of the Spanish Succession, and they have held possession since that time, notwithstanding several desperate attempts to recapture it, *e.g.*, 1789-93.

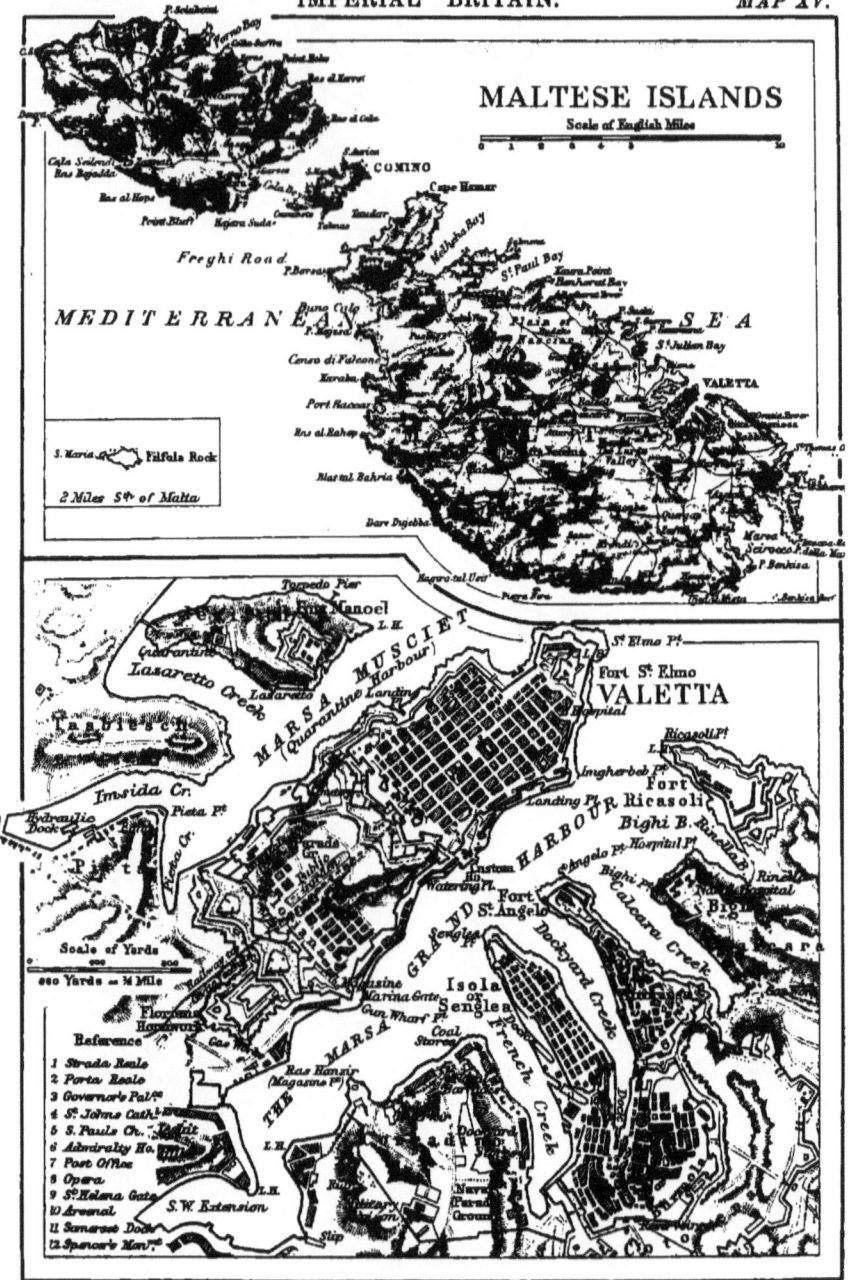

# THE MALTESE ISLANDS.

NAME AND POSITION.—This small group of islands occupy a central position in the Mediterranean Sea, lying midway between Europe and Africa, at a distance of 60 miles from the Island of Sicily, and 180 miles from the Northern Coast of Africa. This splendid position places Malta upon the direct trade route with India and the East of Asia. More than 6,000 vessels call here each year, and, in addition, the excellent harbour of Valetta forms the central station of the British Fleet in the Mediteranean.

*Valetta Harbour, Malta.*

The chief island is Malta, the ancient Melita, where St. Paul suffered shipwreck on his last journey to Rome as a prisoner (Acts xxvii.); and the group includes, besides Gozo and Comino Islands, with two smaller ones, Cominotto, or Little Comino, an islet off the West Coast of Comino, and the Rocks of Filfola and St. Maria lying off the South Coast of Malta.

AREA AND EXTENT.—The combined area of the Maltese Group is about 117 square miles, Malta alone being 95 square miles; Gozo 20 square miles; and Comino, Cominotto, and Filfola from 2 to 2⅓ square miles. Authorities differ as to the length and breadth of Malta. The Government chart makes it about 18½ miles long, by 8½ miles wide; but the extreme width is about 9½ miles in one part.

GENERAL FEATURES.—The islands are chiefly composed of limestone rock, late Eocene or Miocene period, and undoubtedly at a comparatively recent geological period they were joined to the mainland of both Europe and Africa.

Malta is of an irregular oval shape, and its uneven, rugged surface from the coast to the interior may be described as more hilly than mountainous. The calcareous rocks of the coast, in many parts, present a somewhat wild and sterile appearance as they are approached from the sea. In some places on the South Coast these limestone rocks reach to a height of from 300 to 400 feet; and here there are but few harbours. On the contrary, the North and East Coasts are low, and indented with bays or harbours as follows:—

On the North Coast the bays are Mellilia, St. Paul, St. George, St. Julian, with Grand (Valetta) Harbour and Quarantine Harbour. On the East Coast the chief harbour is Marsa Scirocco or South-East Harbour.

Although the surface of the interior is so hilly, it is a strange feature that neither rivers nor streams are to be met with. The highest point of Malta is 730 feet above the sea-level, near to the village of Dingli.

Lying off the North-West Coast of Malta is the small island of Comino, which is still more barren in appearance, inasmuch as it is composed largely of rocks; and still beyond this island lies Gozo, presenting a similar landscape in general features to Malta, with the exception that the

## THE MALTESE ISLANDS. 277

coast-line is steep and rocky throughout. Cominotto, or Little Comino, and Filfola are other rocky islets of this

*Grand Harbour, Valetta.*

group. The narrow straits dividing the islands are called the North and the South Channels.

CLIMATE.—Snow and frost are practically unknown in these islands. The lowest winter temperature registers about 40°-42°. During the summer and autumn there are hot winds, but not of sufficient power to destroy the vegetation, as is generally supposed; so that on the whole they may be considered warm and healthy, resembling more the climate of Northern Africa than Southern Europe. Of late years much has been done to perfect sanitation, and to improve the water supply of the islands, which is naturally limited; the only sources being the natural springs and the artificial collecting rain-tanks, arranged for storage in many parts. The rainy season comes in late autumn, and the change it produces over the whole island is marvellous; for vegetation, which remains dormant during the dry season, as with us in winter, starts again into vigorous and sudden growth.

SOIL AND AGRICULTURE.—It is generally supposed that the soil of Malta was in the past imported from Sicily or Italy, and, so strong has the fiction become, that many text-books assert this as the truth. What has been, and still is, imported is a volcanic product, called "puzzolana," a reddish earth, which is used by the natives for several purposes. The soil of the island is natural to the island. All that has been done has been to collect it from the clefts and depressions where it was not required, and to spread it out in a thick layer in suitable places to form new fields and gardens, or to increase in size those already in existence. The fields of Malta are all small in size, and they are formed by constructing terraces upon the sloping hill sides, being divided by stone walls very similar in appearance to those met with in Ireland. Although the conditions of agriculture are somewhat difficult in operation, the great industry and enterprise of the inhabitants, coupled with the delightful climate following the rainy season, quite make up for all drawbacks, so that it may be considered very good indeed.

PRODUCTIONS.—The products of Malta include all the fruits of Italy and Southern Europe, such as oranges, lemons, grapes, figs, olives, early potatoes, corn, and numerous vegetables.

The once famous Maltese dog is now virtually extinct as a breed in Malta; most of the present dogs are mongrels. There are many kinds of migratory birds, the chief being the quail; but of resident birds there are not many species. Asses and goats are numerous (in 1893, there were 23,932 goats in the islands); and wild bees still frequent all parts.

PEOPLE.—The population in 1896 was about 176,000, excluding the garrison, which numbers about 10,000 more English and Maltese, who are employed by the Government. The average population is well over 1,500 per square mile, which places Malta in the front rank as to density of population among the countries of Europe. Four-fifths of the inhabitants are Maltese, who claim to be descendants of the Phœnicians. Through the knights of St. John of Malta, no doubt they can claim "relationship" with all the nations of Europe, and more especially with the Spanish race. They are remarkable for their frugal and industrious habits, being both courageous and active, and possessing a natural love for the sea, which they regard as their home, second to their beloved island, which they proudly call "Fior del Mondo," or the "Flower of the World." As a race, the Maltese are short in stature, with dark complexions. Their chief employment consists of the cultivation of the island, and they are generally good as cabinetmakers, boat-builders, etc. Lace is still largely made by the women and girls; filigree jewellery is also produced in large quantities. A good number of men and boys are engaged as sailors, while Maltese porters and attendants are to be met with in all the principal Mediterranean ports.

Towns.—The chief town is Valetta, situated upon the Grand Harbour, which opens out to the north-east side of the island. It is the chief naval station of the British Fleet in the Mediterranean, besides being a highly important commercial and coaling station, where a large transit trade is carried on with the Mediterranean ports, both on the European and the African shores. Besides the town of Valetta, there is an arsenal and dockyard, with strong fortifications. The trade and commerce are considerable. There is a railway from this port to the ancient capital, Citta Vecchia, situated in the interior of the island. The mails are sent from London *via* Brindisi.

Exports and Imports.—Malta exports early potatoes, onions, oranges, lemons, lace, jewellery, and fancy articles. Cotton is no longer exported from the island. The imports consist of English and foreign manufactured goods; wood from Austria; charcoal from Italy and Sicily; food supplies, coal, cutlery, bicycles, and machinery of all sorts from Great Britain.

Government.—This is in great measure representative. The Governor, who is *ex-officio* President of the Malta Council, called *the Council of Government*, is appointed by the Crown. He is assisted by a council of twenty members, of whom six are official, and fourteen elected. There is also an Executive Council, which deals with all matters relating to the laws and government of the island.

Religion.—The Maltese are Roman Catholics, and they are under the supervision of the Roman Catholic Bishop of Malta. Owing to the large number of British residents on the islands, this group forms a part of the English Church Diocese of Gibraltar; but the Bishop only visits

Malta from time to time for his official duties, when occasionally he is the guest of the Governor.

HISTORY.—These islands were first colonised by the Phœnicians; but they have passed in succession from them to the Greeks, Carthaginians, Romans, and Saracens. The latter were driven out by the Normans, who retained possession of them for a considerable period. Charles V. ceded them to the Knights of St. John of Jerusalem in 1530. In 1565, the Turks besieged Malta for four months without success. The Knights of St. John gave up possession to Napoleon I. (Buonaparte) in 1798. They were surrendered by the French to Great Britain in 1800, and by the Treaty of Paris, 1814, they finally became a British possession.

# CYPRUS.

POSITION AND EXTENT.—The Island of Cyprus lies in the North-Eastern angle of the Mediterranean Sea, with the coast-line of Asia Minor, some 60 miles distant, on its Northern side, and Syria, 41 miles distant, upon its Eastern end. In shape, it has been described as an irregular parallelogram, with its North-Eastern corner much elongated; but it really more resembles, roughly, a lizard than a regular figure.

The area of the island is 3,584 square miles; the greatest length is 140 miles; and the extreme breadth is nearly 60 miles. The port of Larnaka, on the Southern Coast, is 258 miles from Port Said; and 1,117 miles from Malta. It is the third largest island in the Mediterranean.

GENERAL FEATURES.—Cyprus is certainly a mountainous island. There are two distinct mountain ranges running parallel to each other. The one which extends along the Northern shore, called the Carpas, or Kyrenia Mountains, reaches from the North-Eastern point, Cape St. Andrea, to Cape Kormakiti. The highest point is Mount Buffaventa. This range presents a bold and rugged appearance from the sea, so that this coast contains but few bays or inlets. The second range, in the Southern part of the island, has numerous spurs running at right angles to the main chain upon the Southern side, between which small streamlets —for rivers there are none of importance—rush downward to the sea. Between these two mountain ranges extends the fertile plain of Mesaoria, through which flows the Pedias, and the Potamos streams, the largest in the island. The highest peaks are in this Southern range, *e.g.*, Mount

IMPERIAL BRITAIN.  MAP XVI.

# CYPRUS
Scale of English Miles

*Marina, Larnaka, Cyprus*

Troödos, 6,406 feet (the ancient Olympus); Mount Paputsa, Mount Makhæras, and Mount Stavrovuni.

The coast is naturally bold, and there are fine bays, the chief being Morphou Bay, Famagusta Bay, Larnaka Bay, Akrotiri Bay, with the Gulfs of Episkopi and Khrysokhu. The Capes are St. Andrea, Græco, Gatto, Levgari, Arnauti, and Kormakiti.

CLIMATE.—The range of temperature taken in the shade at Nicosia, 509 feet above the sea, is from 110° to 30°, giving a mean temperature of about 70°. The average rainfall is 17 inches, occurring chiefly in the winter months; but the island suffers severely from drought during the hot weather. On the whole, the climate may be considered both genial and healthy, if we consider the latitude—and this is in great part owing to the sea-breezes—and the altitude of a large portion of the surface.

SOIL AND AGRICULTURE.—In ancient times there were important copper mines, but these have been discontinued for hundreds of years, and the present inhabitants know nothing of the valuable yield of other days. The chief products are now agricultural: wheat, barley, olives, grapes, and carobs or locust beans, are largely cultivated, and the latter are exported to England. Madder, cotton, aniseed, sesame, and silk are produced in smaller quantities. The principal drawbacks to agriculture in Cyprus are—the scarcity of water by reason of the deficient rainfall, and the occasional visits of swarms of locusts, which devour everything before them. To help the former, a new system of irrigation has been established, and every precaution is taken to destroy the young locusts, so that a more hopeful future is looked for, as the soil is rich and fertile. The chief animals of Cyprus are horses, mules, donkeys, cattle, sheep, and goats, and about 1,200 camels are used as beasts of burden. The value of the sponge fisheries on the coast are estimated at

£20,000 per annum. The only wild animals are hares and rabbits, but reptiles and snakes are numerous.

Limasol, Cyprus.

PEOPLE.—The population of Cyprus in 1891 was 209,286. About three-fourths of the inhabitants belong to the

Greek Church, and there are a considerable number of Mahommedans.

The Cypriots, as the natives are called, are now in the minority. Both the Greeks, and the Turks, take the precedence in all matters of trade and the administration of government and law.

TOWNS.—The island is divided into six districts—Nicosia, Larnaka, Limasol, Famagusta, Papho, and Kyrenia—for administrative and legal purposes. "Each possesses a commissioner; a court of law, presided over by an English barrister, who is assisted by two native judges, one being Christian and the other Mahommedan. There is also a supreme court for the whole island, consisting of two English judges."—(*From* "Whitaker's Almanack," 1897.)

The capital is Nicosia (Lefkosia), in the centre of the island, with a population of 12,515. Excellent leather is manufactured here. Larnaka, 7,593, on the South Coast, is the chief port of the island. Limasol, 7,388, also on the South Coast, is chiefly noted for its trade in wine; and Famagusta, now a ruined city, was in earlier times the chief commercial port of the island. There are neither railways nor canals in Cyprus.

COMMERCE.—The chief trade is carried on with England, Turkey, Egypt, Austria, France, Russia, and Italy; and the principal exports are cattle and other animals, cheese, silk, sponges, wines, carobs or locust beans, fruit, wool, and cotton; while the imports are food supplies, manufactured goods, tobacco, colonial produce, timber, and machinery.

GOVERNMENT.—The island is governed as a Crown Colony of Great Britain. It is under the protection and administration of the British arms. "Still it forms part of the Ottoman Empire, but by virtue of a treaty made between England and the Porte, dated 4th of June, 1878, the government is administered by England for so long a time as Batoum and Kars may be kept by Russia." ("Whitaker's Almanack," 1897.) The High Commissioner, or Colonial Governor, is assisted by an executive council of officials. The Legislature consists of the Governor, 6 *ex-officio* members, and 12 elected members, *viz.*, 3 Mahommedans and 9 Christians.

RELIGION.—Both the Orthodox Greek Church and Mahommedanism are well represented, and the English Church people are under the care of the Bishop of Gibraltar. In 1892, 226 Christian and 108 Mahommedan primary schools were in working order. These were aided by Government grants, and attended, the former by 10,555, and the latter by 3,771, scholars.

HISTORY.—The earliest mention of Cyprus was in the 17th century B.C., when Thotmes III., King of Egypt, conquered the island. It next passed to the Phœnicians, the Assyrians, the Persians, and again to the Egyptians, who held it for 240 years, until in 57 B.C. it became a Roman province. In 45 A.D., St. Paul and St. Barnabas visited the island, when Sergius Paulus, the pro-consul, was converted, and Elymas, the sorcerer, was punished with blindness. The Saracens were the possessors for a long period. Richard I. of England defeated the Catapan and took possession of the island for insulting his bride-elect, Berengaria of Navarre, and they were afterwards married at Limasol. The Knights Templar purchased it from Richard I., but being too weak to govern the island, they restored it again to him, whereupon he gave it to Guy de Lusignan, a French crusader. The Lusignan dynasty ruled for nearly 300 years, when the Republic of Venice became masters of the island. In 1571, the Turks captured and became the rulers until the treaty in 1878, when for a second time it passed under the Crown of Great Britain. £5,000 a year are paid out of the revenue to the Sultan of Turkey, this being the sum supposed to represent the excess of revenue over expenditure in the island. Under the present Convention Treaty of 1878, by which England holds possession of Cyprus, at any time she may be called upon to evacuate and restore it to the Porte, as it is held conditionally to the claims of Russia upon Kars and Batoum in Armenia, by reason of conquest in the late war.

THE END.

*Printed by Cowan & Co., Limited, Perth.*

# INDEX.

## A

Aberdeenshire, 208
— Town, 220
Abbotsford, 214
Achill or Eagle Island, 226
Advantages and Uses of Colonies, 10
Agate, Scotch, 198
Agents-General in London, 8
Agricultural Returns, 92, 93
— Depression, 135
Agriculture, Government aid to, 135
— Great Britain and Ireland, 135, 197, 233
Alderney, 267
— Race of, 267
Alum and Jet, 131
American Independence War, 27
Anglesea, 107, 145
Angus, Dr., on English Tongue, 47
Animals, Wild, England and Wales, 136
— — Domestic, 137
— Scotland, Wild, 198
— — Domestic, 234
— Ireland, Wild, 234
— — Domestic, 199
Antimony and Manganese, 130
Archipelago, British, 48
Arctic Explorers, 25
Argyleshire, 210
Army, British, 57
— Board, 57
— Stations, 58
Arran Island, 185, 227
Ascension Island, Admiralty Possession, 7
Aubyns, St. (Jersey), 226
Ayrshire, 211

## B

Balmoral, 193, 208
Banff, 208
Bann, River, Ireland, 230
Barrow, River, Ireland, 230
Battlefields, England and Wales, 175
— Scotland, 221
— Ireland, 252
Battles, Naval, since 1066, 84
Bays and Inlets, England and Wales, 97-100
— Scotland, 179
— Ireland, 225
Bedfordshire, 159
Belfast, 246
Berkshire, 159
Berwickshire or Merse, 212
Birds, British, 136
Birmingham, 170
Blackdown Hills, 115
Blackwater, River, 230
Board of Trade Established, 26
Boundaries, England and Wales, 95
British Possessions, how Acquired, 4
— Flag Planting, 1
Broads, Norfolk, 124-126, 136
Brotherhood of Saint Thomas à Becket, 19
Bubble Bursting, South Sea, 27
Buckinghamshire, 159
Bullers, The, 201
Buteshire, 211
Bute, 185

## C

Cabinet, Gladstone's Definition of, 54
Cabot, John and Sebastian, Discovered New World, 22
Caithness, 205
Caledonian Canal, 190
Cambridgeshire, 158
Cambrian System, 113
Canals, 69

289 T

Capes and Headlands, England and Wales, 97-100
—— Scotland, 178
—— Ireland, 224
Cape Clear Island, 227
Castletown, Isle of Man, 260
Casquets, The, 267
Census Statistics, British Isles, 52
Central Hills, 114
Cereals and Roots, England and Wales, 134
—— Scotland, 200
—— Ireland, 237
Channel Islands, Names and Area, 108, 262
—— Population and Position, 262
—— Climate, 262
—— People and Language, 263
—— Trade and Commerce, 263
—— Government, 263
—— History, 263
Cheshire, 153
Cheviot Hills, 110
Chiltern Hills, 115
Church of England, 77
—— Scotland, 78
—— Ireland, 80, 250
Cinque Ports, 109
Clackmannan, 209
Clay for China, 132
Climate, British Isles, 49, 126
Clyde Falls, 201
Coal-Fields, England and Wales, 129
—— Scotland, 198
—— Ireland, 236
Coastline, England and Wales, 95
— Scotland, 178
— Ireland, 223
Coast Defence, British Isles, 108
— Safeguards, 108
Colonial Institute, 9
Colonies, Representative Government, 6
— Responsible Government, 6
— Crown, 6
Colony, Definition of, 5
Columbus, Christopher, and Discoverer of New World, 22
Comino Island, 275
Cominotto Island, 275
Commerce, 71, 203
Communication, Internal, 60, 200
— External, 70
Comparison, Army and Navy, with Foreign Powers, 56
Conacre or Tenant Right, 234
Constitution, British Empire, 6

Continent, Connexion with, 49
Coolie Labour, 3
Copper and Tin, 130
Cork, 246
Cornwall, 152
Cotswold Hills, 115
Coupée, The (Sark), 268
Counties, England, 143-146
— Scotland, 204
— Wales, 172
— Ireland, 239
County Council, 161
— Names, Derivation of, 147
Cromarty and Ross, 206
Cumberland, 155
Cumbrae, Great and Little, 185
Cumbrian Group, 112
Curiosities, Natural, England and Wales, 132
—— Scotland, 200
—— Ireland, 237
Cyprus Island, Position and Extent, 282
—— General Features, 282
—— Coast, 284
—— Climate, 284
—— Soil and Agriculture, 284
—— People, 285
—— Commerce, 286
—— Government, 286
—— Religion, 287
—— History, 287
—— Treaty, Turkey and England, 287, 288

D

Dates Table, British Possessions, 30-33
Dependency, Definition of, 5
Derbyshire, 155
Devil's Punch Bowl (Ireland), 238
Devonian Range, 114
Devonshire, 151
Distance Table, Ports, British Empire, 42
Dorsetshire, 151
Douglas, Isle of Man, 260
Downs, The, 115
Dublin, 242
Dumbartonshire, 210
Dumfriesshire, 214
Dundee, 220
Durham, 149

# INDEX. 291

## E

East Anglian Heights, 115
East India Company's Charter, 24
Edge Hills, 115
Edinburgh or Mid-Lothian, 212
Edinburgh City, 216
Education Acts, 81
— Elementary, 80, 202, 250
— Secondary, 85, 202, 250
— University, 80, 202, 250
— Grants, 81
— Inspector's Statistics, 81
Elements of British People, 43
Elgin, 206
Elizabethan Discoverers, 24
Ellen's Isle, 195
Emigration, 2
English Garden, 134
English Language, Origin of, 46
Essex, 150
Ethnology, Great Britain, 43, 138
Expenditure, National, 52
— Annual, of British Colonies, 3
Exports and Imports, 72, 139, 140, 141, 213, 251
Extent, British Isles, 50, 95

## F

Famagusta, Cyprus, 286
Father of English Commerce, (Edward III.), 20
Features, Natural, British Isles, 94
Federation, Imperial (John G. Colmer, Esq., C.M.G.), 15
Fifeshire, 208
Filfola Island, 275, 276, 277
Fingal's Cave, 200
Fior-del-Mondo (Malta), 279
First Merchant Ship to India, 23
Fish Markets, 74
Fisheries, Home, 75, 137, 199, 235
Fishermen, Our (H.R.H. Duke of Edinburgh), 75
Fleet, British, 58
Flemings' Early Settlement, Worsted, 19
Foreign Possessions, Great Britain, 3
Forests, 133, 200, 235
Forest Trees, 133, 200, 235
Forfarshire or Angus, 208
Foyers Fall, 201
Franklin, Sir John, 28
Free Trade, 136
— — Measure Island, 28
Fuller's Earth, 132

## G

Geikie's, Professor, Island Theory, 110
Geology, 236
German Merchants of the Steelyard, 19
Giant's Causeway, 237
Gibraltar, Name, Position, Extent, 269
— General Description, 271
— Garrison, 271
— Climate, 272
— Population, Inhabitants, 274
— Government, 274
— History, 274
Glasgow, 218
Gloucestershire, 153
Gog and Magog, 115
Government and Administration, British Empire, 5, 52, 202
Gozo Island, 275, 276
Granite, 131, 197
*Great Harry I.* (Henry V.), 21
Guernsey, 266
— Agriculture, 267
— Political Divisions, 267
— Population, 267

## H

Haddington or East Lothian, 212
Hampshire, 151
Hanseatic League, 20-24
Hartington, Lord : Description of British Empire, 7
Headlands and Capes, England and Wales, 97-100
— — Scotland, 178
— — Ireland, 224
Hebrides, The, 180-183
Heliers, St. (Jersey), 266
Herefordshire, 157
Hertfordshire, 159
Highlands, Farewell to (Sir W. Scott), 186
Hills, England and Wales, 114
— Scotland, 187
— Ireland, 228
Historical Events, Great Britain, 87-89
History of British Commerce, 19
Holyrood Palace, 216
Home Control, 8
House of Commons, 54
— of Lords, 54
Hudson Bay Company, 25
Huntingdonshire, 158

## I

Immigration, British Isles, 3
Imperial Institute, 9
Imports and Exports, British Isles, 72, 139, 140, 141, 203, 251
India Conquest—Clive, Hastings, Wellesley, 27
— Overland Route to, 13, 28, 29
Inhabitants, British Empire, 1
Insects, 137
Inverness, 206, 220
Ireland, 223
— Name, Shape, Area, Extent, Position, Coastline, 223
— Physical Features, 228
— Climate, Soil, and Agriculture, 233
— Natural Productions, 234
— Population, 238
— Industries, 241
— Government, 248
— Revenue and Commerce, 250
— History, 251
Iron, 130, 198
Islands, of the World, Comparison, 48
— Smaller Coast, England and Wales, 51, 102
— Scotland, 180
— Ireland, 226
Italian and Flemish Merchants, 19

## J

Jersey Island, 264
— Area, Coastline, Surface, 264
— Agricultural Products, 264
— Political Division, Commerce, 266
— Population, 266
Jet and Alum, 131

## K

Kent, 150
Keys, House of, 261
Kincardine, 208
Kinross, 209
Kirkcudbright, 214
Knights of St. John of Jerusalem, 281

## L

Lakes, England and Wales, 124
— Scotland, 190, 194, 196
— Ireland, 231, 232
Lanarkshire, 210
Lancashire, 154
Languages, British Isles, 87, 238
Larnaka, Cyprus, 286
Law, General, British Empire, 7
Lead and Zinc, 130
Leeds, 172
Leicestershire, 156
Leith, 218
Leven, Loch, 196
Lifeboat Institution, 108
Liffey, River, Ireland, 230
Limasol, Cyprus, 286
Limerick, 248
Lincolnshire, 150
Linlithgow, 210
Literature, Victorian, 76
Liverpool, 168, 172
Liverpool Channel, 124
Llanberis, Lake, 125
London, City of, 162-8
— County of, 164
Londonderry, 248
Longman, Professor — Commerce, (Edward III.), 21

## M

Magna Charta, Commerce, 19
Mail Intelligence, British Possessions, 34-7
Maltese Islands, Name, 275
— — Position, Area, Extent, 275
— — General Features, 276
— — Climate, 278
— — Productions, 279
— — People, Population, 279
— — Towns, 280
— — Exports and Imports, 280
— — Government and Religion, 280
— — History, 281
Man, Isle of, Position, 108, 255
— — Area and Shape, 255
— — Physical Features, 255
— — Mr. Hall Caine's Description, 255
— — Mountains, 257
— — Rivers and Glens, 258
— — Climate, 258
— — Soil and Agriculture, 258
— — Dr. Tellet's Report, 259
— — Animals, 260
— — People and Language, 260
— — Commerce, 261
— — History, 261
Manchester, 170
— Ship Canal, 69, 143
Manganese and Antimony, 130

# INDEX.

Mannanin, Magician, 258
Manufactures and Trade, 141, 142, 148, 174-6, 241
Manufactured Articles—Forbidden Importation, 22
Mariners' Compass Invented, 21
Meiklejohn, Prof., on Submarine Plateau, 49
Melrose Abbey, 214
Mercator Navigation Chart, 24
Merchant Adventurers, 20
Merchants of the Staple, 20
Middlesex, 161
Minerals, England and Wales, 132
— Scotland, 197
— Ireland, 236
Mineral Springs, 132, 200, 237
Mistress of Sea, Britain, 25, 56
Mixed Races, British Empire, 2
Monmouthshire, 153
Moors, 115
Mountain Systems, England and Wales, 110
— — Scotland, 187
— — Ireland, 228

## N

Nairn, 206
National Debt, 52
— Symbols, 84
Nation of Shopkeepers, 127
Natural Products, England and Wales, 127-132
— — Scotland, 197
— — Ireland, 234
Naval Stations, 59, 242
— Yards and Depots, 60
— Prisons, 60
— Training Institutions, 60
Navigable Rivers, 69
Navigation Act I., 21
— Chart, England and Wales, 102
Navy Estimates, 59
— Strength of, 58
Neutral Ground (Gibraltar), 269
Newspaper Press, 76
Nicosia (Cyprus), 286
Norfolk, 150
Northamptonshire, 158
Northumberland, 149
Nottinghamshire, 155

## O

Orkney Islands, 180-182
Oxfordshire, 160

## P

Paper Tax Withdrawal, 76
Paris, Treaty of, 27, 281
Passenger Steamship Lines, 38-41
Patron Saints (British Isles), 84
Paul, St., Visit to Cyprus, 287
— — Shipwreck, Malta, 275
Peebles, 212
Peel, Isle of Man, 260
Penal Settlements, 5
Pennine Range, 110
Penny Postage Rates, 68
Perthshire, 209
Peter Port, St., Guernsey, 267
Pilgrim Fathers, 25
Plains, England and Wales, 116
— Scotland, 190
— Ireland, 229
Plumbago, 130
Population, British Empire, 2
— British Isles, 51, 138
— Largest Centres, 138
— in Towns, 162
Position, British Empire, 1
— British Isles, 50, 95
Post and Cable Rates, British Possessions, 34-37
Postal Service, 67
Prophecy, Prof. Seeley's, 12

## Q

Queen Anne, British Commerce, 26
— Berengaria of Navarre, 287
— Catherine of Braganza, 5
— Elizabeth, Rise of Colonial Empire, 4, 24
— Mary, British Commerce, 24
— Mary of Scots, 196
— Victoria's Accession, 82-89
— — British Commerce, 28
— — Empress of India, 89
— — Family, 82
— — Jubilee and Diamond Jubilee, 89
— — Reign of Literature, 76
— — Visits Channel Islands, 264

## R

Race, British Isles, 2, 43
— Ireland, 238
— of Alderney, 267
Railways, England and Wales, 60
— Scotland, 66

## INDEX.

Railways, Ireland, 67
— Light, 61
— From Metropolis, 61
— Not touching Metropolis, 66
— Electric, 66
Rainfall, British Isles, 50
Ramsay, Isle of Man, 260
Rathlin Island, 226
Registrar-General's List, 79
Religion, National, British Isles, 77
Religious Bodies, 79
Renfrew, 210
Reptiles, 137
Restrictions of Foreign Money (Henry IV.), 21
— — Goods, 21
Revenue, British Empire, 52
Review, Commercial Progress, 29
Rivers, England and Wales, 118
— Scotland, 191
— Ireland, 229
Roads, British Isles, 70, 204
Roadsteads, England and Wales, 101
Roots and Cereals, 134
Ross and Cromarty, 206
Roxburghshire, 213
Royal Exchange, 24
— Family, 82
— Other Persons, 84
— Palaces, 84
Rutlandshire, 158

### S

Salt, Common, 130
— Rock, 130
Sark, Description, 268
— Population, 268
Scilly Islands, 105, 152
Scotland, Physical Features, 177
— Climate, 196
— Agriculture, 197
— Political Divisions, 204
— Trade and Manufactures, 221
— History, 222
Seaports, England and Wales, 143
— Scotland, 202
— Ireland, 241
Selkirkshire, 213
Seven Years' War, 27
Shannon, River, 229
Sheadings (Isle of Man), 260
Sheffield, 172
Shetland Islands, 180
Shipping Register, Lloyd's, 72
Shires and Counties, 143

Shropshire, 156
Skye, Caverns of, 201
Slate, 138, 198
Somersetshire, 153
Spanish Succession, War of, 26
Sponge Fisheries, 284
Staffordshire, 155
State Officers and Stipends, 55
Stirlingshire, 210
Stone, 131
Stratified Rocks, 128
Straits, England and Wales, 100
— Scotland, 179
— Ireland, 225
Suffolk, 150
Suir, River, 230
Sun Never Sets on British Empire, 1
Surface Features, England and Wales, 109
— — Scotland, 185
— — Ireland, 228
Surrey, 160
Sussex, 151
Sutherland, 206

### T

Telegraph Service, 68
Temperature, Mean, 127
Tonnage, Ships passing Suez Canal, 10
Trade Notes—Statistics, 90
— and Manufactures, 141, 241
Trinity House Founded, 23
Trossachs, 188, 196
Tunnage and Poundage, 20
Tynwald Hill Parliament, 258, 261

### U

Utrecht, Treaty of, 26

### V

Valentia Island, 227
Valetta (Malta), 276
Vale of Clyde, 190
Valleys, England and Wales, 117
— Scotland, 190
— Ireland, 229
Vasco de Gama, 23
Vegetation, England and Wales, 134
— Scotland, 199
— Ireland, 235
Venetian Republic, Trade with, 20
Victorian Ministries, 54

## INDEX.

### W

Wales, Counties, 174
— Area, 174
— Mining Interests, 174
— Manufactures, 174
Wars, British, 86
Warwickshire, 156
Waterford, 248
West African Coast Trade, 24
Westmoreland, 155
Whale Fisheries Established, 24
Wight, Isle of, 104, 151
Wigtonshire, 214
William the Conqueror, 46
Wiltshire, 160

Wolds, Lincolnshire and Yorkshire, 115
Woolwich Dockyard Established, 23
Worcestershire, 157
World's Workshop, The, 138

### Y

Yorkshire, 149

### Z

Zinc and Lead, 130

*Printed by Cowan & Co., Limited, Perth.*

# *The Imperial Press,*
## LIMITED.

Telegrams:
"Letters, London."

**Registered Offices:**
### 21 SURREY STREET, STRAND, LONDON, W.C.

THE large amount of influential support which has been obtained for the important undertaking of "THE IMPERIAL PRESS," and the prospect of wide-reaching results, from the efforts of its Committees, in the direction of promoting the Unity and Prosperity of the British Empire, have suggested the great desirability of extending the sphere of its usefulness. The Organising or Executive Committee have therefore determined to seek the co-operation of a much larger number of Members.

It will be readily admitted that no more powerful influence than that of an EDUCATIVE PRESS could possibly be brought to bear in furtherance of the great objects sought to be attained. By Books: such as those of "THE IMPERIAL LIBRARY," by Magazines, by Newspapers, and by other means within the compass of LITERATURE and ART, it is believed that a substantial impetus will be given to the great movement now progressing for adding further solidity and strength to the magnificent Empire of Her Majesty the Queen.

By multiplying centres of influence in all parts of this Empire, an important stride will be made towards the rapid accomplishment of the objects of "THE IMPERIAL PRESS": and this can best be brought about, the Committee believe, by a considerable enlargement of the Shareholding body.

## THE OBJECTS

for which THE IMPERIAL PRESS, LIMITED, has been formed, are set forth in the following Extracts from its Memorandum of Association :—

(*a*) To establish a great commercial enterprise which, whilst producing profit for its originators, shall seek especially to promote, by the powerful influence of the Press, objects conducive to the moral, educational, material, and social prosperity of the British Race in all parts of the world.

(*b*) To carry on in Great Britain and Ireland, throughout the British Empire, and elsewhere, the business of Printers, Publishers, Bookbinders, Booksellers, and any other business or undertaking connected therewith, or in any way incidental to Science, Art, and Literature.

(*c*) And for that purpose to purchase or otherwise acquire the proprietorship or copyright in any work of Science, Art, or Literature, and in any book, or printed or written article, or the title or titles thereof, or any artistic or literary contribution whatsoever, and to re-sell the same, or any portion thereof.

(*d*) To purchase or otherwise acquire any books, magazines, or other periodicals, whether for use or for re-sale, and likewise any stereotype, letterpress, engraved or other blocks or stones, or anything whatsoever for printing or reproducing books, magazines, periodicals, or other works of Science, Art, or Literature.

(*e*) To carry on the business of General Advertising Agents and Advertising Contractors.

(*f*) To purchase, have, or otherwise acquire any property, land, buildings, manufactories, letters-patent, machinery, plant, licenses, concessions, grants, or monopolies, or to re-sell the same, or any of the same.

(*g*) To enter into partnership or into any other arrangement for sharing profits, obtaining union of interests or co-operation with any person or company, carrying on, or about to carry on, any business or transaction that may seem conducive to the Company's objects, or any of them. And for such purposes to provide or advance money to assist any such person or company, and to guarantee the performance of contracts effected through the Company's Agency or otherwise.

(*h*) To do all such other things as may be necessary or incidental or conducive to the before-mentioned objects, or any of them.

(*i*) To amalgamate with any other similar undertaking or company upon the terms of payment in shares or money.

There are Trade Contracts of which each applicant for shares may obtain a copy, or inspection, on enquiry at the Company's Offices. A Duplicate of the Contract registered may also be seen.

## THE OBJECTS OF
# THE IMPERIAL PRESS,
### *LIMITED,*

Have been warmly commended by a considerable number of public men (in addition to those who form its General Committee) competent to form a sound judgment as to its merits; as an instance of which the following opinion of a very representative man is given:—

**LORD CHARLES BERESFORD,**

in a letter to the Editor, says:—

"I wish your scheme every possible success. I think there is ample scope for 'THE IMPERIAL PRESS, LIMITED,' to educate people on Imperial matters, and to make them see that the Empire means more than these little Islands. Then there is the question of the Navy, for which I am always working; and if you can only make people realise that our Navy is the buttress which supports the bridge between the various parts of the Empire, and that, if that buttress is weak or inefficient, the whole structure will crumble, you will be doing a most excellent work. I think that your idea of sandwiching these very practical lessons, in 'The Imperial Magazine,' between more palatable and entertaining matter, is well planned, and deserves success."

# The Imperial Library,

## CONDUCTED BY FRANCIS GEORGE HEATH,

Will be issued in a series of Volumes which, elegantly bound, will be published from time to time.

---

"The Imperial Library" is to consist of works of far-reaching interest, giving information upon every subject concerning our great Empire—all designed to aid the noble movement, now progressing, for strengthening the ties which unite the Mother Country to the splendid Colonies which are the power and the pride of "Greater Britain."

The great and far-reaching object for which "The Imperial Library" has been founded is to bring home to the minds of the millions of our splendid Empire a knowledge of what they, as citizens in their huge commonwealth, are so proud to possess; and thus, it is hoped, may be built up, by gradual means, and at a cost that may come (by easy instalments) within the pecuniary resources of the humblest of intelligent readers, a storehouse of information collected with one object and under one system; and ultimately, it may reasonably be hoped, there will be produced an Encyclopædia Britannica such as no private person at present possesses.

---

London: THE IMPERIAL PRESS, Limited, 21 Surrey Street, Victoria Embankment, W.C.

## APPLICATION FORM FOR MEMBERSHIP

OF

# THE IMPERIAL PRESS, Ltd.

*Registered under the Companies' Acts, 1862 to 1890 (whereby the liability of Members is limited to the amount of their Shares), with a capital of £25,000, divided into 25,000 Shares of £1 each (with power to increase).*

N.B.—The Application Form (which can be copied), with the remittance, should be sent, in the first instance, direct to the Bankers.

2s. 6d. per Share is payable on application, and 5s. per Share on allotment, and the balance by calls of 2s. 6d. per Share, as required, at one month's notice of call.

TO THE EXECUTIVE COMMITTEE OF "THE IMPERIAL PRESS, LIMITED."

Registered Offices :—21 SURREY STREET, STRAND, LONDON, W.C.

GENTLEMEN,
   I desire to become a member of "THE IMPERIAL PRESS, LIMITED," and to assist in any way in my power the objects of the undertaking; and having paid to your Bankers, THE LONDON AND WESTMINSTER BANK, LIMITED, Lothbury, London, E.C., the sum of £.................. being a deposit of.........on an application for .........Shares of £1 each in the above-named Company, I hereby apply for that number of Shares on the terms and conditions of the Company's Memorandum and Articles of Association and Prospectus, and subject to its contracts; and I agree to accept the same, and to make the payments above-mentioned; and I authorise you to place my name on the Register of Members of the Company, in respect of the Shares so allotted.

*Name in full,*......................................................

*Address,*.............................................................

*Description,*........................................................

*Usual Signature,*.................................................

*Date,*...... ..........................................

Dedicated by Express Permission to
HER MAJESTY THE QUEEN-EMPRESS.

# "Imperial Defence,"

BY

### Sir Geo. S. Clarke, K.C.M.G., F.R.S., R.E.,

CONCERNS THE

DEFENCE OF THE BRITISH EMPIRE,

Is Illustrated by Eight Engravings, and Two Coloured Maps, and

### IS NOW READY.

In One Handsome Volume, Cloth Gilt, with Special Emblematic Design.

Part I.—THE EMPIRE.    Part II.—TRADE.
Part III.—THE NAVY.    Part IV.—THE ARMY.
Part V.—IMPERIAL ORGANISATION.

### PRICE, 7/6.    POST FREE, 8/-.

### *THE TIMES,*

Writing in 1897, said :—"The conductors of the 'Imperial Library' may be congratulated on having secured the services of Sir George Clarke to contribute an inaugural volume on 'Imperial Defence.' No writer of our time is better qualified to do justice to so inspiring a theme, or has shown a more comprehensive grasp of its real dimensions and conditions. The growth of that Imperial sentiment which makes for unity, and passionately repudiates all thought of separation, is perhaps the most significant characteristic of the reign whose splendid achievements and long duration the whole Empire is now on the eve of celebrating. If the note of the last century was Imperial expansion, that of the present is Imperial concentration. We have, indeed, extended the bounds of Empire in these latter days far more widely than our forefathers did. But the world has grown smaller since the close of the last century, and with the contractions of time and space—which we owe to science and to mechanical enterprise—has grown a deeper sense of kin and a larger wisdom in framing that Imperial body politic of which it is the soul. It is, therefore, not without a deep significance that Sir George Clarke's stimulating essay on 'Imperial Defence' should be dedicated in this year of jubilee 'to the Queen-Empress, by Her Majesty's most gracious permission.' . . . The method pursued by Sir George Clarke is unimpeachable, and the principles enunciated by him are justified by history, and now accepted by the highest authorities of the State. In the coming pan-Britannic festival of the Empire, the wise counsels preferred in this luminous exposition of the things which belong to its peace should not pass unheeded. There is no time like the present to take thought for the common defence of what all the subjects of the Queen now regard as their common and inalienable patrimony ; and we know not where to look for better assistance than is to be found in this masterly essay for giving such thought precision and such action consistency."

LONDON : THE IMPERIAL PRESS, LIMITED, 21 SURREY STREET,
VICTORIA EMBANKMENT, W.C.

## Press Opinions of "Imperial Defence"—*Continued.*

### SPECTATOR.

"A very useful text-book, not only on the subject of defence, but also on the growth and actual extent of the British Empire as it exists to-day. The chapters that Sir George Clarke devotes to the actual condition of our navy and army give a very lucid and clear aspect of our system of defence and its practical working. But by far the most interesting feature of his book is the able manner in which he discusses the wider question of Imperial organisation, and succeeds in enforcing the lesson of the great risks that the country has run in the past, and of the absolute necessity for exercising a wiser and more far-seeing prudence in the future."

### MORNING ADVERTISER.

"The publishers are to be congratulated on such an excellent start to their undertaking, and the public on the existence of such a practical work."

### ARMY AND NAVY GAZETTE.

"A volume that condenses with admirable lucidity the main features of the question. The book is a veritable armoury from which arguments may be drawn, and out of which reasonable judgments may be evolved. Appropriately, it opens with a survey of what we may call the genesis of the Empire, and deals with the purpose and significance of wars. . . . We hope for a wide sale for the book."

### SCOTSMAN.

"Sir George S. Clarke's book on Imperial Defence inaugurates a series of volumes to be called 'The Imperial Library,' and it says much for their prospect of success. . . . A man who wishes to be well-informed upon its subject will find it relieve him from the weariness of much research in blue-books, and it cannot but do good by spreading abroad a knowledge of the most pressing questions of contemporary politics."

### PUBLISHERS' CIRCULAR.

"Readers will find that the author has treated the subject with the exhaustiveness which comes of perfect mastery, and his style is clear and agreeable."

### DAILY GRAPHIC.

"Of the capacity of Sir George Clarke to write on the subject of Imperial Defence, no one who is familiar with his essays and papers on various aspects of the main subject can for a moment doubt. He has as clear a grasp of the conditions of the problem as any public man, and he has, in addition, an admirable facility for lucid exposition. Both these features will be found in the present volume. . . . Sir George Clarke's book will be found most valuable by all readers who wish to form a clear conception of the conditions underlying the successful defence of the British Empire."

LONDON: THE IMPERIAL PRESS, LIMITED, 21 SURREY STREET, VICTORIA EMBANKMENT, W.C.

## Some Press Opinions of "Imperial Defence"—*Continued.*

### COMMERCE.

"Magnificently got up, and printed in the most excellent way, on paper which it is a pleasure to handle, this volume is one of the most important contributions to the subject it deals with yet published. . . . A word of praise is due to Mr. Francis G. Heath for the compilation of a full index."

### LEEDS MERCURY.

"The writer justifies his claim to be regarded as a man of letters as well as of action. The plates and diagrams are beautifully produced."

### MELBOURNE ARGUS.

"There could be no more auspicious season for the inauguration of 'The Imperial Library' than the year in which we celebrate the sixtieth anniversary of the reign of Victoria, and there could be no happier beginning of such a series than that which has been made by Sir George Clarke in his admirable volume on Imperial Defence."

### BIRMINGHAM DAILY GAZETTE.

"This book, from its very title-page to the end, teems with interesting information, set forth in interesting fashion, and of supreme importance to every Englishman."

### STATIST.

"Sir George Clarke has written a little book on the problems of Imperial Defence which can confidently be recommended to those who have not studied the subject, and yet wish to have a clear idea of it."

### JOURNAL OF THE ROYAL COLONIAL INSTITUTE.

"This is the work of an expert whose views upon this great question of Imperial Defence have been so much before the public during recent years. Sir George Clarke has made a special study of the subject, and has so been enabled to set forth the conditions of the national problem, and to point out the road towards a solution."

### DUNDEE COURIER.

"No more appropriate or more serviceable addition to 'The Imperial Library' could be obtained than this instructive and interesting book."

### LIVERPOOL COURIER.

"When the history of the reign of Queen Victoria comes to be written, one of its notable features will undoubtedly be the conception and growth of the Imperial idea, and may we hope the full realisation of that idea. To further that realisation is the chief object of 'The Imperial Press, Limited,' and one of the means towards this end is the publication of such books as this of Sir George Clarke, which forms the first of 'The Imperial Library.' . . . On this subject no higher authority could be found."

### MANCHESTER GUARDIAN.

"The first volume of the new 'Imperial Library' is a work on Imperial Defence, by Lieut.-Col. Sir George Clarke, K.C.M.G. If all the works in 'The Imperial Library' are as sound and reasonable as this, the new series is destined to do much service in popularising the intelligent and sober-minded study of Imperial questions."

LONDON: THE IMPERIAL PRESS, LTD., 21 SURREY STREET, W.C.

# IMPERIAL AFRICA.

A Description of the History, Geography, Commerce, Government and Prospects of the
BRITISH POSSESSIONS IN AFRICA,
With Notes on Anthropology, Natural History, Native Customs, and Languages.

(*IN THREE VOLUMES, with Illustrations and Maps.*) Price 12/6 Each.

Vol. I.—BRITISH WEST AFRICA. (*Now Ready*)
Vol. II.—BRITISH EAST AFRICA. Vol. III.—BRITISH SOUTH AFRICA.

BY

MAJOR A. F. MOCKLER-FERRYMAN, F.R.G.S., F.Z.S., &c.,
of the Oxfordshire Light Infantry,
Author of "Up the Niger," "In the Northman's Land," &c.

Vol. I. DEDICATED, by Permission, to FIELD-MARSHAL LORD WOLSELEY.

## BRITISH WEST AFRICA.

With Nine Coloured Maps and Numerous other Illustrations.
Price 12/6.

The first volume contains a complete description—geographical and historical—of the British possessions in West Africa, with a detailed account of all important events that have occurred from the earliest times to the present day. No pains have been spared to make this volume not only interesting to the general reader, but also valuable as a work of reference to the student of the several African problems. In it will be found discussed at length such matters as Slavery, the Liquor Traffic, Mission Work, Commerce, the Claims of European Rivals, and the Manners and Customs of the Numerous Tribes.

Contents.—Chapter I. Introductory—II. Gambia—III. Sierra Leone—IV. The Gold Coast—V. Ashanti—VI. The Two Ashanti Expeditions—VII. Lagos—VIII. The Niger and its Early Explorers—IX. Further Explorations of the Niger—X. The Travels of Barth and Baikie—XI. The Commencement of Trade on the Niger—XII. Nigeria—XIII. The Fulah Empire—XIV. The Fulah Empire (continued)—XV. The Royal Niger Company, Chartered and Limited--XVI. The Niger Coast Protectorate—XVII. Native Tribes and Customs—XVIII. Samory and Rabeh—XIX. Slavery and the Slave Trade—XX. Religion and Missionaries—XXI. France and Germany in West Africa—XXII. West African Products—XXIII. Folk Lore—XXIV. Conclusion.

N.B.—Subscribers to the Three Volumes of "Imperial Africa" will obtain them for 30s., post free, if prepaid and ordered at once direct from the Publishers, but if ordered singly the price will be 12s. 6d. each as published.

---

(Now Ready.)
IN ONE VOLUME. *Price* 7/6.

## BIRDS OF THE BRITISH EMPIRE,
FULLY ILLUSTRATED.

By DR. W. T. GREENE, F.Z.S.

Author of
"The Song Birds of Great Britain," "Favourite Foreign Birds," "The Birds of my Garden," "Parrots in Captivity," "The Amateur's Aviary of Foreign Birds," "Feathered Friends : Old and New," "The Grey Parrot," etc.

"The book is an Education in itself and a welcome addition to ' The Imperial Library.'"
*European Mail.*

---

LONDON : THE IMPERIAL PRESS, LIMITED,
21 SURREY STREET, VICTORIA EMBANKMENT, W.C.

# Imperial Britain,

A Comprehensive Description of the Geography, History, Commerce, Trade, Government, and Religion of the British Empire.

### In 2 Volumes, price 7/6 each.

With Maps and other Illustrations.

---

NOW READY.
VOL. I.
### THE BRITISH EMPIRE IN EUROPE.

VOL. II.
*(In preparation.)*
### THE BRITISH EMPIRE IN ASIA, AFRICA, AMERICA, AND AUSTRALIA.

BY
THE REV. THEODORE JOHNSON, M.A.,
Late Chief Diocesan Inspector of Schools for Rochester Diocese, and Author of
"A Geography and Atlas of the British Empire," "A Handbook of English History," "The Parish Guide," etc., etc.

---

## *THE FEDERAL DEMOCRACY,*

BY
DR. JETHRO BROWN,
Principal of the Tasmanian University, and

THE HONOURABLE ANDREW INGLIS CLARK,
Attorney-General for Tasmania.

---

A New (Illustrated) Edition of
## MY GARDEN WILD.
By FRANCIS GEORGE HEATH.
*Will be ready shortly.   Price 5/-*

---

A New Edition is also in preparation of
## TREE GOSSIP.
By FRANCIS GEORGE HEATH.

---

LONDON : THE IMPERIAL PRESS, LIMITED, 21 SURREY STREET, VICTORIA EMBANKMENT, W.C.

# WORKS BY FRANCIS GEORGE HEATH.

(NOW READY, price 7/6, Coloured Plates Entirely Redrawn.)

# THE FERN WORLD

BY

## FRANCIS GEORGE HEATH,

Editor of the New Edition of "Gilpin's Forest Scenery."

Author of

"Our Woodland Trees," "The Fern Paradise," "Sylvan Spring," "Autumnal Leaves," "The Fern Portfolio," "Where to find Ferns," "My Garden Wild," "Trees and Ferns," "Tree Gossip," "Burnham Beeches," "The English Peasantry," "Peasant Life in the West of England,"
etc., etc.

New and cheaper Edition (being the eighth), price 7s. 6d., containing 12 Coloured Plates and numerous Wood Engravings.

*⁎* "THE FERN WORLD" has been sold in every English-speaking country in the world.

## CONTENTS.

PART I.—THE FERN WORLD.—Introduction—The Germs of Fern Life—Conditions of Growth—Structure—Classification—Distribution—Uses—The Folk-lore of Ferns.

PART II.—FERN CULTURE.—Introduction—Soil and Aspect—General Treatment—Propagation—A Fern Valley—Subterranean Fern Culture—A Fern Garden—Fern Rockery—A Fern House—Pot Culture of Ferns—Ferns at Home.

PART III.—FERN HUNTING.—Introduction—Fern Holidays—Fern Collecting—Frond Gathering.

PART IV.—SOME RAMBLES THROUGH FERNLAND.—Introduction—Down a Combe to the Sea—The Valleys of the Lyn—The Valley of the Rocks—Clovelly—Sea and Sky and Waving Green—Torbay—The South-east Coast of Devon—The Home of the Sea Fern.

PART V.—BRITISH FERNS: Their Description, Distribution, and Culture.

LONDON: THE IMPERIAL PRESS, LIMITED, 21 SURREY STREET, VICTORIA EMBANKMENT, W.C.

## SOME PRESS OPINIONS OF
# THE FERN WORLD.

**THE SATURDAY REVIEW**:—"The work may be said to comprise the whole grammar and dictionary of the fern world—a delightful addition to the naturalist's library."

**THE ATHENÆUM**:—"The book contains good, well-written descriptions of our native ferns, with indications of their habitats, the conditions under which they grow naturally, and under which they may be cultivated."

**THE BRITISH QUARTERLY REVIEW**:—"The book is beautifully illustrated. The ferns are photographed and coloured with an excellency we have never seen surpassed. The volume is a very charming one, and is as fascinating for the general reader as it is useful for the amateur cultivator. Vivid and felicitous descriptions of natural scenery, ouches of poetry, accounts of rambles, a pervading glow of enthusiasm, and an easy, sparkling style combine with the useful information to make the volume one that even those most insensible to the charms of nature will be glad to possess."

**THE WORLD**:—"It is equally charming and useful. No work of the kind could advance a more substantial claim to popularity of the best kind."

**THE STANDARD**:—"The execution of the work is in every way worthy of the past fame and the present aims of the author."

**THE MORNING POST**:—"The illustrations in the 'FERN WORLD' are simply perfection."

**THE SPECTATOR**:—"Many lovers of the quieter aspects of nature will thank us for directing their attention to Mr. Heath's 'FERN WORLD.'"

**THE DAILY TELEGRAPH**:—"The name of its author is a guarantee for the practical value of 'THE FERN WORLD,' whilst its elegant appearance and copious illustrations furnish their own recommendation."

**JOHN BULL**:—"'THE FERN WORLD' is one of the most charming books upon a charming subject which it has ever been our lot to meet with."

**LIGHT**:—"We should infinitely prefer to spend the summer or autumn holidays with Mr. Heath's charmingly-written apotheosis of ferns than with any work of current fiction that we know of. . . . Even for the reader who cares little or nothing for ferns there is much to captivate and hold the interest and imagination in this book."

**THE ILLUSTRATED LONDON NEWS**:—"'THE FERN WORLD' is both instructive and delightful in the highest degree, combining exact botanical description with the most inviting and enchanting accounts of many a ramble in the sweetest rural haunts. . . . But in this delightful book the study of botanical, generic and specific varieties has obtained a fascinating and most helpful method of representation. This is done by means of twelve of the finest plates, from photographs of fronds, collected and grouped by the author, which are unquestionably the most beautiful, vivid and faithful pictures of plant life that have ever yet appeared in any work of this class. They have all the freshness of the living hues of nature."

**THE QUEEN**:—"'THE FERN WORLD' is a beautiful, instructive and bewitching book."

LONDON: THE IMPERIAL PRESS, LIMITED, 21 SURREY STREET, W.C.

*IN PREPARATION.*

# Autumnal Leaves.

### By FRANCIS GEORGE HEATH.

New and Cheaper Edition, price 7s. 6d., containing twelve coloured plates of autumn-tinted leaves and numerous wood engravings.

### SOME PRESS OPINIONS OF "AUTUMNAL LEAVES."

**Spectator**:—"This charmingly-illustrated volume will delight many eyes."

**Saturday Review**:—"The present charming volume is in every way attractive."

**Harper's Magazine**:—"Perhaps the most novel and pleasing of all the numerous books Mr. Francis George Heath has written."

**Queen**:—"Mr. Heath's writings on the poetry of forest and field are fascinating in the highest degree. 'Autumnal Leaves' stands unrivalled."

**Pall Mall Gazette**:—"The coloured representations of various autumn leaves have been produced with immense care and marvellous accuracy. . . . The result is a facsimile—as perfect, perhaps, as imitative art could make it—of every detail in the original foliage. . . Mr. Heath is above all things a master of word painting, who can make minute and deft description do duty instead of palette and colour-box in a way that is quite surprising for its vivid and graphic effect."

**Tablet**:—"Mr. Heath has now passed from the tender blooms of spring to the sunset-dyed glories of autumn; but we recognise in the book before us the mind of long ago. There is the same tender regard for all that in nature lives; the same keen insight for revealing wonders unseen by the casual passer-by; the same power of holding his readers' deepest attention; and the same gift of adorning each subject to which he sets his hand."

LONDON : THE IMPERIAL PRESS, LIMITED, 21 SURREY STREET, VICTORIA EMBANKMENT, W.C.

*IN PREPARATION.*

# Burnham Beeches.

### By FRANCIS GEORGE HEATH.
### NEW EDITION.

CONTENTS.—1. Remnants of the Sylvan Past—2. Burnham Forest—3. The Beeches—4. Burnham and its Common—5. A Ramble to Burnham—6. The Railway—7. The Walk—8. The Woods.

"**BURNHAM BEECHES**" is illustrated by eight beautifully-executed wood engravings, and a Map of Burnham Beech-woods and Common.

The late LORD BEACONSFIELD, in a letter to the author written from Hughenden Manor, December 28th, 1880, says: "Your life is occupied with two subjects which always deeply interest me: the condition of our peasantry and trees. . . With regard to trees, I passed part of my youth in the shade of Burnham Beeches, and have now the happiness of living amid my own 'green retreats.' I am not surprised that the ancients worshipped trees. Lakes and Mountains, however glorious for a time, in time weary—sylvan scenery never palls."

### SOME PRESS OPINIONS OF "BURNHAM BEECHES."

**Illustrated London News**:—"The Burnham Beeches were saved by the liberality of the London City Corporation, prompted thereto by an accomplished writer of pleasant books about trees and ferns and rural delights, Mr. Francis George Heath, who addressed the public authorities with earnest letters of remonstrance. . . A charming little volume."

**Globe**:—"Writing with even more than his usual brilliancy, Mr. Heath here gives the public an interesting monograph of the splendid old trees. . . . This charming little work."

**Guardian**:—"A charming little volume, illustrated by some choice engravings of woodland scenery, besides four faithful transcripts of the Beeches in their spring, summer, autumn, and winter dress."

**Daily News**:—"We have here a pretty description of the Beeches and surrounding neighbourhood, with its associations, picturesque, topographical, and biographical."

**Spectator**:—"A most readable account of the Beeches. . . There are some very pretty illustrations. Let our readers enjoy Mr. Heath's book now, and go to see the Beeches themselves in the summer."

**Record**:—"The charm of style and perfection of illustration."

LONDON: THE IMPERIAL PRESS, LIMITED, 21 SURREY STREET,
VICTORIA EMBANKMENT, W.C.

# THE IMPERIAL MAGAZINE

(REGISTERED)

WILL BE ONE OF THE FORTHCOMING PUBLICATIONS OF

## THE IMPERIAL PRESS, LIMITED,

and will be commenced as soon as arrangements can be made for it.

---

"THE IMPERIAL MAGAZINE" is to be a beautifully and profusely illustrated Shilling Monthly. Besides Fiction—which will be a powerfully-attractive feature—it will deal with Biographical and Descriptive subjects, covering the fields of Recreation, Literature, Science, and Art in so comprehensive a manner as to possess interest for English readers everywhere.

*To promote the unity of the British Empire, to open up to British readers at home the beautiful scenery and the magnificent natural resources of our Colonies will be especial aims of the conductors of the Magazine, and to endeavour to bring about a federation of English-speaking people in all parts of the world is also an object that will be kept steadily in view.*

On the next page will be found a reduced facsimile of the proposed design for the cover of

"THE IMPERIAL MAGAZINE."

LONDON: THE IMPERIAL PRESS, LIMITED, 21 SURREY STREET, VICTORIA EMBANKMENT, W.C.

Reduced Design for Front Cover.

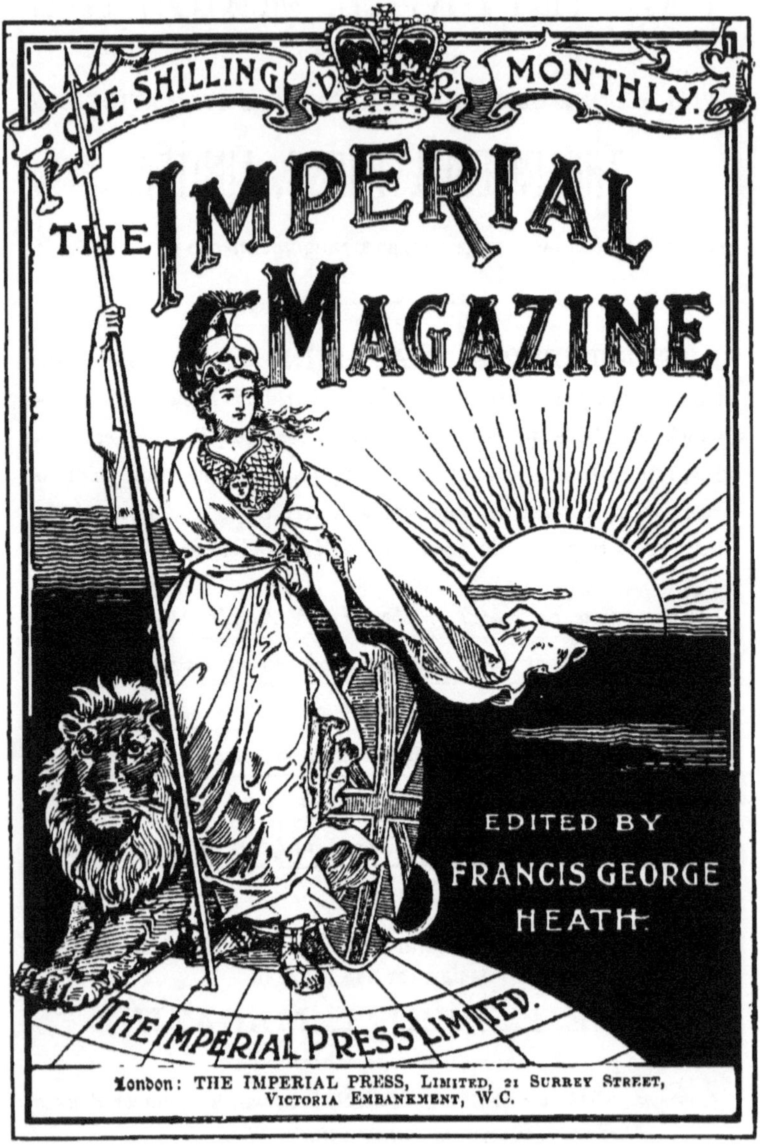

www.ingramcontent.com/pod-product-compliance
Lightning Source LLC
Chambersburg PA
CBHW031425230426
43668CB00007B/444